"This book is a remarkable piece of apologetic reasoning, which uses a format that is both textually rich and diagrammatically wise. I know of nothing else like it and I am thankful to the God of truth and reason for its appearance. It will open doors to apologetics in a new way that will help many Christians and non-Christians. Bravo!"

Douglas Groothuis, PhD
Professor of Philosophy, Denver Seminary
and author of *Christian Apologetics*

"Robert Velarde is a meticulous Christian thinker and gifted writer. His newest work, *A Visual Defense: The Case For and Against Christianity*, again demonstrates Velarde's ability to understand all sides of an issue, to fairly critique the nonbiblical claims, and to explain and defend the Christian position."

Alex McFarland
Director for Christian Worldview and Apologetics
North Greenville University, South Carolina

A VISUAL DEFENSE

THE CASE FOR AND AGAINST CHRISTIANITY

ROBERT VELARDE

Kregel
Publications

A Visual Defense: The Case For and Against Christianity
© 2013 by Robert Velarde.

Published by Kregel Publications, a division of Kregel, Inc., P.O. Box 2607, Grand Rapids, MI 49501.

All Scripture quotations, unless otherwise indicated, are from The Holy Bible, English Standard Version® (ESV®), copyright © 2001 by Crossway, a publishing ministry of Good News Publishers. Used by permission. All rights reserved.

Scripture quotations marked NASB are from the New American Standard Bible®. Copyright © 1960, 1962, 1963, 1968, 1971, 1972, 1973, 1975, 1977, 1995 by The Lockman Foundation. Used by permission. www.Lockman.org

Scripture quotations marked NIV are from the Holy Bible, New International Version®, NIV®. Copyright © 1973, 1978, 1984 by Biblica, Inc.™ Used by permission of Zondervan. All rights reserved worldwide. www.zondervan.com

ISBN 978-0-8254-3926-1

Printed in the United States of America
13 14 15 16 17 / 5 4 3 2 1

Contents

Preface   7

Part 1: Introduction

  1: Understanding Argument Diagrams   11

  2: Is Apologetics Necessary?   17

  3: Is Intellect Essential to the Christian Life?   23

  4: How Are Faith and Reason Related?   31

Part 2: Arguments for God and Christianity

  5: Christianity Is True   39

  6: The Theistic God Exists   49

  7: Truth Is Objective, Absolute, Universal, and More   59

  8: Objective Moral Values Exist   67

  9: Christianity Is Beneficial   75

  10: Christ Rose from the Dead   83

  11: Christ Is the Only Way of Salvation   91

  12: The Argument from Desire   97

  13: Pascal's Anthropological Argument   103

  14: Christianity Best Explains Evil   109

  15: Hell Is Justifiable   117

Part 3: Arguments Against God and Christianity

  16: God Does Not Exist (Atheism)   125

  17: Nontheistic Evolution Is True (God Is Unnecessary)   133

  18: Belief in God/Christianity Is Delusional   139

  19: Evil Exists, So God Does Not Exist   145

  20: Christianity Is Harmful   153

  21: Monistic Pantheism Is True   161

  22: All Religions Are Essentially True (Christianity Is Not Unique) 167

  23: Evil Is an Illusion   173

  24: Christian Hypocrisy Shows That Christianity Is False   179

  25: Religious Experience Is Subjective and Cannot Be Tested   185

Conclusion   193

Glossary   195

Annotated Bibliography   199

Subject Index   205

Name Index   207

About the Author   208

Preface

When we want to correct someone usefully and show him he is wrong, we must see from what point of view he is approaching the matter, for it is usually right from that point of view, and we must admit this, but show him the point of view from which it is wrong. This will please him, because he will see that he was not wrong but merely failed to see every aspect of the question.

–Blaise Pascal, *Pensées* (701/9)

My purpose in this book is threefold: to help the reader (1) learn to think critically; (2) make the case for the Christian worldview; and (3) seek to understand opposing viewpoints. Regarding critical thinking, part 1 provides background on the value of logical discourse, the necessity of defending the faith (apologetics), the life of the intellect in relation to the Christian worldview, and a brief tour through the relationship between faith and reason.

But our overview of critical thinking is far from limited to part 1, as parts 2 and 3 continue to examine and analyze various arguments for and against Christianity. As a committed Christian, I do not want to tear down Christianity and leave its followers without hope. Rather, I desire to demonstrate that Christianity not only can make a robust, positive case for its truth but also can withstand the harshest intellectual attacks. It does no good to the cause of Christ to avoid grappling with challenges to our faith. In reality, much harm can come from such avoidance, since those who follow such a path may lack a solid foundation regarding why they believe what they believe.

Part 2 makes the case for the Christian worldview via eleven argument maps. These diagrams present a visual approach to understanding argument forms including conclusions and premises, as well as objections and rebuttals that arise in the normal course of reasoned dialogue. Note that the diagrams make no attempt to be exhaustive. Such an endeavor would quickly result in lengthy sheets of paper and diagrams that a book cannot accommodate. Consequently, *the diagrams in this book are broad overviews of various arguments for and against Christianity.* In some instances the reader may not consider some of the points central or may note omissions; feel free to think through alternatives and responses to them. At any rate, the arguments presented in part 2 largely fall into positive apologetics—that is, they make a positive case for the Christian worldview. However, even these arguments must grapple with criticisms and challenges, so there is an ongoing interplay with competing ideas.

In part 3 we turn to ten arguments against Christianity. Although the atheistic worldview is stressed due to its current prominence in Western culture, at times we also explore the worldview of monistic pantheism, which remains a powerful draw for millions of people.

Thus, this book primarily addresses three worldviews overall: Christian theism, atheism, and pantheism. There are, of course, other worldviews, but in the assessment of the author, the three addressed represent the primary live options in the world, with many sub-worldviews under them. As such, theism, atheism, and pantheism serve as umbrellas over various offshoots. The arguments in part 3 are not to be approached lightly, either intellectually or spiritually. If one is weak in the faith to begin with, it is best to begin with part 2, which will edify the Christian in the truth of the Christian worldview.

Keep in mind, too, that the argument maps in this book are highly intellectual in their content and nature. But the Christian life is about far more than logical argumentation and analysis. We must not neglect its spiritual side. There is a time and a place for defending the faith, but we cannot always live in that world or in that frame of mind. As C. S. Lewis wisely stated, "A man can't be always defending the truth; there must be a time to feed on it."[1]

Part 3 calls us to seek to understand opposing viewpoints. Often, to our detriment, we become entrenched in our own worldview without considering its place in the broader scheme of the pursuit of intellectual truth. This is not to say that, as Christians, we should avoid understanding and believing in our worldview; rather, it is to say that too often we neglect to see other perspectives, quickly dismissing arguments without even assessing them. Consequently, part of our goal in this book is to learn to consider various options and viewpoints when it comes to understanding reality.

As a former atheist and, for a short time, a monistic pantheist, I have attempted to fairly represent the arguments and worldviews in the associated diagrams. This, however, does not mean that all the diagrams are flawless. Indeed, disagreements about the strengths and weaknesses of certain arguments and approaches are inevitable. Moreover, different theists, atheists, and pantheists may have differing ideas as to what arguments, if any, form the key foundations of the relevant worldview under discussion. Nevertheless, it is my hope that the diagrams and related text offer helpful insights as we seek to understand reality as best we can.

A few final points must be noted or reiterated. First, I am unashamedly a Christian theist, and as such I will defend the Christian worldview vigorously. Second, although I will approach the defense of the faith from what is typically called the position of classical apologetics, this does not mean that there is little or no value in this work for Christian thinkers who hold to other views of apologetic methodology, such as evidentialism, presuppositionalism, Reformed epistemology, cumulative case apologetics, and other forms of defending the faith (see the glossary for brief definitions of these types of apologetics). Third, the argument maps are key to our threefold approach. While the accompanying text is of much value in understanding the diagrams, readers should begin each chapter by carefully viewing and considering the flow of thought represented in the diagrams themselves. To this end, we now turn to chapter 1, where our method of mapping is further explained.

---

1. C. S. Lewis, *Reflections on the Psalms* (New York: Harcourt, 1958), 7.

PART I

Introduction

CHAPTER I

Understanding Argument Diagrams

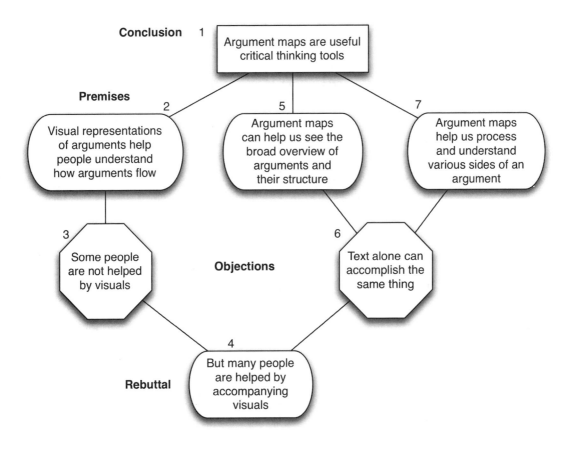

Argument diagrams are crucial to this book. Therefore, this chapter will explain the rationale and structure of the diagrams as well as help the reader interpret the sample diagram at the beginning of this chapter.

An argument diagram visually represents the parts of a logical argument. Such diagrams are also called argument maps. Keep in mind that we are using the word *argument* in relation to logical reasoning, not as in a fight or squabble of some kind.

A logical argument consists of propositions—what we might call truth claims about reality. The argument maps in this book begin with the *conclusion* of the argument, then are followed by *premises* (propositions that claim to support the conclusion). The premises are then followed by *objections*—ideas or even emotional reasons why someone might object to a premise. The objections are then followed by *rebuttals*, wherein the supporter of the conclusion responds to the objection. In some cases the rebuttals are followed by further objections. Obviously, arguments can go back and forth in this manner—objection, rebuttal—for quite some time, so for our purposes the argument diagrams are limited to one page.

Some diagrams include an assumption(s), noted next to the conclusion. This means that the conclusion itself relies on key assumptions or presuppositions. Since every argument relies to some extent on some assumptions and presuppositions, the diagrams will not always note such assumptions. Only where certain assumptions are worth noting are they included in the diagram in question.

Take a moment to look over the diagram at the beginning of this chapter. Make sure you can find the conclusion, premises, objections, and rebuttals. Note the shapes too. The conclusion is always at the top in a rectangular box, while premises and rebuttals have rounded corners. Objections take the form of octagons, as in stop signs. You'll also see that the shapes are connected with lines. These lines represent associations between the ideas represented. For instance, three lines are leaving the conclusion and pointing to three supporting premises for the argument. In turn, these premises are connected via lines to related objections, and so forth.

Finally, take note of the numbers on the argument map. These numbers relate to text in the book. For instance, as we work our way through the sample diagram in the following pages, when you see bold text beginning with a number, the text beside this heading refers to the box next to the number on the diagram. Number 6, then, is followed by text relating to the objection, "Text alone can accomplish the same thing." Many of the argument diagrams in later chapters can involve as many as two dozen or so numbers, so it is important to understand the relationship between the numbers and the text.

While this resource is not a primer on logic, it is important to understand that logical argumentation fits well with the Christian worldview (see chapters 3 and 4). The Bible clearly supports the use of logic both implicitly and explicitly. It contains numerous logical truth claims communicated in reasonable language that relies on the laws of logic.

God's Word is also explicit in its support of logic. In Isaiah 1:18, for instance, we read, "Come now, and let us reason together, says the Lord" (NASB). In Matthew 22:37, Jesus admonishes his followers to love God with heart, soul, and mind. The passage uses the Greek word *dianoia*, translated as *mind*, which refers to deep thought, implying the use of logical thinking in order to gain understanding. Moreover, Jesus often interacted with his critics by utilizing various logical forms of argumentation, such as a fortiori arguments, appeal to evidence, escaping the horns of a dilemma, reductio ad absurdum argumentation, and more.[1]

The Bible never encourages believers to shun the intellect (although we often behave in such a way, much to the detriment of the case for Christianity). Ignoring reasoning and emptying the mind are Eastern meditative ideas, supposedly useful in seeking enlightenment, rather than Christian precepts. In short, biblical Christianity is a thinking religion. This does not mean there is no room for feeling or religious experience. Both reason and emotion play critical roles in the Christian life. The point, however, is that the Bible never requires believers to discard the life of the mind, but in fact strongly encourages it.

1. Argument maps are useful critical thinking tools

Here we begin to discuss the argument diagram in question (at the beginning of this chapter). Note that the heading includes the number associated with the conclusion, signifying that text below this heading will relate to the conclusion. In this case our conclusion is, "Argument maps are useful critical thinking tools." The evidence in support of this conclusion is found in points 2, 5, and 7—the boxes below the conclusion in the diagram.

2. Visual representations of arguments help people understand how arguments flow

Due to space limitations, the content in most boxes, including the premises, is limited, so the associated text is where ideas are amplified as necessary. The premise here claims, "Visual representations of arguments help people understand how arguments flow." Here is where the text would add supporting information or reasoning behind the premise in question. In this instance we could cite research documenting the value of visual learning, as well as the benefit of utilizing argument maps and diagrams.

3. Some people are not helped by visuals

This is the first objection to the argument. Since it is connected by a line to point 2, we know that the objection is specifically to the premise in point 2. We also know that it is an objection because of the octagonal shape. Keep in mind that arguments in part 2 argue in favor of Christianity, while arguments in part 3 argue against it. Therefore, we must pay attention to the parts of the argument, such as objections, since we will at times, for the sake of argument, defend an alternative worldview such as atheism or pantheism. The objection here notes, "Some people

---

1. See Groothuis, *On Jesus*, chapter 3; and Dallas Willard, "Jesus the Logician," *Christian Scholars Review* 28, no. 4 (1999), 605–14, available at http://www.dwillard.org/articles/artview.asp?artID=39.

are not helped by visuals." In the text, the objector may go on to cite documentation or offer further evidence in support of the objection. For instance, he may claim that the blind are not helped by visuals or that some people prefer text over visuals.

4. But many people are helped by accompanying visuals

The supporter of the conclusion now offers a rebuttal to the objection in point 3: "But many people are helped by accompanying visuals." Further documentation may be offered, or perhaps a partial agreement with the objection. For example, it might be noted that even though it is true that the blind or others are not helped by visuals, argument maps are still useful critical thinking tools (point 1, our conclusion).

5. Argument maps can help us see the broad overview of arguments and their structure

We now direct our attention near the top of the diagram as we return to another premise: "Argument maps can help us see the broad overview of arguments and their structure." Being able to see the broad overview and flow of a conclusion, premises, objections, and rebuttals, will help us to grasp the main points of an argument more quickly, including what we may deem strengths and weaknesses of its structure.

6. Text alone can accomplish the same thing

Point 6 objects to our conclusion and to premises 5 and 7, since it is connected to point 5 and point 7. In other words, one objection (point 6) can at times respond to more than one premise. The objector may here tout the value of text in and of itself, demonstrating its claimed superiority to visuals or diagrams. Notice that the rebuttal to point 6 leads to point 4, demonstrating that an individual rebuttal may also respond to more than one objection.

7. Argument maps help us process and understand various sides of an argument

As noted in the preface, one of the goals of this book is to emphasize the importance of understanding various sides of an argument, not just our own position. The text associated with point 7, then, would underscore this belief.

This concludes our tour of the sample argument diagram at the beginning of this chapter. At the end of each chapter, you'll find discussion questions suitable for individuals or groups (such as classrooms), as well as suggested assignments.

DISCUSSION QUESTIONS

1. Visualizing argument forms presents us with a different way of understanding arguments and their structures. What do you find helpful and/or unhelpful about argument maps? Why?
2. Would you find it difficult to create your own argument map or not? What would you find difficult or easy about creating your own argument map?
3. If you were to make an argument map, would you begin with your conclusion or your premises? Why would you approach your map that way?
4. Do you find it difficult to come up with objections that others might have to your conclusions and premises? What might make it easier for you to better understand other worldviews such as atheism and pantheism?
5. Critical thinking is a key aspect of creating, understanding, and evaluating an argument map. How would you characterize your skills in the area of critical thinking? What might you do to improve your abilities in this area?

SUGGESTED ASSIGNMENTS

1. Practice creating some simple argument maps. Pick a few conclusions or premises and make an argument map on paper. Assess how your maps turned out and improve them if you can.
2. Most conclusions in any argument map have some assumptions or presuppositions associated with them. Given the conclusion, "Christianity is true," make a list of what assumptions and presuppositions you believe go along with the conclusion. Do the same for the conclusion, "God does not exist."
3. Play the role of a contemporary atheist. List your best arguments against religious belief. Sketch an argument map that includes your arguments. Now take the position of a Christian theist and list your best arguments for your faith. Sketch an argument map that includes your arguments.

CHAPTER 2

Is Apologetics Necessary?

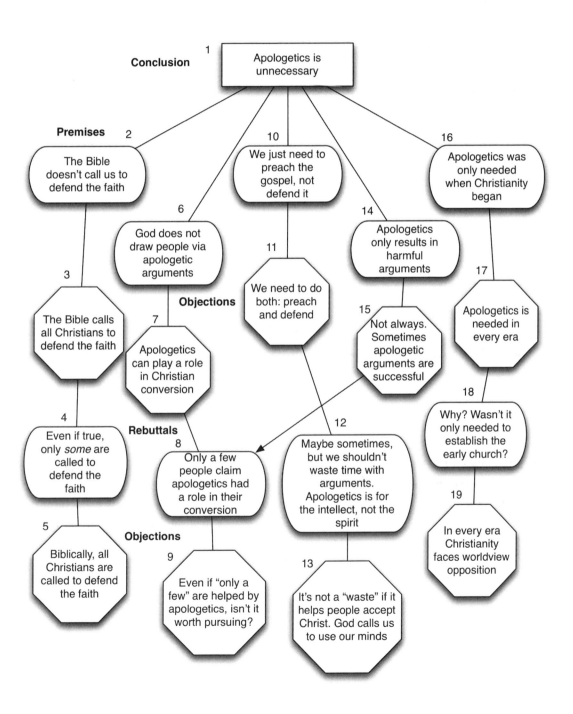

Conclusion

1 — Apologetics is unnecessary

Premises

2 — The Bible doesn't call us to defend the faith

10 — We just need to preach the gospel, not defend it

16 — Apologetics was only needed when Christianity began

6 — God does not draw people via apologetic arguments

14 — Apologetics only results in harmful arguments

Objections

3 — The Bible calls all Christians to defend the faith

7 — Apologetics can play a role in Christian conversion

11 — We need to do both: preach and defend

15 — Not always. Sometimes apologetic arguments are successful

17 — Apologetics is needed in every era

Rebuttals

4 — Even if true, only *some* are called to defend the faith

8 — Only a few people claim apologetics had a role in their conversion

12 — Maybe sometimes, but we shouldn't waste time with arguments. Apologetics is for the intellect, not the spirit

18 — Why? Wasn't it only needed to establish the early church?

5 — Biblically, all Christians are called to defend the faith

Objections

9 — Even if "only a few" are helped by apologetics, isn't it worth pursuing?

13 — It's not a "waste" if it helps people accept Christ. God calls us to use our minds

19 — In every era Christianity faces worldview opposition

1. Apologetics is unnecessary (Conclusion)	The conclusion dismisses the rational defense of the Christian faith as unnecessary. If true, then we don't need logical argumentation to convince others of the existence of God or the truth of Christianity.
2. The Bible doesn't call us to defend the faith (Premise)	The supporting premise argues that the Bible does not call us to defend the faith. The New Testament calls us to faith, not reason (see chapter 4). In fact, using arguments to support the faith may be a sign of lack of faith.
3. The Bible calls all Christians to defend the faith (Objection)	This is substantiated by a number of biblical verses such as 1 Peter 3:15: "But in your hearts honor Christ the Lord as holy, always being prepared to make a defense to anyone who asks you for a reason for the hope that is in you; yet do it with gentleness and respect." Nothing here states that making a defense (an apologetic) is unbiblical, or only for a select few, or only for the historical time of the apostles. Moreover, we find apologetics throughout the New Testament, especially, for instance, in the book of Acts. In Acts 17, Paul offers a sustained apologetic for Christianity in opposition to beliefs such as Stoicism, Epicureanism, and paganism.
4. Even if true, only *some* are called to defend the faith (Rebuttal)	But, this rebuttal argues, even if the preceding objection is true, not everyone is called to defend the faith, only some, such as those specially called to apologetics. And even in such cases, it's better to rely on a simple gospel presentation and faith alone. Pastors and teachers may be called to defend the faith at times, but most Christians don't need to bother with the defense of the faith.
5. Biblically, all Christians are called to defend the faith (Objection)	We may not all be experts or pastors or teachers, but every Christian is called to defend his or her faith. Passages such as 1 Peter 3:15 or the rest of the New Testament do not limit defending the faith to a select few, such as certain Christian callings or professions. We should all know what we believe and why we believe it and be prepared to defend it.

For example, 1 Peter 3:15 is clear in its apologetic calling to all Christians: "But in your hearts honor Christ the Lord as holy, always being prepared to make a defense to anyone who asks you for a reason for the hope that is in you; yet do it with gentleness and respect." Note a few important points indicated by the verse. First, apologetics is a holy endeavor wherein the

Christian should focus on honoring Christ. Second, preparation to defend the faith is paramount. Third, apologetics should not neglect the hope that Christian truth offers. Fourth, apologetics is not to be done in a manner that is unworthy of God, but "with gentleness and respect."

6. God does not draw people via apologetic arguments (Premise)

Apologetic arguments may be interesting to some people (mostly intellectual Christians), but in the real world God does not draw people to himself via apologetic arguments. Instead, God uses people who just preach the gospel (point 10) and who reach people's emotions, not their intellects (see chapter 3).

7. Apologetics can play a role in Christian conversion (Objection)

Point 6 is simply not true. God does use apologetic arguments as part of his way of drawing people to himself. Examples include C. S. Lewis and, more recently, popular apologist Lee Strobel, as well as the author of the book you are now reading. True, the Holy Spirit draws people in various ways, but apologetic arguments may appeal to the intellect and consequently break down barriers that keep someone from believing in God and Christianity.

In addition, apologetic arguments can strengthen the faith of believers, edifying them in their beliefs by offering good reasons for what they believe. This can prevent some Christians from falling away from faith due to a lack of proper grounding in the truth of their beliefs.

8. Only a few people claim apologetics had a role in their conversion (Rebuttal)

Even if some people claim apologetics had a role in their conversion, these are isolated incidents and not the norm. In the New Testament, people like Peter preached and thousands came to faith, but Peter did not need to offer arguments for God's existence or the resurrection. Most people don't come to faith because of arguments, but because of emotional reasons. Therefore, apologetics is not really that important.

9. Even if "only a few" are helped by apologetics, isn't it worth pursuing? (Objection)

First, it may be that far more people come to faith because apologetics helped them than we know. Second, "only a few" lives brought into God's eternal kingdom because of apologetics is enough to warrant its use. Third, we've already established that apologetics is biblical (point 3), so there's no good reason not to implement it in our case for the faith. Fourth, Peter is the same apostle who wrote 1 Peter 3:15, so he believed in offering answers and reasons for the faith.

The passages involving Peter preaching and thousands coming to faith must be interpreted in context. For instance, he was already preaching to theists (Jews), so there would be no reason to offer arguments for the existence of God. Besides, the new Christians did point to the reality of the resurrection of Christ as evidence of the truth of their faith, going so far as to call Christ's postresurrection appearances as proof of the truth of Christianity (Acts 1:3).

Fifth, those who come to faith because of emotional reasons are to be welcomed with open arms, but even they should have reasons for why they believe what they believe. Otherwise they are susceptible to falling away from faith because of unanswered doubts, something apologetics can help them overcome.

10. We just need to preach the gospel, not defend it (Premise)

The New Testament Christians just preached the gospel and people either accepted it or rejected it. We don't need to get fancy with apologetic arguments—it's God's job to convince people's hearts, not ours.

11. We need to do both: preach and defend (Objection)

It is not true that New Testament Christians only preached the gospel without defending it. See, for instance, *The Defense of the Gospel in the New Testament* by F. F. Bruce and *The Apologetics of Jesus* by Norman Geisler and Patrick Zukeran. God indeed convinces hearts, but he also convinces minds and cares about our intellects, and he wishes us to use our minds (chapter 3). Evangelism and apologetics are complementary.

12. Maybe sometimes, but we shouldn't waste time with arguments. Apologetics is for the intellect, not the spirit (Rebuttal)

It's more important to reach the heart, which demonstrates our faith, not win arguments in order to try to convince people. Why waste time with so many arguments, when the gospel by itself can have a powerful impact?

13. It's not a "waste" if it helps people accept Christ. God calls us to use our minds (Objection)

God cares about our hearts *and* our heads, desiring that we use both in our worship of him and in our search for truth (chapter 3). Therefore, it is not a "waste" to use such arguments. Some people are more open to intellectual arguments for faith than they are to emotional appeals that lack an intellectual foundation. It's true that the gospel by itself can have a powerful impact, and we should never neglect it, but it's also true that some people struggle with intellectual obstacles to the faith, which apologetics can help them overcome.

14. Apologetics only results in harmful arguments (Premise)

Nothing really good comes from harmful apologetic arguments that breed bickering, strife, and more heat than light, so why bother?

15. Not always. Sometimes apologetic arguments are successful (Objection)

It is true that some people are more enamored with winning arguments and being clever apologists than they are with effectively sharing and defending their faith. This is unfortunate, but such negative examples do not require entirely dismissing the rigorous intellectual defense of the faith via apologetics. According to 1 Peter 3:15, we are to defend the faith "with gentleness and respect." If we do so, adding a good dose of humility, then apologetics can be God-honoring.

16. Apologetics was only needed when Christianity began (Premise)

Apologetics may have been important when Christianity began, but it's not needed anymore (at least not as much as some people think). God needed to establish Christianity in its early days, so he allowed Jesus' followers to use reason and apologetics, but apologetics is not really needed anymore.

17. Apologetics is needed in every era (Objection)

Wherever competing worldviews exist, the rational defense of Christianity is necessary. Today in Western culture, Christianity faces numerous competing worldviews—pantheism, atheism, and Islam, to name a few. Even if there were no competing worldviews, apologetics can still contribute to glorifying God and edifying his people.

18. Why? Wasn't it only needed to establish the early church? (Rebuttal)

This rebuttal simply reiterates point 16.

19. In every era Christianity faces worldview opposition (Objection)

See point 17.

DISCUSSION QUESTIONS

1. What do you consider essentials of the Christian faith that apologists must defend?
2. Where does the Bible support the use of apologetics?
3. What issues in apologetics interest you the most?
4. Are there any apologetics issues that cause you to doubt your faith? If so, what can you do to address your concerns?
5. What objection in the argument diagram do you resonate with the most? The least?

SUGGESTED ASSIGNMENTS

1. Write a paper on Paul's address in Acts 17:16–32. Describe his apologetic and evangelistic approach.
2. Perform a research study on the history of apologetics, noting various key developments. Consult, for instance, *A History of Apologetics* by Avery Cardinal Dulles; *Faith Has Its Reasons* by Kenneth Boa and Robert Bowman; *Christian Apologetics: An Anthology of Primary Sources* edited by Khaldoun Sweis and Chad Meister; or the two volumes in *Christian Apologetics Past and Present* by William Edgar and K. Scott Oliphint.
3. Referring only to the diagram in this chapter, write your own text to go along with each point without consulting the text in this chapter.
4. Pick one of the objections (3, 7, 11, 15, or 17) and create a list of points supporting it. Then assess strengths and weaknesses of the objection.

CHAPTER 3

Is Intellect Essential to the Christian Life?

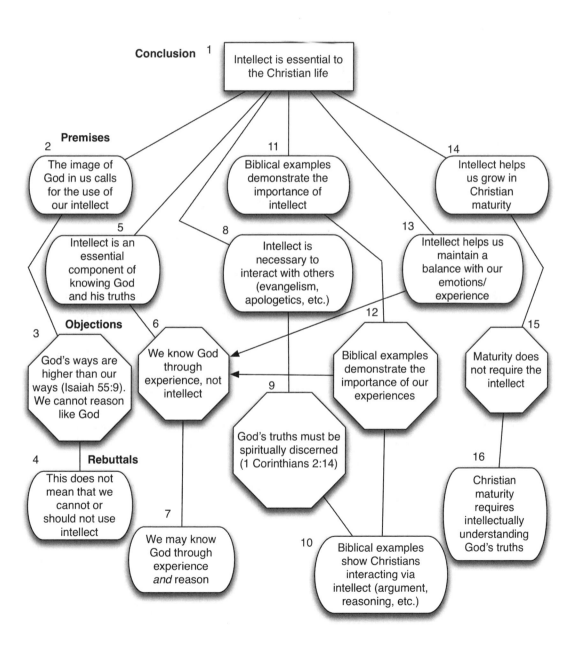

Conclusion 1

Intellect is essential to the Christian life

Premises

2 The image of God in us calls for the use of our intellect

5 Intellect is an essential component of knowing God and his truths

11 Biblical examples demonstrate the importance of intellect

14 Intellect helps us grow in Christian maturity

8 Intellect is necessary to interact with others (evangelism, apologetics, etc.)

13 Intellect helps us maintain a balance with our emotions/experience

Objections

3 God's ways are higher than our ways (Isaiah 55:9). We cannot reason like God

6 We know God through experience, not intellect

12 Biblical examples demonstrate the importance of our experiences

15 Maturity does not require the intellect

Rebuttals

4 This does not mean that we cannot or should not use intellect

9 God's truths must be spiritually discerned (1 Corinthians 2:14)

16 Christian maturity requires intellectually understanding God's truths

7 We may know God through experience *and* reason

10 Biblical examples show Christians interacting via intellect (argument, reasoning, etc.)

1. Intellect is essential to the Christian life (Conclusion)

The conclusion values the life of the mind in relation to Christian belief. But is intellect really essential to the Christian life? Critics of this conclusion offer a multitude of objections (points 3, 6, 9, 12, and 15). If, however, the conclusion is true, then it is beneficial for Christians to cultivate the intellect in the Christian life. Doing so will result in many positive benefits to culture at large and to the church. Moreover, by using our God-given intellects, we may glorify our Creator who is the source of our reasoning abilities. Intellect, in addition, need not negate our emotions. We are not logic machines, but neither are we to fully embrace the spectrum of our emotions without applying our powers of thought.

2. The image of God in us calls for the use of our intellect (Premise)

This premise points to the *imago Dei*, noting that God's image in us calls for the use of our intellect. Genesis 1:26–27 informs us we are made in God's image. Theologians interpret this fact as encompassing a number of areas including our creative imagination, moral awareness, and intellectual capacity. By using our minds in relation to our faith, we honor God.

3. God's ways are higher than our ways (Isaiah 55:9). We cannot reason like God (Objection)

This objection points to biblical evidence demonstrating that God is "higher" than us, and therefore, applying our minds to matters of faith is needless and hopeless. We can never achieve anything close to the intellect of God, so we need not attempt to do so. In fact, some may even argue that attempting to use our intellect in such a manner may dishonor God and cause pride in us. Others claim that since God is in such a higher category than us, we can never reason like him. What if God is beyond reason? Why should we play by the rules of our human logic?

4. This does not mean that we cannot or should not use intellect (Rebuttal)

Using Isaiah 55:9 to claim that Christians need not use reasoning is invalid. Doing so fails to take into account the whole of Scripture. While it is true that God as Creator is in a different class than limited human creatures, this does not mean that God has not called us to reason for our faith (see the other premises, for instance). We acknowledge that God is all-powerful and sovereign, but this does not mean that we cannot use our God-given reasoning abilities constructively. As far as God being "beyond reason," this is a false view (see point 11).

Furthermore, "human logic" is not a creation or invention of human beings but is rooted in God's very nature. God is the source of the foundational laws of logic, and throughout its pages the Bible demonstrates God's adherence to fundamental laws of logic, such as the law of identity, the law of noncontradiction, and the laws of rational inference. Without logic, we could not understand the Bible and neither could it have been created. The Bible contains logically coherent sentences in order to communicate God's truths. In doing so, it adheres to foundational laws of logic.

For instance, many passages describe the nature of God, including his attributes. In order to do so, these passages use the law of identity (A is A). Whenever we read that God is like something, the law of identity is at play, describing what God is like using language we can understand.

Moreover, whenever we read that God is *not* like something, the law of noncontradiction is being utilized (A is not non-A). See, for example, Numbers 23:19, where we are told, "God is not a man, that he should lie, nor a son of man, that he should change his mind" (NIV). Again, in 2 Corinthians 1:18, Paul states, "our message to you is not 'Yes' and 'No,'" which also supports the law of noncontradiction.

5. Intellect is an essential component of knowing God and his truths (Premise)

Without utilizing intellect, we could not know anything meaningful about God. God has made us to know via intellect. Some may argue that our intellect is so depraved as to leave us without viable recourse in using it properly. While it is true that we are fallen beings and depravity does impact our intellectual capacities, it is not true that we are completely unable to use our intellect in the pursuit of truth or in the defense of the faith. Biblical examples support the Christian use of the intellect (point 11).

6. We know God through experience, not intellect (Objection)

But we know God through experience, not intellect. Intellect can fail us, as was even noted in point 5. Since our intellect is fallen and depraved, we have no guarantees that we are reasoning properly or coming to right conclusions. It is, therefore, more reliable to turn to experience as our guide. Through personal religious experience, we can know much about God without appealing to the intellect.

7. We may know God through experience and reason (Rebuttal)

There is nothing in the conclusion that excludes well-founded religious experience in relation to knowing God or playing a role in faith (see chapter 25). Both may play an important role in the Christian life.

8. Intellect is necessary to interact with others (evangelism, apologetics, etc.) (Premise)

Intellect is essential to the Christian life because through it we interact with others, including fellow Christians and non-Christians, via evangelism, apologetics, and more. In order to share even the basic message of the gospel we must use intellect. Even if we think we are avoiding "doctrine" or "theology," the very act of sharing even the basics of the gospel involves us in intellectual questions about what we are sharing. Both evangelism and apologetics, then, require the use of the intellect.

9. God's truths must be spiritually discerned (1 Corinthians 2:14) (Objection)

But what of passages such as 1 Corinthians 2:14: "The natural person does not accept the things of the Spirit of God, for they are folly to him, and he is not able to understand them because they are spiritually discerned." Doesn't this mean that attempting to use intellect when sharing or defending the faith is fruitless? Instead, it is the Holy Spirit who draws people, not our intellectual arguments.

10. Biblical examples show Christians interacting via intellect (argument, reasoning, etc.) (Rebuttal)

In response to objections 9 and 12, those who hold such positions must either deny the biblical evidence in support of reasoning or turn to another solution, such as our experiences. Biblical examples demonstrate the value of the intellect (point 11) as well as showing that early Christians valued this approach. One need only turn to the pages of the book of Acts, where Christians are found reasoning with non-Christians (Acts 17:2, 17; 18:4, 19; 19:8; 24:25). Such reasoning involved careful dialogue and intellectual persuasion, as exemplified by the apostle Paul in his encounter with the Athenians in Acts 17. Paul proclaimed and defended the truth of Christianity intellectually.

As far as a response to point 12 is concerned, the Matthew 22:37–38 passage is in context about loving God, but it does nevertheless stress the use of the intellect in relation to loving God. By extension, we can apply the use of the intellect to other areas such as evangelism and apologetics, as many biblical examples demonstrate. Moreover, Paul's apologetic in Acts 17 was not a failure, as some of his hearers became Christians (Acts 17:34). We must also keep in mind that Paul was not preaching to theists, but to nontheists. Therefore, it was expected that not as many would respond to his message. The fact that "some men joined him and believed him" is a testimony to the power of the gospel message to reach minds and hearts.

11. Biblical examples demonstrate the importance of intellect (Premise)	See point 10 for a list of a number of verses in Acts that demonstrate the importance of the intellect. To this we may also add passages such as Isaiah 1:18 where God says, "Come now, and let us reason together, says the Lord" (NASB). God values the power of reasoning, going so far as to invite humans to reason with him. Lest we think this is an isolated Old Testament anomaly, we also have the very words of Christ supporting the life of the mind: "And He said to him, 'You shall love the Lord your God with all your heart, and with all your soul, and with all your mind. This is the great and foremost commandment" (Matt. 22:37–38 NASB). In other words, our entire being, including the mind, must be involved in demonstrating our love for God. Christ, too, demonstrated the importance of reasoning in relating to others, often integrating many logical argument forms in his dialogues.[1]
12. Biblical examples demonstrate the importance of our experiences (Objection)	See points 6 and 7. It may be argued that many biblical examples of Christians using their intellects in defense of the faith resulted in failure, such as Acts 17. As far as Matthew 22:37–38 is concerned, those who object to the use of the intellect may argue that the passage relates only to our love for God, not to sharing or defending our faith with others.
13. Intellect helps us maintain a balance with our emotions/ experience (Premise)	God did not make us only logical or only emotional. While it is true that some possess inherent tendencies toward logic or emotion, God made us in a way that includes both reason and emotion in our being. The danger in becoming too intellectual is that we might neglect our experiential, emotional love of God; but there is also the danger of becoming so emotionally centered that we neglect to truly grasp God via our intellect. Given that much of conservative Western Christianity has turned away from intellectual pursuits, the current condition of much of the church demands a revival of the intellectual life. We should not do so at the expense of the emotions; however, intellect helps us maintain a balance with our emotions and experience of God.

---

1. See, for instance, *On Jesus* by Douglas Groothuis, *Habits of the Mind* by James Sire, and *The Apologetics of Jesus* by Norman Geisler and Patrick Zukeran.

14. Intellect helps us grow in Christian maturity (Premise)	If all we did was pursue our emotional experience of God, we would quickly become emotionally drained or burned out. Human beings were not made to constantly run on high emotions. Intellect, then, can help us grow in Christian maturity. Moreover, worship of God need not be confined to worship services or specific times of emotional worship. Intellectual pursuits can form a part of our worship of the holy God. As we learn more about God and his ways intellectually, we grow in Christian maturity individually and, in turn, help others learn as well.
15. Maturity does not require the intellect (Objection)	But what if maturity does not require the intellect? In Revelation we read of God's people constantly worshiping him with songs and praises, not studying and cloistered in libraries around books worshiping God with their intellects. People can be mature Christians without the intellect.
16. Christian maturity requires intellectually understanding God's truths (Rebuttal)	See point 5. Biblical depictions of eternal worship of God need not exclude the intellect. Given the biblical evidence in support of the intellectual life (point 11), it is reasonable to conclude that even in heaven we will continue intellectual pursuits and value the life of the mind. Maturity, moreover, cannot solely focus on our experiences (point 14). Throughout history, people of God have worshiped and glorified him with their intellects, leaving the church and the world richer for having done so, not poorer. If some of the greatest minds of history are Christians, and some of the greatest contemporary minds in different fields are also Christians, this honors God and the church as well as helping fellow believers grow in Christian maturity.

DISCUSSION QUESTIONS

1. Do you tend to gravitate more to the intellectual or experiential aspects of the Christian life? What might you do to find a better balance?
2. How does the image of God in us relate to the life of the mind?
3. Are there situations where our human emotions are more valuable than our intellect?
4. What does 1 Corinthians 2:14 mean in relation to apologetics? Given the broader context of what Scripture says about apologetics, such as 1 Peter 3:15, how should we address the "natural person" who rejects God's truths?
5. What are three specific things you can do to help yourself grow in intellectual maturity as a follower of Christ?

SUGGESTED ASSIGNMENTS

1. Read *Love Your God with All Your Mind* by J. P. Moreland, then write a critique and evaluation of it.
2. Read *Habits of the Mind* by James Sire and write a summary of the main points in each chapter.
3. Select an area of apologetic interest that you know little about and research a recent Christian book on the subject that you will commit to reading within a month.
4. Find out if there is a group in your church already established or if you can establish one for the purposes of intentionally seeking to grow intellectually as Christians. Subjects you may choose include theology, apologetics, philosophy, other religions, or understanding worldviews.
5. Compile a list of biblical passages that address questions regarding the life of the mind, and study those passages in context. See, for example, Romans 12:2, Matthew 22:37–38, and 1 Peter 3:15, and study the context and message of the passages, consulting biblical commentaries for further insights.

CHAPTER 4

How Are Faith and Reason Related?

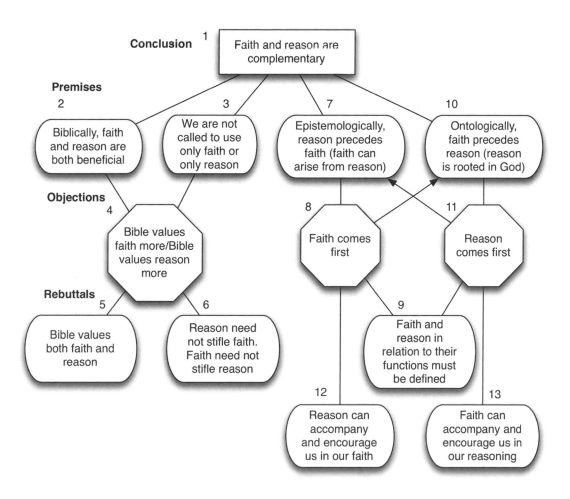

Conclusion   1

Faith and reason are complementary

Premises

2

Biblically, faith and reason are both beneficial

3

We are not called to use only faith or only reason

7

Epistemologically, reason precedes faith (faith can arise from reason)

10

Ontologically, faith precedes reason (reason is rooted in God)

Objections

4

Bible values faith more/Bible values reason more

8

Faith comes first

11

Reason comes first

Rebuttals

5

Bible values both faith and reason

6

Reason need not stifle faith. Faith need not stifle reason

9

Faith and reason in relation to their functions must be defined

12

Reason can accompany and encourage us in our faith

13

Faith can accompany and encourage us in our reasoning

1. Faith and reason are complementary (Conclusion)

The issue of the relationship between faith and reason involves different theological approaches and solutions. The view taken in this argument map is that faith and reason are complementary. In other words, rather than being in opposition or competition, faith and reason complement one another and are both of value theologically, philosophically, and apologetically. Moreover, there are no marked imbalances in this complementary relationship between faith and reason, such as a view of epistemology that places reason as supreme (as in rationalism) or one that places faith as supreme (as in empiricism or experience). Both forms of reasoning can contribute to our understanding of reality.

2. Biblically, faith and reason are both beneficial (Premise)

In examining the biblical record, we find evidence of both faith and reason being beneficial. Christians are not called to blind faith or to reason only. Indeed, our reasoning abilities, while still present and capable, are fallen and thus more prone to error than God originally intended. Yet although the image of God in us is marred, including our intellectual capacities, it is not erased. Especially for the Christian relying on God, our reasoning capabilities should be employed to seek the glory of God and should be guided by precision and a desire for clear thinking. Reason allows us to understand theological concepts, interact with non-Christians, and more. Faith, however, also plays a critical role. At some point our evidences will fall short of the ideal, thus requiring faith.

3. We are not called to use only faith or only reason (Premise)

As noted briefly in point 2, we are not called to use only faith or only reason. The two are intertwined, so to speak, in a complementary manner. Faith and reason both serve their purposes in God's plan.

4. Bible values faith more/ Bible values reason more (Objection)

Some object by noting that the Bible values either faith more or reason more. Those who argue for the former point to key passages involving faith, which appear to elevate it above human reason. For instance, Hebrews 11:6 informs us that "without faith it is impossible to please God" (NIV). Others who would defend the latter position argue that the Bible values reason more. Passages such as Matthew 22:37–38, for instance, call us to love God with "all your mind." If either of these views is exclusively correct, then it is not possible that faith and reason are complementary, or at least not to the extent made by the conclusion in point 1. One may be more valuable than the other.

5. Bible values both faith and reason (Rebuttal)

The Bible, however, can value both faith and reason without either viewpoint being mutually exclusive. Hebrews 11:6, for example, need not exclude the life of the mind or its value (see chapter 3). Hebrews 11 underscores the value of faith, but not at the expense of reason. The passage quoted continues, "for whoever would draw near to God must believe that he exists." But this does not mean that we cannot believe God exists based on reasoned arguments for his existence (chapter 6). Faith without reason in such cases may amount to blind faith, which does not correspond with God's desire for us to use our minds (Matt. 22:37–38) or to "examine everything carefully" (1 Thess. 5:21 NASB).

6. Reason need not stifle faith. Faith need not stifle reason (Rebuttal)

Moreover, reason need not stifle faith or vice versa. Reason can bolster our faith, edifying believers in the truths of the faith by offering sound intellectual support for the existence of God, the historicity of Christ, and more. Reason can also help us interact with non-Christians, as evidenced in many passages in Acts where Paul "reasoned" not only with Jews and God-fearing Greeks but also with nontheists (pagans, polytheists, Stoics, and Epicureans).

The first followers of Christ never told someone who did not believe to "just believe" without appealing to some kind of evidence, such as the testimony of the resurrection. One may also have great faith yet still rely on reason to support such faith.

7. Epistemologically, reason precedes faith (faith can arise from reason) (Premise)

Does reason precede faith or does faith precede reason? In relation to knowledge (epistemology), reason appears to precede faith, which can arise from reason. We apprehend and understand doctrinal truths, for instance, with our reason. Believing that God exists requires that we understand the concept of God in a theistic context before we can have faith in such a being. Thus, faith can arise from reason.

However, we must be careful to note that both faith and reason come from God. As such, any faith that reason produces is the result of God working in our lives. Left to ourselves, human beings are incapable of truly apprehending God or his truths.

8. Faith comes first (Objection)	This objection argues that faith comes first, clearly indicating that reason is subordinate to belief, or at least comes later.
9. Faith and reason in relation to their functions must be defined (Rebuttal)	If we understand the roles of faith and reason in relation to their functions (epistemology, ontology [see glossary]), then the apparent difficulty of reconciling points 8 and 11 can be explained and surmounted. Reason comes first epistemologically speaking, while faith comes first ontologically speaking. Note: Epistemology has to do with knowledge, while ontology is related to being.
10. Ontologically, faith precedes reason (reason is rooted in God) (Premise)	The fact that God exists necessarily precedes any knowledge we can have of him. Consequently, in this ontological respect, faith precedes our reason, knowledge, and understanding of God.
11. Reason comes first (Objection)	This point would seem to follow from point 7, at least in reference to epistemology.
12. Reason can accompany and encourage us in our faith (Rebuttal)	As noted earlier, reason can accompany and encourage us in our faith as well as help us dialogue with non-Christians. This last point is particularly important. Non-Christians are obviously not yet adherents of the Christian worldview and therefore cannot be expected to accept Christ on the basis of unsubstantiated faith (though God can certainly lead non-Christians to himself however he wishes). Offering reasons and evidence for faith can help guide non-Christians toward truth, thus encouraging faith by providing a foundation for it.
13. Faith can accompany and encourage us in our reasoning (Rebuttal)	Conversely, faith can accompany and encourage us in our reasoning. If we truly believe in the living God and all that his attributes encompass, then we can be reassured in our intellectual endeavors, knowing that God has sanctioned the use of the intellect for the furtherance of his truths.

DISCUSSION QUESTIONS

1. Which resonates with you more, faith or reason? Why do you think this is?
2. When it comes to believing in God, do you believe faith precedes reason or that reason precedes faith? How so?
3. How might an overemphasis on either faith or reason have positive or negative results in your Christian walk?
4. How does the question of the relationship between faith and reason relate to the task of apologetics?
5. What biblical figure comes to mind when you think of a person of faith? What biblical figure comes to mind when you think of a person of reason? What qualities do these individuals exhibit?

SUGGESTED ASSIGNMENTS

1. Research the view of faith and reason expounded by Augustine and Aquinas and prepare a short report on the subject. Seek to critically and biblically evaluate your findings.
2. Perform a Bible study on faith and reason, noting relevant passages and their contextual meanings.
3. Select a Christian proponent of fideism—the view that religious truth is based solely on faith, not reason—and evaluate his or her position in relation to faith and reason (for instance, Søren Kierkegaard or Karl Barth).

PART 2

Arguments for God and Christianity

CHAPTER 5

Christianity Is True

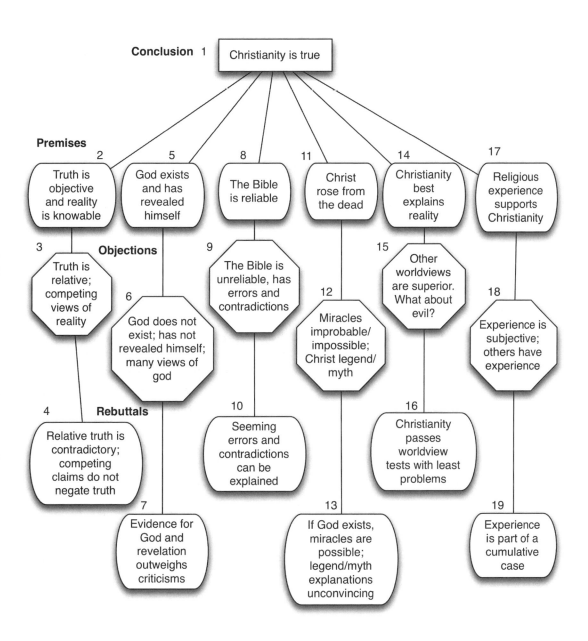

Conclusion 1
Christianity is true

Premises

2 — Truth is objective and reality is knowable

5 — God exists and has revealed himself

8 — The Bible is reliable

11 — Christ rose from the dead

14 — Christianity best explains reality

17 — Religious experience supports Christianity

Objections

3 — Truth is relative; competing views of reality

6 — God does not exist; has not revealed himself; many views of god

9 — The Bible is unreliable, has errors and contradictions

12 — Miracles improbable/impossible; Christ legend/myth

15 — Other worldviews are superior. What about evil?

18 — Experience is subjective; others have experience

Rebuttals

4 — Relative truth is contradictory; competing claims do not negate truth

7 — Evidence for God and revelation outweighs criticisms

10 — Seeming errors and contradictions can be explained

13 — If God exists, miracles are possible; legend/myth explanations unconvincing

16 — Christianity passes worldview tests with least problems

19 — Experience is part of a cumulative case

1. Christianity is true (Conclusion)

This argument map presents a case for Christian theism. Some people will add to or merge its elements while others will modify them. Fideists, for instance, might disagree with the entire endeavor of making a rational case for Christianity; for them, the conclusion itself is absolute in the diagram. But some apologists may choose to make a softer argument, claiming instead that Christian theism is not absolutely true but most likely true, especially in comparison with other worldviews. This lack of absolute certainty in the conclusion need not mean that the Christian has doubts about the faith or is uncertain regarding its veracity, but may merely serve as a stronger rhetorical position in making the case for Christianity.

Regardless of whether the conclusion is presented as "Christianity is true" or some variation of "Christianity is most likely true," the supporting premises remain valuable. It should be stressed, however, that the conclusion is presented as a truth claim, not a taste claim. In other words, the proposition that Christianity is true is either true or false; it is not a mere matter of preference or taste. What we are seeking to determine is whether or not the Christian worldview corresponds to reality or not.

2. Truth is objective and reality is knowable (Premise)

While there have always been skeptics throughout history, until fairly recent times most people would have agreed that truth is objective and reality is knowable. Unfortunately, this is not necessarily the case in the early twenty-first century. With the rise of relativistic thinking, postmodernism, and skeptical epistemology, the contemporary apologist must be able to defend the objectivity of truth, present a biblical view of truth, and defend reality as knowable. If someone already agrees that truth is objective and reality is knowable, such as most other non-Christian theists, then the apologist need not take the time to go over this premise unless confusion arises.

Nevertheless, this is a significant premise. In order for Christianity to be true, truth must be objective and reality must be knowable. In other words, this premise not only provides a prerequisite to the viability of the Christian worldview but also serves as a support for the conclusion (see chapter 7).

3. Truth is relative, competing views of reality (Objection)

We cannot here anticipate every response to point 2, which claims that "truth is objective and reality is knowable." Many scientifically minded atheists, for instance, will readily agree with point 2. Their disagreements will arise when it is claimed that Christianity is true. Such atheists understand antithesis (noncontradiction) and accept that if Christianity is true, then atheism is false (and vice versa). Variations of pantheists are more likely to argue, somewhat paradoxically, that truth is relative. Others may take a more pluralistic approach, claiming that since there are many competing views of reality, we really can't know which view is true; or that all religious views of reality somehow mean the same thing and point to the same thing. We will address these points somewhat in point 4.

4. Relative truth is contradictory; competing claims do not negate truth (Rebuttal)

This is in response to point 3, "Truth is relative, competing views of reality." As we have suggested earlier, it is somewhat contradictory to claim with seeming certainty that truth is not relative, since that is itself presented as a truth claim, and an absolute one at that.

Here the Christian must make the case for the objectivity of truth, presenting and defending the biblical view of truth. One way to do this is to examine the leading viable theories of truth, such as the correspondence view, coherence view, and pragmatic view (see glossary). All of these views of truth have serious deficiencies, with the exception of the biblical, correspondence view. If this is the case, then the objective view of truth, as championed by the biblical view of truth, offers a far more reasonable and compelling explanation of truth. Another approach is to contrast an objective view of truth with alternatives, such as a relative view of truth. In practice, a relative view of truth cannot sustain itself because, for one, if it is believed that the relative view of truth is, in fact, true, then that very claim defeats the relative view of truth.

Moreover, the fact that there are competing views of reality does not make them either all false or all true. They may indeed all be false, but they cannot all be true since many of them are contradictory. For instance, God cannot both exist and not exist, be impersonal and personal, or reveal himself and not reveal himself. The law of noncontradiction helps us discern truth (see chapter 2).

Sifting through so many competing worldviews, both religious and nonreligious, may be confusing and difficult, but that does not mean that truth is unattainable. Sometimes it is hard to reach, but it is not unreachable.

5. God exists and has revealed himself (Premise)

Some apologists separate this premise into two parts: (1) God exists, and (2) God has revealed himself. To keep it simple, both points are included here in one premise. In order for Christianity to be considered true, God must exist. Without a transcendent God, Christianity collapses into a man-made philosophy. Unless a theistic God exists, miracles in the Christian sense are impossible and, moreover, Christ cannot be a member of the Godhead. It is the job of the apologist, when necessary, to make the case for the existence of the theistic God on which Christianity is dependent.

The revelation portion of this point involves whether or not God has revealed himself, and if so, how? Christian thinkers believe that God has revealed himself via both general and special revelation. General revelation refers to God's revelation in nature and in human moral conscience, while special revelation typically refers to God's Word and the person of Christ. Some thinkers emphasize one form of revelation over the other, while others give both forms equal weight.

6. God does not exist, has not revealed himself, many views of God (Objection)

This objection is in some ways similar to the objection in point 3 that there are many views of reality. One part of the objection in point 6 is that there are many views of God, which is supposed to cause doubt regarding Christianity's claims to truth. The other part of this point is simple. If one claims firmly that God does not exist, or probably does not exist, then point 5 has little weight. Obviously, if God does not exist then he cannot in any way reveal himself. Others may claim that some "God" or something like "God" exists, but he either does not reveal himself at all or he reveals himself in ways different from Christian claims.

7. Evidence for God and revelation outweighs criticisms (Rebuttal)

This rebuttal is in response to point 6, which in turn is in response to point 5. There is a rich history of Christian responses to the claim that God does not exist and has not revealed himself. As such, the Christian must draw on this rich history in responding to criticisms regarding God's existence.

Typical arguments are grouped into one of four catego-

---

1. Cosmological arguments argue from the fact of the universe to the reality of a God behind it; teleological arguments claim that evidence of design, such as design in nature, is evidence of a designer; axiological arguments make the case that evidence of moral standards point to a transcendent source of morality (God); and ontological arguments, though somewhat abstract for the layperson, claim that the very idea of God must require his existence.

ries: cosmological (universe), teleological (design), axiological (moral), and ontological (being).[1] But many other arguments for God exist as well as variations of the four broad categories.

As to the claim that there are many views of God, how does this have any bearing on whether or not God exists? One must dig deeper and ask the critic what he or she means. For instance, the argument beneath this claim may be that God is too hidden and, as such, has not adequately revealed himself to make his existence clearly known. Or the argument may be that if God really does exist, then why has he allowed so many competing views of himself to circulate throughout human history and in various cultures?

8. The Bible is reliable (Premise)

Some apologists place more weight than others on the reliability of the Bible in making the overall case for Christianity. However, it makes sense to incorporate reliable Scriptures as part of the case for Christian theism. If, for instance, the Bible contains errors even in areas that are not directly about theology, then the question often arises in the mind of the critic, "If the Bible is not reliable in this area, then how can I trust it in areas of faith?" Consequently, more conservative apologists typically will make a case for the reliability, authority, and inerrancy of the Bible.

When making the case for Christian theism, one may choose to emphasize the reliability of the New Testament, since that is where we find material about the person of Christ. As a subset of this approach, one may choose to focus on the reliability of the four gospels. In any event, in order for us to viably test and evaluate the truth claims of Christianity, we must have a reliable source of those claims. How is the Bible said to be reliable? Various apologetic approaches exist, but most commonly the extensive manuscript evidence in support of the accuracy of the Bible is offered as evidence of its reliability, since this demonstrates that the text has remained unchanged over the centuries (with the exception of minor copyist errors known as variants that do not alter the substance of the text). Some also point to the archaeological and historical evidence that supports rather than contradicts the Bible, thus demonstrating that the Bible contains an accurate record of people, places, and events. Internal consistency of the biblical text is another example of its reliability, while others may add key prophetic elements.

9. Bible is unreliable, has errors and contradictions (Objection)

Surprisingly, this objection may at times come from other theists, such as Muslims or Jews. In the case of Muslims, for instance, while they will revere the Old and New Testaments, in reality they will often criticize the New Testament for being filled with errors and consequently unreliable. Atheists, too, may object to the reliability of the Bible, often claiming it is full of contradictions, historical errors, scientific shortcomings, or other defeaters.

10. Seeming errors and contradictions can be explained (Rebuttal)

Responding to point 9 is often a matter of simply knowing the information available in making the case for biblical reliability. Often, a seeming contradiction is just that—*seeming*. Further inspection and analysis will clear up most claims of alleged contradictions.

Keep in mind, too, that often it is our theology or our interpretation of the Bible that is wrong, not the Bible itself. Still, the honest Christian must leave room for falsifiability. We need not take the blindly dedicated position that the Bible is beyond inspection or reproach. We may hold this view personally as Christians, but when interacting with non-Christians, we should allow room for "testing" Scripture, being open to honest criticisms and willing to seek out honest answers.

In addition, it is often the Christian's job to make a positive case for biblical reliability and to always ask the critic for a specific example of an error or contradiction. Most such criticisms are readily addressed using rudimentary principles of biblical interpretation (hermeneutics).

11. Christ rose from the dead (Premise)

The resurrection of Christ is central to Christianity. Without it, Christianity collapses. See the diagram on the resurrection in chapter 10 for more on this premise.

12. Miracles improbable/ impossible, Christ legend/myth (Objection)

Most contemporary objections to miracles are rooted in eighteenth-century Enlightenment criticisms, such as those of David Hume. If miracles are improbable or impossible, then Christianity is stripped of its miracles, including the resurrection. But without these miracles, Christianity becomes meaningless.

Other critics argue that even if Christ did exist, the New Testament records of him are likely legendary or even mythical. This includes the resurrection account, which some say bears striking resemblances to similar claims of pagan religions that predate Christianity.

13. If God exists, miracles are possible; legend/myth explanations unconvincing (Rebuttal)

Recall that this rebuttal is in response to criticisms of the claim that Christ rose from the dead (point 11). A deist, for instance, believes that God exists, but does not believe that God is active (immanent) in the world and, therefore, the deistic God does not perform miracles in history (though ironically, deists accept that God created the universe—surely an event worthy of the miraculous!).

Typically, however, the criticisms in point 12 are raised by skeptics, atheists, and secular humanists. Their claim, usually related to point 6, is that because God does not exist in the first place, he cannot perform miracles. The job of the Christian, then, is to make the case for the existence of God as well as the case for miracles.[2]

He or she must also be able to articulate why claims that Jesus was a myth or legend fail. For instance, there is ample evidence for the historicity of Christ. And not enough time passed from the time of Christ to the recording of the New Testament for myth or legend to develop.

14. Christianity best explains reality (Premise)

This is a broad but important premise. Those who claim Christianity is true should do so in part because that worldview offers the best explanation of reality. If a competing worldview, such as atheism or pantheism or their variations, offers a superior explanation of reality, then why should Christians continue to defend a worldview that is less than the best explanation of reality?

This premise may encompass a number of other areas of inquiry including metaphysics, epistemology, ethics, and so forth. For instance, does Christianity best explain the meaning of life? Or the reality of evil and suffering? These and other "big questions" are encompassed in this premise.

15. Other worldviews are superior. What about evil? (Objection)

Obviously, those who reject Christianity must believe their worldview is superior to the claims of Christian theism. This is a logical rejection *if* it is true that other worldviews are superior to Christianity and in reality *do* offer better explanations of reality.

A common point here is that the reality of the Christian God cannot be satisfactorily reconciled with the reality of evil

---

2. On miracles, see *Miracles* by C. S. Lewis, *In Defense of Miracles* edited by R. Douglas Geivett and Gary Habermas, and *Miracles and the Modern Mind* by Norman Geisler.

and suffering in the world. Since evil and suffering appear random, and there are signs of gratuitous evil, it makes more sense that God does not exist. So claim the typical atheist critics. A pantheist may take a different approach, denying the reality of evil entirely by calling it mere illusion while still believing that her worldview best explains reality.

The problem of evil is underscored in this objection because it is often brought up against Christianity (see chapter 14).

16. Christianity passes worldview tests with least problems (Rebuttal)

When others claim that alternative worldviews offer better explanations of reality, the Christian must offer reasons why Christianity in fact offers the best explanations and why the explanations of other worldviews are deficient. Christianity, for example, is a robust worldview that passes several worldview tests, such as logical consistency, historical investigation, correspondence with reality (e.g., empirical facts), support from many lines of evidence and reasoning, and existential livability.

To name just a few serious problems with competing worldviews, both atheism and pantheism offer deficient explanations of evil as well as of morality in general, including its source, objectivity, and meaning. Atheism has no logical grounds for calling anything good or evil, since it denies the reality of a transcendent God and says human existence is the result of an undirected, impersonal process. Monistic pantheism denies that evil actually exists, despite much evidence to the contrary.

17. Religious experience supports Christianity (Premise)

Sometimes apologists shy away from religious experience as part of a case for Christian theism. At times this is warranted. For example, we do not want to make religious experience the cornerstone of a case for Christianity. If we do, then how do we resolve conflicts with others who have experiences based on worldviews that contradict Christianity? How do we explain the religious experience of a Hindu, Buddhist, Muslim, or adherent of any number of religious viewpoints? So religious experience is not sufficient in itself to make a strong case for Christianity; however, it may serve as part of a cumulative case for it (see chapter 25). In other words, in conjunction with points 2, 5, 8, 11, and 14, religious experience can indeed bolster the overall case for the truth of the Christian worldview.

18. Experience is subjective; others have experience (Objection)	This objection tends to isolate religious experience as being the supreme or sole argument in support of belief. This is not the case. Nevertheless, the objection can have a degree of merit, especially in cases where Christians overemphasize experience as the only or best test of truth. This is because other worldviews can indeed point to experience too. If a Hindu, Buddhist, or atheist claims that his personal experience verifies his worldview, while a Christian does the same, how, then, can one determine which, if any, of these worldviews is true?
19. Experience is part of a cumulative case (Rebuttal)	The Christian should not make point 17 a stand alone argument for Christianity. However, a religious experience argument for Christianity can be incorporated as part of a cumulative case for Christian theism. In such a context, it becomes a valid and useful part of a larger whole.

Since religious experience alone cannot be the ultimate test of the truth or falsity of any worldviews, we must carefully examine other factors such as that raised in point 14: Which worldview offers the best explanation of reality? This does not mean that the worldview that offers the best overall explanation of reality will have no deficiencies, but it should mean that as a whole its deficiencies are not nearly as challenging as the deficiencies found in competing worldviews, including those whose practitioners claim religious experiences to validate them.

Objection 18 assumes that the Christian is presenting the premise from religious experience (point 17) as a stand-alone argument for Christianity, but this is not true (or, at least, it should not be). What the Christian should argue is that religious experience has a valid place as part of a broader argument for Christianity, not that religious experience is the sole argument for the truth of Christianity. It is true that others have religious experiences as well, but one must also take into account other arguments supporting the truth claims of other religions. When assessed as a whole, which worldview offers the best explanation of reality? (See point 14.)

DISCUSSION QUESTIONS

1. Six premises are presented in the diagram in overall support of the truth of the Christian worldview. Which premise resonates with you the most? The least? Would you add additional premises? If so, what are they?
2. Which objection to Christianity in the diagram do you find the strongest? Why? How would you respond to it?
3. Which objection to Christianity in the diagram do you find the weakest? Why do you think someone would hold to that particular objection?
4. Examine the rebuttals, then imagine that you are continuing to add to the argument diagram. What objections would fall under each rebuttal?
5. How certain do you believe we can be when it comes to the conclusion, "Christianity is true"? Can we be certain or is it based on a degree of probability?

SUGGESTED ASSIGNMENTS

1. Read *The God Who Is There* by Francis Schaeffer or *Total Truth* by Nancy Pearcey, then write a report emphasizing how these works contribute to the overall case for the validity of the Christian worldview in light of contemporary challenges.
2. Research and write a paper on general revelation and special revelation, noting in particular their relationship to apologetics and concluding with a defense of your position on the matter. You may wish to begin by consulting a few works of systematic theology and/or theological dictionaries.
3. Write a report on the New Testament documents, specifically seeking to build an apologetic case for their reliability.

CHAPTER 6

The Theistic God Exists

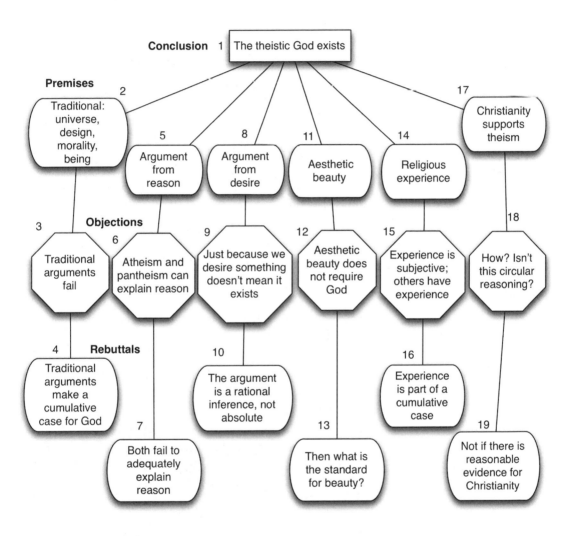

Conclusion 1 The theistic God exists

Premises

2 Traditional: universe, design, morality, being

5 Argument from reason

8 Argument from desire

11 Aesthetic beauty

14 Religious experience

17 Christianity supports theism

Objections

3 Traditional arguments fail

6 Atheism and pantheism can explain reason

9 Just because we desire something doesn't mean it exists

12 Aesthetic beauty does not require God

15 Experience is subjective; others have experience

18 How? Isn't this circular reasoning?

Rebuttals

4 Traditional arguments make a cumulative case for God

7 Both fail to adequately explain reason

10 The argument is a rational inference, not absolute

13 Then what is the standard for beauty?

16 Experience is part of a cumulative case

19 Not if there is reasonable evidence for Christianity

1. The theistic God exists (Conclusion)

The conclusion claims the one theistic God exists. What makes the "theistic God" distinct? The God of theism is infinite, intelligent, creative, moral, personal, transcendent, immanent, the Creator, and possesses a variety of *omni* attributes, such as omnipotence, omnipresence, omniscience, and omnibenevolence.

By definition, this conclusion excludes atheism (no god exists) and pantheism (an impersonal divine force exists), the two primary worldviews addressed in this book. It also excludes polytheism, since we are making the case here for the monotheistic God of theism. Deism, however, may fit within theism, though not in the same sense as taken by Christians, Muslims, and Jews, because deists deny that God is active in his universe (immanent) via special revelation or miracles.

Christianity requires the existence of the theistic God, for without the theistic God Christianity cannot adequately explain its Scriptures, miracles, or the resurrection of Christ, much less offer a meaningful and true worldview that corresponds to reality.

2. Traditional: universe, design, morality, being (Premise)

These four lines of argumentation form a family of traditional arguments for the existence of God. Critics must keep in mind that defeating *one form* of any of these arguments does not necessarily mean that *all forms* of these arguments are, consequently, defeated.

Arguments from the existence and origins of the universe are known as cosmological arguments. In brief, they argue from the reality of the existence of the universe to the claim that the explanation for the universe is God. One form of this argument, for instance, claims that everything that has a beginning has a cause. Since the universe has a beginning, it had a cause. The best explanation of this cause is that it is something personal rather than impersonal, and as such, it is God.

The second family of arguments emphasizes design and purpose in the universe. These arguments are known as *teleological* arguments for God. They maintain that the universe displays evidences of design; things that show evidences of design have a designer; and therefore, the universe has a designer (God).

Moral arguments for God are sometimes referred to as axiological arguments. They claim that universal moral laws exist. But if they do, then there must then be a universal moral law giver (God); otherwise, there is no real or meaningful source for morality. Alternative worldviews—naturalism, for instance—offer no satisfactory basis for moral laws. If, however, God exists, then moral standards make far more sense.

Arguments from being, or *ontological* arguments, originated with Anselm but have since been developed by other Christian thinkers such as Alvin Plantinga. Norman Geisler summarizes one form of the ontological argument as follows:

> Once we get an idea of what God is, that idea necessarily involves existence. There are several forms of this argument, but let's just talk about the idea of God as a perfect Being.
>
> 1. Whatever perfection can be attributed to the most perfect Being possible (conceivable) *must* be attributed to it (otherwise it would not be the most perfect being possible).
> 2. Necessary existence is a perfection which can be attributed to the most perfect Being.
> 3. Therefore, necessary existence must be attributed to the most perfect Being.
>
> Geisler restates the argument as follows:
>
> 1. If God exists, we conceive of Him as a necessary Being.
> 2. By definition, a necessary Being must exist and cannot not exist.
> 3. Therefore, if God exists, then He must exist and cannot not exist.[1]

Arguments in point 2 represent typical methods of making the case for Christian theism. As we shall see, other methods are also available, a few of which are noted in points 5, 8, 11, 14, and 17. Note, too, that often these arguments, as well as others listed under "Premises," often work together in order to build a cumulative case for the existence of the theistic God. These arguments at times complement one another, each supporting one or more attributes of the theistic God in making their case.

---

1. Geisler and Brooks, *When Skeptics Ask*, 24–25. For a more thorough introduction to the ontological argument, see Groothuis, *Christian Apologetics*, chapter 10.

3. Traditional arguments fail (Objection)

As noted earlier, the critic of the four families of traditional arguments for God's existence must defeat specific forms of these arguments. There are far too many potential objections, and we cannot address them all here. However, under point 4 we will offer a brief summary of common objections to the most typical forms of cosmological, teleological, axiological, and ontological arguments.

4. Traditional arguments make a cumulative case for God (Rebuttal)

The cosmological argument—Critics will at times take issue with the claim that the universe had a beginning, despite the fact that contemporary science as a whole agrees that it did. Such critics offer alternative theories that go against mainstream scientific thinking. The apologist must respond with further scientific evidence, or perhaps supplement such evidence with philosophical arguments, in support of the cosmological argument.

Big Bang cosmology, for instance, is strong scientific evidence that the universe had a beginning. Although other theories have been offered, none have the same extensive support or evidence behind them. The multiverse theory, for instance, which posits many universes, is an ad hoc theory that lacks substantiation. Granting that the universe had a beginning, the options for explaining that beginning are severely limited. It makes far more sense to posit a Beginner (God) than to point to nothing as the origin of its beginning (atheism), or to an impersonal force (pantheism).

Teleological or design arguments—Critics will often take the approach of David Hume or various other common objections to design. Design, they will claim, is only *apparent* design, not *actual* design. Consequently, what we are mistaking as design either on a macroscopic level, such as the universe and objects in it, or on a microscopic level, such as elements of microbiology, are not really true design at all, but only apparent design. But as proponents of the Intelligent Design movement have argued extensively, biological evidence of design is overwhelming. Specified complexity, for example, argues that certain molecular machines could not have developed without being designed since they require all their parts, fully formed, to function at all. Taken as a whole, Christian theism, including a universe created and designed by God, makes far more sense of reality than alternatives.

Arguments from morality—Atheistic critics may claim that morality is relative or that morality is the result of the undirected process of naturalistic evolution. As such, it can be explained within that naturalistic system without requiring a theistic God.

The pantheist may take issue with claims to absolute moral laws, maintaining that there really is no such thing as good or evil since all is one and all is divine. But in so doing, the pantheist loses all moral ground, reducing to ethical relativism, and, consequently, is unable to offer any judgments or moral distinctions about reality (see chapters 21 and 23).

Without a transcendent moral lawgiver, absolute, meaningful moral standards cannot exist. God provides this transcendent source for morality as well as the foundation for human morality. No other worldview offers a better explanation of morality. An atheistic universe—which by definition arose without the involvement of a personal deity of any kind, but rather, through impersonal chance, time, and an undirected process—leaves little if any room for morality, which dictates personal moral interactions.

5. Argument from reason (Premise)

Popularized by C. S. Lewis in his book *Miracles* (though he is not the originator of the argument), the argument from reason claims that if we are merely the products of randomness rather than intelligence, as naturalism claims, then why do we think our reasoning abilities actually have the power to arrive at truth?

Lewis makes the point that "strict materialism refutes itself for the reason given long ago by Professor Haldane: 'If my mental processes are determined wholly by the motions of atoms in my brain, I have no reason to suppose that my beliefs are true. . . . And hence I have no reason for supposing my brain to be composed of atoms.'"[2]

6. Atheism and pantheism can explain reason (Objection)

Atheists may argue that the undirected process of evolution can indeed explain reason, while pantheists may claim that reason is possible because a divine, albeit impersonal, mind or force exists. An atheist may argue that the human ability to reason is a helpful evolutionary development, allowing human beings to survive and thrive. If so, then God is not necessary as an explanation of human reasoning abilities. The pantheist, believing in the reality of a divine mind, may merely point out that this divine mind, which we are all part of, imbues each of us with the capacity to think.

2. Lewis, *Miracles*, 22.

7. Both [atheism and pantheism] fail to adequately explain reason (Rebuttal)	Atheism lacks an adequate foundation to explain the reliability of human reason. If, as atheism claims, human beings are the result of an undirected and impersonal process, then how is it possible that we have developed rational mental processes at all? And if we have developed these processes without the existence of a personal God or transcendent mind, then how can we even trust our reasoning abilities? Pantheism does not have as much difficulty explaining reason as atheism does. Nevertheless, pantheists also face the problem of personality in relation to reason. If the divine force is impersonal, as forms of pantheism claim, then how is it that we have developed thoughts that are of a personal nature?
8. Argument from desire (Premise)	Also addressed throughout the writings of C. S. Lewis (though again, he is not the originator), the argument from desire has its early roots in thinkers such as Augustine and Pascal. In short, it claims that human beings have an innate longing or desire for an elusive something that nothing on earth is capable of truly satisfying. This desire points to a corresponding reality in the universe. Since other of our desires and longings are fulfilled somehow in this world—for instance, hunger is satisfied by the reality of food—we can reasonably expect that this desire, too, is matched with a reality that can fulfill it. Thus, spiritual longing points to the reality of the theistic God.
9. Just because we desire something doesn't mean it exists. (Objection)	This objection is fairly self-contained, so only a few words are in order. The objection claims that the existence of a theistic God is unnecessary in order to explain desire and longing. Maybe our longing is, for instance, an evolutionary mechanism for spurring human beings to continue to desire to live. Or, from a pantheistic perspective, perhaps this desire or longing is a result of the impersonal divine force spurring us on to seek enlightenment. Again, some persons may claim that they do not experience this desire or longing in the first place; consequently, the argument is invalid.
10. The argument is a rational inference, not absolute (Rebuttal)	The argument from desire (point 8) is not intended as an absolute argument for the theistic God, but instead serves as a rational inference based on the evidence that people often desire or long for something elusive that nothing this world can adequately satisfy. Consequently, it is probable that this elusive satisfaction is found only in the theistic God.

11. Aesthetic beauty (Premise)	This argument claims that aesthetic beauty points to the reality of the theistic God. As Peter Kreeft and Ronald Tacelli put it, "There is the music of Johann Sebastian Bach. Therefore there must be a God. You either see this one or you don't."
12. Aesthetic beauty does not require God (Objection)	But can't human beings appreciate artistic beauty without appealing to God? There may be some evolutionary explanation for the reality of beauty and human reactions to it.
13. Then what is the standard for beauty? (Rebuttal)	Then what is the standard for beauty? It is more likely that such a standard is rooted in a transcendent source (i.e., God) than in any alternatives. Otherwise, beauty serves no real function when it comes to survival of the fittest (naturalism) or within a worldview that sees everything as divine and therefore offers no real foundation for moral or aesthetic distinctions (pantheism). It is more sensible to accept the reality of aesthetic beauty given a universe with a good, transcendent God who created human beings with the capacity for creativity, imagination, and the intellectual capacity to implement works of artistic beauty for God's glory.
14. Religious experience (Premise)	This premise is also given in the argument map that makes the case for Christian theism (chapter 5). We will not reiterate in detail points covered in the other diagram. In summary, while inconclusive on its own, religious experience may serve as supporting evidence for a theistic God. Moreover, if scores of human beings throughout history have claimed to experience this metaphysical being, then their claim lends credence to this theistic God's existence. This is not a conclusive argument per se. Nevertheless, it can serve as a supporting argument combined with other premises for the theistic God.
15. Experience is subjective; others have experience (Objection)	See chapter 25, where it is argued that religious experience can indeed contribute to an overall case for Christian theism, demonstrating the reality of changed lives. The primary objection here is that anyone from any worldview can claim experience and use this as evidence for the worldview in question. But if anyone can claim experience as a trump card of truth, so to speak, then it would seem that experience loses objective value as evidence for any belief.

16. Experience is part of a cumulative case (Rebuttal)	See chapter 25, where it is argued that religious experience can fit into a cumulative case for Christian theism, being one of many lines of argumentation.
17. Christianity supports theism (Premise)	If key aspects of the Christian worldview are true, then they lend support to the existence of the theistic God. For instance, if miracles occur and are, by nature, supernatural, then their reality points to the theistic God. More specifically, the resurrection of Christ points to the reality of the theistic God (see chapter 10).
18. How? Isn't this circular reasoning? (Objection)	This response relates to point 17, "Christianity supports theism." As stated under point 17, Christianity necessitates the reality of the theistic God. Consequently, if, for instance, Christian miracles are true, then this bolsters the case for the reality of the existence of God.
	Some, however, claim that this is circular reasoning. The Christian is appealing to Christianity in order to demonstrate the existence of God, which, in turn, is integral to Christianity.
19. Not if there is reasonable evidence for Christianity (Rebuttal)	If there is sufficient reasonable evidence in support of Christianity, then the argument is not circular. In other words, if it can be shown that the biblical record is reliable, that Christ rose from the dead, and that other claims of Christianity are trustworthy, then all of this evidence can converge to demonstrate the high probability that Christianity is true. However, if the Christian can offer reasonable evidence in support of its claims to the miraculous, such as the resurrection of Christ, then the argument for the theistic God is not circular but a reasonable inference on the basis of various Christian evidences including miracles, internal consistency, coherence with known facts of history, its existential viability, and more.

DISCUSSION QUESTIONS

1. Which argument for the existence of God do you find most convincing? Why?
2. Which argument for the existence of God do you find least convincing? Why?
3. Do arguments for God conclusively provide proof of his existence? Why or why not? What are the implications of your conclusions?
4. Given contemporary criticisms of Christianity, which argument do you think would resonate most with a New Atheist?

5. Do traditional arguments for God's existence (point 2) work together to build a case for God's existence, or are the arguments self-contained and distinct?

SUGGESTED ASSIGNMENTS

1. Write a report on one form of the cosmological argument (e.g., the kalam argument; see glossary).
2. Write a report on the design argument, selecting a specific form of the argument (e.g., a fine-tuning argument for God).
3. Read chapter 3 of the book *Miracles* by C. S. Lewis, where he presents an argument from reason. Do you find his case convincing?
4. Read *C. S. Lewis's Dangerous Idea* by Victor Reppert and write a report assessing his presentation of various arguments from reason.

CHAPTER 7

Truth Is Objective, Absolute, Universal, and More

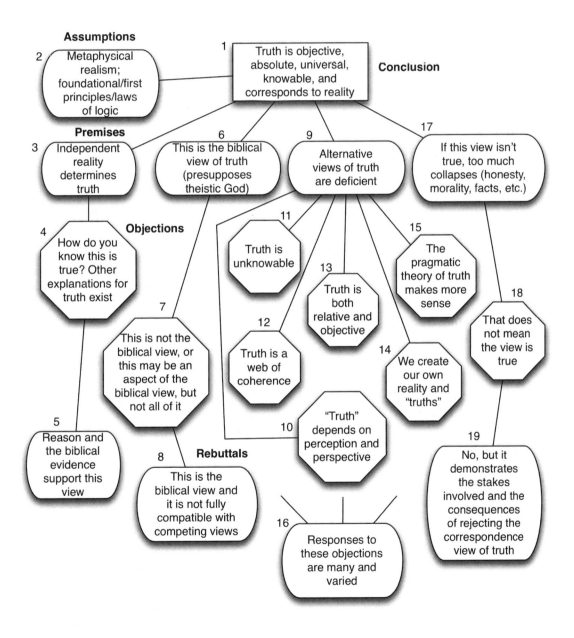

Assumptions

2 Metaphysical realism; foundational/first principles/laws of logic

1 Truth is objective, absolute, universal, knowable, and corresponds to reality

Conclusion

Premises

3 Independent reality determines truth

6 This is the biblical view of truth (presupposes theistic God)

9 Alternative views of truth are deficient

17 If this view isn't true, too much collapses (honesty, morality, facts, etc.)

4 How do you know this is true? Other explanations for truth exist

Objections

11 Truth is unknowable

15 The pragmatic theory of truth makes more sense

7 This is not the biblical view, or this may be an aspect of the biblical view, but not all of it

13 Truth is both relative and objective

18 That does not mean the view is true

12 Truth is a web of coherence

14 We create our own reality and "truths"

5 Reason and the biblical evidence support this view

10 "Truth" depends on perception and perspective

8 This is the biblical view and it is not fully compatible with competing views

Rebuttals

16 Responses to these objections are many and varied

19 No, but it demonstrates the stakes involved and the consequences of rejecting the correspondence view of truth

1. Truth is objective, absolute, universal, knowable, and corresponds to reality (Conclusion)	This conclusion adheres to the biblical view of truth, concluding with a belief in the veracity of the correspondence view of truth (see glossary). Since truth is objective, it is beyond our subjective views and thus is what is really true.

The nature of truth as absolute does away with relativistic views of truth, while truth as universal means that it applies to all people at all times and in all ways, not just to some areas of reality or some worldview perspectives. The fact that truth is knowable means that we can grasp truth, counter to views of truth that claim it is unknowable or indefinable.

Truth corresponds to reality, thus adhering to realism, and more specifically, to the correspondence view of truth. |
| **2. Metaphysical realism; foundational/first principles/laws of logic (Assumptions)** | Assumptions related to the conclusion in point 1 are many. First, realism is assumed to be true, though not without evidence. Realism, which is required by the correspondence view of truth, *necessitates a reality that exists and that human beings can make sense of by reasoned observations.* In other words, a reality exists and we can make meaningful and accurate statements about it—truth claims, propositions.

Other assumptions include foundational first principles such as the laws of logic (A is A [identity], A is not non-A [non-contradiction], and laws of rational inference). |
3. Independent reality determines truth (Premise)	We do not "make up" what is true or false, but what is true or false depends on the independent facts of reality.
4. How do you know this is true? Other explanations for truth exist (Objection)	This is an objection to realism and to the correspondence view of truth in general. The "other explanations for truth" encompass objections such as those noted in points 10 through 15 and are addressed in point 16.
5. Reason and the biblical evidence support this view (Rebuttal)	The very nature of the objection in point 4 suggests skepticism expressed with a degree of paradoxical certainty and an appeal to "other explanations" of truth. In other words, the objection itself seems to support point 3, as the person making the objection seems to acknowledge that an appeal to external reality can help us arrive at truth. Moreover, if other explanations exist, and if one or more of the alternative explanations is viewed as true, then at least the objector believes that some knowledge or truth exists that is superior to that in point 3.

The main rebuttal, however, is a basic defense of the correspondence view of truth. In short, we all reason in ways that presuppose the correspondence view of truth (i.e., truth corresponds to reality). We know that a lie does not correspond to what is true and is, in fact, false when it comes to reality. We also know that telling the truth does correspond to reality.

To attempt any serious thinking or dialogue in relation to questions of truth will at some point presuppose and utilize the correspondence view of truth. Even those who disagree with this point of view will essentially default to the position that their alternative view is true and the correspondence view is false, but this very default is a tacit acceptance of the correspondence view.

6. This is the biblical view of truth (presupposes theistic God) (Premise)

Point 1 supports the biblical view of truth, which, in turn, presupposes the theistic God. If the theistic God exists (chapter 6), then reality is under his purview, including our ability to reason and arrive at conclusions. The Bible clearly teaches that truth is objective, absolute, universal, knowable, and corresponds to reality.

7. This is not the biblical view, or this may be an aspect of the biblical view, but not all of it (Objection)

Those who object may argue that the correspondence view is not the biblical view, opting instead, for example, for the coherence view or even a postmodern view. Or they may say that the correspondence view may be one aspect of the biblical view but not all of it, thus allowing for other views of reality and truth to either override the correspondence view, replace it, or minimize its all-encompassing significance (other views are noted in points 10–15). The correspondence view of truth may be deemed too narrow-minded, intolerant, and unloving and, as a result, is rejected or at least not fully embraced. Some influenced by postmodern ideas may reject the biblical view of truth because they do not believe any single metanarrative or view of truth can suffice to explain all of reality.

8. This is the biblical view and it is not fully compatible with competing views (Rebuttal)

See point 16. In short, the biblical evidence overwhelmingly supports the correspondence view of truth. While aspects of the coherence view of truth (point 12, and see glossary) may serve as one test for the truth of a worldview, as a whole the coherence view of truth is insufficient. In short, if the correspondence view of truth is indeed true, then alternative views are by definition false (point 9).

9. Alternative views of truth are deficient (Premise)	This premise does not directly support the conclusion in point 1, but if true, it does eliminate competing views of truth. If such competing views are indeed deficient, and if the view in point 1 is superior, then it is more reasonable to hold to the conclusion in point 1 than to hold to any competing view or views of truth. In keeping with the approach of reasoning to the best explanation, we need not state with 100 percent certainty that the conclusion in point 1 is absolutely true; we need only reason that it offers a far superior explanation of reality than competing views, and therefore, we do far better to hold to this view than its alternatives.
Objections 10–15	A few words are in order in reference to the objections in points 10 through 15. Although six objections are presented, they may be categorized under four broad families of objections or alternatives to the correspondence view of truth. These four categories include postmodern views of truth (10, 11), New Age views of truth (10, 13, 14), coherence views of truth (12), and pragmatic views of truth (15).
10. "Truth" depends on perception and perspective (Objection)	Depending on how this view is articulated, it may fall into postmodern or New Age views of truth. The postmodernist will deny the reality of any one overarching view of truth (metanarrative), thus viewing truth as a matter of perception and perspective. The New Age adherent may hold to a nuanced form of this same view, noting that all roads lead to the same reality or that blind men touching different parts of an elephant all had the "truth" from their point of view (see chapter 22).
11. Truth is unknowable (Objection)	This view fits well within certain kinds of postmodern thinking, which may at times come across as skepticism. If truth is ultimately unknowable, then there is no way to truly and decisively determine whether anything really corresponds to what is true or not. Thus, no one can claim that a particular view of reality or truth is the only correct view, since ultimately truth is beyond us.
12. Truth is a web of coherence (Objection)	This view objects to the correspondence view by offering the alternative view of truth as a coherent web, so to speak. If truths cohere well within a given worldview, the worldview may be said to be true. As Douglas Groothuis puts it, "Coherence theories of truth argue that what makes a statement or

belief true is its coherence or consistency with other beliefs. If my 'web of belief' is large and internally consistent—that is, if none of my beliefs contradict each other—my beliefs are true. A belief is false if it fails to cohere with the rest of my beliefs."[1]

13. Truth is both relative and objective (Objection)

This objection makes clear its disagreement with truth as objective, absolute, and corresponding to reality. It fits well within New Age approaches, which tend to minimize logical consistency in favor of relativistic subjectivity in relation to questions of truth. Thus, the apparently contradictory views of truth as relative and truth as objective are embraced.[2]

14. We create our own reality and "truths" (Objection)

This view likewise fits with the New Age perspective. If we create our own reality, then reality is not subject to some grand or absolute standard since it can change. God, then, or the divine force or power in the universe, may fluctuate depending on how we as a whole "create" reality.

15. The pragmatic theory of truth makes more sense (Objection)

An idea or worldview that "works" can be said to be pragmatic and therefore true. If a "truth" benefits us, then it can be said to be "true."

16. Responses to these objections are many and varied (Rebuttal)

Responses to objections 10–15 are many and varied. As noted earlier, these objections fall under four broad families of objections: postmodern, New Age, coherence, and pragmatism. Recall that point 9 finds all the alternatives deficient in comparison to the view of truth concluded in point 1 (the biblical, coherence view of truth).

Detailed responses to each of points 10–15 would fill a separate book or even multiple books. Nevertheless, listed here are some salient responses to the points in question. Regarding point 12, truth is not a web of coherence because even though truth claims within a particular web may cohere within themselves, they may in fact contradict known facts that exist outside the web of coherence. What about point 13? Is truth both relative and objective? This violates the law of

---

1. Groothuis, *Christian Apologetics*, 132. Groothuis holds to the correspondence view of truth and in this quote is merely describing the coherence view, not defending it.
2. In an effort to avoid conflict, New Age adherents will at times jettison reason, in particular the law of noncontradiction, in order to espouse their view that there are no real distinctions in reality between right or wrong, good or evil, or truth or non-truth. But if this position is carried to its logical conclusions, New Age adherents are left with a world of philosophical anarchy where no real truth can exist, including their own claim that the New Age worldview is true.

noncontradiction (A is not non-A). An impersonal divine force cannot also be a personal, transcendent being, for instance. Point 14 is popular among adherents of the new spirituality or New Age. Unfortunately, the fact that we do not create our own reality is readily apparent on a daily basis. We cannot cross a busy highway in the blind belief that we can create a clear path across. If we attempt to do so, reality will crush us. We cannot create a reality where we can walk on water, as reality will cause us to sink. As for the pragmatic theory of truth (point 15), its emphasis is on what "works," but what works may not be true. We may find phrenology to be a helpful and beneficial practice to guide and improve our health, but basing our medical condition and treatment on a pseudoscience that is not true is not helpful.

17. If this view isn't true, too much collapses (honesty, morality, facts, etc.) (Premise)

The consequences of the view of truth presented in point 1 are monumental if the view is not correct. Too much collapses if it falls. Fundamental moral principles, such as honesty and moral goodness, lose objective meaning and value. Moreover, objective facts also lose value, thus resulting in the collapse of fields such as science, which depends on the correspondence view of truth in order to support its foundational methodology. Scientific experiments and the scientific method rely on the correspondence view of truth. The stakes are too high for reality if the biblical correspondence view of truth is not in fact true.

18. That does not mean the view is true (Objection)

But we can't claim that point 1 is true simply because we are afraid of the consequences. What if point 1 is false? Do we hold to it despite contrary evidence? Point 17 seems a weak reason to support point 1.

19. No, but it demonstrates the stakes involved and the consequences of rejecting the correspondence view of truth (Rebuttal)

The stakes are too high to merely dismiss point 1 without sufficient, supportable warrant. Besides, point 17 is not the only argument supporting point 1. We must also consider point 3, point 6, and the fact that if competing views are deficient, and if a solid case can be made for point 1, then point 1 seems the most viable explanation of reality as we know it. If that is the case, then it is wise to maintain the view that truth is objective, absolute, universal, knowable, and corresponds to reality.

DISCUSSION QUESTIONS

1. If someone were to ask you, "What is truth?" how would you respond?
2. Given all the alternatives and possibilities when it comes to understanding reality, how is it possible for anyone to make sense of reality and come to truth? What obstacles might need dismantling before someone is able to seek and grasp truth?
3. What is meant by the claim that truth is "universal"?
4. What is wrong with the coherence view of truth?
5. If the conclusion in the diagram is true how can one avoid the charge that such a view is intolerant and narrow-minded?

SUGGESTED ASSIGNMENTS

1. Do a Bible study on truth, noting its contextual meaning and its application for Christian life and ministry today.
2. Read chapters 6 and 7 in *Christian Apologetics* by Douglas Groothuis and write a report summarizing the arguments presented in those chapters.
3. Given popular culture's emphasis on tolerance and relativism, research and prepare a practical guide to sharing your faith with relativists. See Beckwith and Koukl, *Relativism*, for instance, as one source on the topic.
4. Select one classic and one modern or contemporary Christian thinker and compare their respective views of truth, assessing both in the light of biblical revelation. Consider, for instance, Augustine, Aquinas, Kierkegaard, Pascal, C. S. Lewis, Francis Schaeffer, William Lane Craig, and Alvin Plantinga.

CHAPTER 8

Objective Moral Values Exist

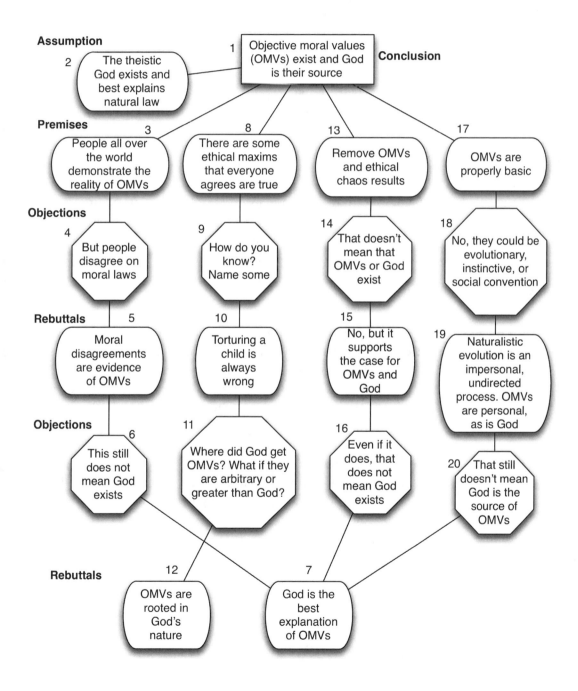

Assumption

2 The theistic God exists and best explains natural law

1 Objective moral values (OMVs) exist and God is their source

Conclusion

Premises

3 People all over the world demonstrate the reality of OMVs

8 There are some ethical maxims that everyone agrees are true

13 Remove OMVs and ethical chaos results

17 OMVs are properly basic

Objections

4 But people disagree on moral laws

9 How do you know? Name some

14 That doesn't mean that OMVs or God exist

18 No, they could be evolutionary, instinctive, or social convention

Rebuttals

5 Moral disagreements are evidence of OMVs

10 Torturing a child is always wrong

15 No, but it supports the case for OMVs and God

19 Naturalistic evolution is an impersonal, undirected process. OMVs are personal, as is God

Objections

6 This still does not mean God exists

11 Where did God get OMVs? What if they are arbitrary or greater than God?

16 Even if it does, that does not mean God exists

20 That still doesn't mean God is the source of OMVs

Rebuttals

12 OMVs are rooted in God's nature

7 God is the best explanation of OMVs

1. Objective moral values (OMVs) exist and God is their source (Conclusion)	Here we have a conclusion that is in two parts: "objective moral values exist" *and* "God is their source." If the conclusion were only "objective moral values exist," then it is logically possible that a nontheistic worldview could agree with the conclusion itself, although probably not with all of the premises. Some atheists, for instance, agree that OMVs exist but deny a theistic source for them. The point of this argument map is to demonstrate that OMVs depend on some form of theism for their source.
2. The theistic God exists, and best explains natural law (Assumption)	Point 1 assumes that the theistic God exists. This assumption is not unfounded but is drawn from various lines of reasoning (see chapter 6).
3. People all over the world demonstrate the reality of OMVs (Premise)	This premise claims that human ethics the world over, historically and today, demonstrate that OMVs exist. Though various cultures and customs exist, at their core all cultures and customs appeal at some point to OMVs. When disputes arise, for instance, and those involved in the disputes appeal to a moral standard, they are demonstrating the reality of OMVs. This is how C. S. Lewis begins his argument from morality to God in *Mere Christianity*.
4. But people disagree on moral laws (Objection)	This objection is to point 3. The claim is that moral laws are not objective because people disagree about these laws the world over. Doesn't this disagreement clearly demonstrate that supposed OMVs are not truly objective? After all, if everyone agreed on OMVs, then why do we see so much disagreement throughout cultures and history? For instance, why in one culture is it acceptable to have more than one mate while in other cultures it is not? By offering counterexamples, the critic seeks to demonstrate that OMVs do not really exist because he or she can show many exceptions.
5. Moral disagreements are evidence of OMVs (Rebuttal)	This rebuttal, stated rather briefly in the diagram, points out that moral disagreements, rather than arguing against OMVs, actually argue for them. Such disagreements demonstrate that a higher moral standard is being appealed to whenever moral disagreement exists. Rather than being a detriment to a case for OMVs, then, moral disagreements demonstrate their reality.

6. This still does not mean God exists (Objection)	The fact that moral disagreements exist does not mean that they are evidence of OMVs or that God is their source. Instead, they may just signify that human beings have disagreements. There is nothing wrong with fitting this into an evolutionary explanation, for instance. If animals disagree and fight, why does this need to mean that OMVs are real?
7. God is the best explanation of OMVs (Rebuttal)	Points 3, 8, 13, and 17 do not *prove* the existence of God per se, but they do point to God as the best explanation of OMVs, offering a cumulative case in favor of OMVs and God as their source. There will always be those who disagree with various points of any argument we present, but this does not mean that we give up on making our case. God is the best explanation of OMVs because they are personal in nature, requiring personal interactions and thus ruling out atheism's and pantheism's impersonal explanations of reality.
8. There are some ethical maxims that everyone agrees are true (Premise)	Certain ethical maxims exist that everyone agrees on, thereby demonstrating the reality of OMVs.

Objections to this premise, addressed later, can include the claim that the premise is simply not true or is greatly exaggerated. One may object to the word "everyone" in the premise. Does it imply that just one counterexample can refute the premise? What if we can produce a human being who disagrees with an ethical maxim that most others agree is universally true?

Such an occurrence need not overturn the premise, though enough people disagreeing with a supposed ethical maxim may weaken point 8. But approaching this objection from a Christian perspective, one might argue that in a fallen world full of depraved souls, it is quite possible to find isolated anomalies—that is, morally malfunctioning individuals who disagree with certain supposed maxims. These anomalies, however, are by definition not the norm, but deviations or aberrations from the expected moral standard. To draw a parallel, isolated individuals may claim the earth is flat, but such claims are anomalous and do not discredit accepted geological fact. |
| **9. How do you know? Name some (Objection)** | This objection is to point 8. The critic rightly asks, "How do you know?" in relation to the claim that "there are some ethical maxims that everyone agrees are true." The critic may be an ethical or cultural relativist, believing that moral claims are relative rather |

than objective; or he may simply be pressing the case by seeking further evidence for the premise in point 8. "Name some," again, is seeking evidence to evaluate point 8 further.

10. Torturing a child is always wrong (Rebuttal)

Here the supporter of the conclusion offers an ethical maxim that everyone supposedly agrees is true. Recall earlier, however, that the fact that some isolated individuals may disagree with this maxim does not invalidate its truth as an OMV. The existence of such isolated individuals merely demonstrates that there are isolated anomalies. On the whole, however, the vast majority of human beings will agree that torturing an innocent child is always wrong.

11. Where did God get OMVs? What if they are arbitrary or greater than God? (Objection)

This is a restatement of the classic Euthyphro dilemma, found in Plato's dialogues where, in context, it refers to the "gods" (polytheism). Nevertheless, the objection has been applied to theism. In short, the claim is that if God appeals to moral standards that are higher than him, then God's power and self-sustaining existence are somehow in question, since at least some OMVs are greater than God or beyond him. On the other hand, if God merely declares certain moral behaviors to be right or wrong, then God seems arbitrary. Could he not just as easily have decreed that torturing an innocent child is right?

12. OMVs are rooted in God's nature (Rebuttal)

OMVs are not beyond God or arbitrarily chosen by him. Instead, they are inherent to his overall nature, which is good, loving, and holy. As such, OMVs are rooted in and flow from the very nature of God, being who he is by definition. The solution is not to accept either alternative of the Euthyphro dilemma, but to escape the horns of the dilemma by seeking a *tertium quid* (third solution). The theist claims that moral goodness is not dictated by an external source or in an arbitrary sense but is rooted in God's very nature. God is good by definition and in his very being. Thus, if God is the source of OMVs, then they are neither arbitrary nor greater than him, but part of what makes God who he is. The solution lies in the character of God.

13. Remove OMVs and ethical chaos results (Premise)

This may serve more as a supporting premise than a stronger, primary premise. By itself, the premise does little to either prove or disprove the conclusion. Since its focus is on the consequences of a lack of OMVs and God as their source, it may be seen by critics as an *irrelevant thesis*, meaning that it has no direct bearing on whether or not OMVs exist. Undesirable consequences do not require that we adopt a position that avoids those consequences. We seek truth, not deluded comfort.

Nevertheless, the premise may serve as a supporting premise, suggesting that a dangerous, slippery slope results if we jettison OMVs and God as their source. While this does not mean that God must therefore exist, it does follow the logical consequences of a worldview that wishes to retain some semblance of morality while at the same time excluding God as the source of such moral laws.

14. That doesn't mean that OMVs or God exist (Objection)

If OMVs are disregarded as false, then the argument claims "ethical chaos results," but as this objection puts it, "That doesn't mean that OMVs or God exist." It is a valid criticism and must be responded to rather than dismissed or avoided.

15. No, but it supports the case for OMVs and God (Rebuttal)

If we strip ethics of OMVs, moral chaos will result. This by itself does not mean that OMVs must exist and must be rooted in God, but it does lend support to the conclusion; alternative explanations of morality will break down, resulting in moral chaos. Combined with the other premises, the best explanation of morality points to OMVs, which find their source in God. In other words, transcendent-derived morality is preferable to non-transcendent-derived morality.

But the critic is correct that this does not mean, consequently, that one must therefore accept the OMV/God conclusion merely because it makes us more comfortable. As such, further evidences must combine in order to make a stronger case for the conclusion.

16. Even if it does, that does not mean God exists (Objection)

Here the responses appear to be breaking down into statements rather than coherent objections, which happens at times during discussion and argumentation. We must seek to determine how we might support our original conclusion that OMVs exist and God is their source. Since point 13 offers a supporting premise, we may seek to bolster our overall case by dedicating our discussion to strengthening our other premises. This does not mean that we must abandon point 13 entirely, but it does mean that if this premise is no longer serving to further a healthy discussion, we may wish to bolster our case by concentrating on other premises.

17. OMVs are properly basic (Premise)	This is somewhat more complicated to demonstrate as a premise. It relates in some ways to so-called Reformed epistemology when it comes to the nature of knowledge of God. Some thinkers, notably Alvin Plantinga, argue that certain beliefs, such as belief in God, need not require various lines of evidences in their support, but may in fact be *properly basic*. This means, in part, that such beliefs are foundational. If this is true, then certain beliefs are properly basic because they are the result of properly functioning human minds. This premise claims that OMVs are properly basic to human beings.
18. No, they could be evolutionary, instinctive, or social convention (Objection)	Here the response both disagrees with the premise in point 17 and also offers alternative explanations for OMVs that find their source in God. Three alternatives are offered: evolution, instinct, and social convention. Point 19 will need to respond to the objection to OMVs being properly basic, thus making a case for morality being properly basic, and also respond to each of the trio of alternative explanations offered in this point.
19. Naturalistic evolution is an impersonal, undirected process. OMVs are personal, as is God (Rebuttal)	The original premise pointed to OMVs as "properly basic," but the objection was raised against the concept of properly basic moral beliefs, and three alternatives to explaining morality were offered. First, it will be prudent for the person defending the conclusion to offer evidence in support of OMVs as being properly basic. Second, an evaluation of each of the three proposed alternatives must be offered (only brief responses are provided here; for additional responses, see the bibliography).

Does naturalistic evolution explain morality? Some critics may favor relativistic or subjective ethics, thus denying objective morality altogether. If this is the case, the response must seek to demonstrate that OMVs exist.

Other critics may claim that naturalistic evolution can explain morality. Various responses may be utilized. For instance, naturalistic evolution is an impersonal, undirected process, yet we are to suppose that this impersonal, undirected process results in moral behavior that governs personal interactions. How is this so? Why is it so?

We may also incorporate the argument from reason, arguing that since we cannot even trust human reason, we cannot trust an impersonal, undirected process to explain morality either. Besides, according to naturalistic evolution, our primary purpose (if we can even call it that) is survival, not truth or |

morality. Yet many human beings are willing to give their lives altruistically, though if naturalistic evolution is true, such behavior deviates from the path to human survival. Why rescue someone from a burning building? Why save a drowning man? Why do anything that normally passes for heroic moral behavior if in fact we are working against the goals of naturalistic evolution and our own survival?

What about instinct and social convention? Instinct cannot adequately explain moral values. Often we must choose between what we call instincts. One instinctive choice may actually place us in danger. We may struggle, briefly, with such apparent instincts—for example, when choosing to run into a burning building in order to save a life. One instinct tells us to flee, while another tells us to forge ahead with the rescue. As C. S. Lewis argued, "But you will find inside you a third thing which tells you that you ought to follow the impulse to help, and suppress the impulse to run away. Now this thing that judges between two instincts, that decides which should be encouraged, cannot itself be either of them."[1]

Does our upbringing and/or education account for our moral proclivities and, consequently, need not appeal to the existence of OMVs or God as their source? Is social convention enough to explain moral values without appeal to God? The fact that we have learned moral values does not mean that they are *only* social conventions. If natural law is true, for instance, then God has instilled within everyone a capacity to grasp, to some degree, moral values.

20. That still doesn't mean God is the source of OMVs (Objection)

The objector may remain defiant of alternative explanations that are better than his own, but that does not nullify the case the arguments can make for the conclusion we are seeking.

DISCUSSION QUESTIONS

1. Imagine you hold to atheism. Where does your morality come from?
2. How would you respond to a critic who claimed that objective moral values are nothing more than evolutionary by-products?
3. Where did God get objective moral values?
4. If objective moral values exist, then why do so many people disagree about what's right and wrong?

---

1. Lewis, *Mere Christianity*, 22 (book I, chapter 2).

5. What's wrong with the claim that naturalistic evolution can explain objective moral values?

SUGGESTED ASSIGNMENTS

1. Read book one of *Mere Christianity* and write a report on Lewis's approach to the argument from morality. Compare it with Paul Copan's chapter on a moral argument for God in *To Everyone an Answer*.
2. Select a contemporary atheist critic of the moral argument and write a report describing and evaluating that person's perspective.
3. Research and write a report on the Euthyphro dilemma, giving special attention to a response from the point of view of Christian theism. See, for instance, the original dialogue of Plato in *Euthyphro*, apologist Greg Koukl's overview of it,[2] and Scott Rae's section on it under "Divine Command Theory" in his book *Moral Choices*.
4. Make a case for the claim that moral values are essentially the same throughout history and across cultures. Be sure to address objections to your perspective. See, for instance, the appendix to *The Abolition of Man* by C. S. Lewis.

---

2. See Gregory Koukl, "Euthyphro's Dilemma," *Stand to Reason* website, http://www.str.org/site/News2?id=5236.

CHAPTER 9

Christianity Is Beneficial

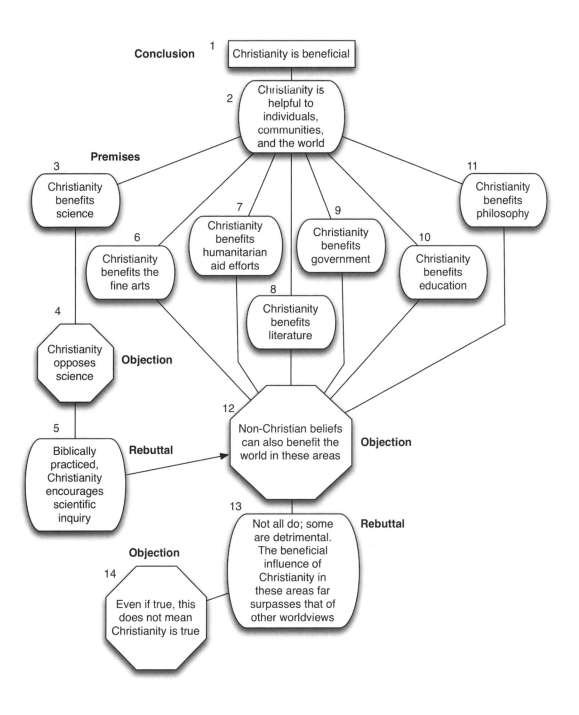

Conclusion 1 | Christianity is beneficial

2 | Christianity is helpful to individuals, communities, and the world

Premises

3 | Christianity benefits science

11 | Christianity benefits philosophy

7 | Christianity benefits humanitarian aid efforts

9 | Christianity benefits government

6 | Christianity benefits the fine arts

10 | Christianity benefits education

4 | Christianity opposes science — **Objection**

8 | Christianity benefits literature

5 | Biblically practiced, Christianity encourages scientific inquiry — **Rebuttal**

12 | Non-Christian beliefs can also benefit the world in these areas — **Objection**

13 | Not all do; some are detrimental. The beneficial influence of Christianity in these areas far surpasses that of other worldviews — **Rebuttal**

14 | Even if true, this does not mean Christianity is true — **Objection**

1. Christianity is beneficial (Conclusion)

Is Christianity really a benefit, or is it harmful (chapter 20)? This question may be asked in relation to individuals as well as to society as a whole, and by extension, the world. We may also ask the question in relation to history. Were there times when Christianity was less than beneficial, even harmful?

While we cannot address all of the concerns related to the question, we will explore some here and others in chapter 20. The conclusion of this diagram views Christianity favorably, claiming that Christianity is good and advantageous. Rather than bringing harm to the world, it offers benefits, which the supporting premises categorize into a number of areas.

2. Christianity is helpful to individuals, communities, and the world (Premise)

This is the major premise supporting the conclusion. If it is true, adhering to the reality of what we know of Christianity, then it easily supports the conclusion regarding Christianity being a benefit.

3. Christianity benefits science (Premise)

Although the remaining premises are in no particular order, we begin with the topic of Christianity and its benefits to science. Contrary to much contemporary belief that Christianity and science are interminable enemies, history as well as the foundations of the Christian worldview tell a far different story.

Historically, Christians set the foundations for modern science and the scientific method because of intellectual curiosity rooted in the theistic worldview. If an orderly designer (God) created our universe, then by extension it would benefit us to study what God has made in order to learn more about him and his creation. Thus the orderly investigation of reality began because of Christian curiosity inspired by the grandeur of creation.

This is not to say that other worldviews and religions have no basis in scientific study, but it is a fact of history that Christians spurred the modern scientific revolution.[1] Biblically speaking, Christianity supports the intellectual life (chapter 3), encouraging the use of the mind in order to discover truth (what corresponds with reality; chapter 7).

4. Christianity opposes science (Objection)

Critics sometimes make the claim that Christianity opposes science. Some soften the claim a bit by stating that while Christianity is not overtly hostile toward science, it does not embrace science, the scientific method, or reason (see chapter 4).

---

1. See resources in the bibliography supporting such claims, including two books by Rodney Stark: *For the Glory of God* and *The Victory of Reason*.

Rather, Christianity is said to be based on faith, often portrayed as blind faith, while science is the voice of cool reasoning and pure intellect. The critics present a dichotomy between science and faith, viewing the latter as being in the realm of personal opinion at best or folly at worst.

5. Biblically practiced, Christianity encourages scientific inquiry (Rebuttal)

As has been shown in point 3, biblical Christianity encourages the life of the intellect, including scientific inquiry. Claims to the contrary are typically based on popular contemporary portrayals of the "war" between Christianity and science in relation to questions such as Darwinian evolution (chapter 17) and the "fairy tale" account of creation as found in the book of Genesis. As a result, Christians are ridiculed for belief in a supernatural creator and portrayed as scientific simpletons, desperately clinging to outmoded ancient myths about creation rather than facing the "facts" that modern science offers. But, as the cosmological argument demonstrates (chapter 6), Christians are far from unscientific dupes, and the biblical account of creation, which maintains that the universe had a beginning, agrees with much modern scientific consensus.

More broadly, true Christianity contributes to objective truth-seeking, which is what science claims to be all about: following the evidence wherever it leads, even if our presuppositions or preconceptions differ from the results we obtain.

6. Christianity benefits the fine arts (Premise)

Because of the beliefs of Christianity, its followers have provided countless beneficial contributions to the fine arts. These artistic contributions, spurred by belief in God and all that the Christian worldview entails, have produced paintings, sculptures, music, literature, architectural marvels, and more. The world is artistically richer because of the depth and commitment of Christian artists throughout history. Remove Christianity from the historical record and much of the artistic beauty the world has produced vanishes. Remove God from the historical record and even more of that beauty disappears. If only atheistic art is left, much of what remains may indeed reach levels of artistic and technical brilliance, but it will rest on a foundation of despair, disorder, confusion, and anger. Moreover, any seemingly ethical benefits it offers will have no real foundation (chapter 8).

7. Christianity benefits humanitarian aid efforts (Premise)

Christians are called to compassion—called to help others, even enemies. The foundation of Christian ethics, as Augustine argued long ago, is love. More specifically, it is God's love. A worldview that calls its followers to love God and love neighbor results in humanitarian aid efforts. From Christianity's inception, Christians have responded to this call, rescuing discarded infants from death, establishing orphanages, building hospitals, offering assistance to those wounded on the battlefield, feeding the hungry, clothing the poor, and much more. This does not mean that non-Christians do not have the capacity for compassion or to help others; they do because of God's image in them. But it does highlight how distinctly Christian values and ideals have spurred beneficial humanitarian aid efforts.

8. Christianity benefits literature (Premise)

The world of literature is vast, spanning the centuries and producing not only Christian works of inestimable value, but also non-Christian writings of beauty, intellectual rigor, and imagination that explore the great questions of life. Christianity, though, has left its distinct literary mark. Men and women moved by their belief in God and the Christian worldview have written works that touch on universal human themes while also communicating Christian truths imaginatively. Examples are plentiful: Augustine's *Confessions* and *City of God*, Dante's *Divine Comedy*, John Milton's *Paradise Lost*, John Bunyan's *Pilgrim's Progress*, and many more.

9. Christianity benefits government (Premise)

"Can anything benefit government?" some may ask. Differing Christian traditions and interpretations of the role of faith in relation to government exist, and we cannot settle such disagreements here. Nevertheless, the Christian influence on government has resulted in democratic freedoms that many today take for granted, often forgetting the Christian roots of those freedoms, such as freedom of religion and equal rights.[2]

Without Christian influence on governments, cruel leadership, constant oppression, and worse are the result. Since Christians believe in God and that humans are made in God's image, every human life is of eternal value. Consequently, when such Christian principles are applied to government, the results are beneficial.

---

2. See, for instance, *How Christianity Changed the World* by Alvin Schmidt and *Christianity on Trial* by Vincent Carroll and David Shiflett for specific details on Christianity's positive influence on government and democracy.

10. Christianity benefits education (Premise)	Education, too, has benefited immensely from the influences of Christianity throughout the centuries. The Christian belief in the importance of the intellect in service to God has resulted in an abundance of educational benefits. From Christianity's ancient origins, its adherents were interested in both learning and teaching—and not just for men, as was common in ancient times, but also for women, thus resulting in some of the first educational settings open to both sexes without prejudice. Christian education transcended ethnic barriers and class distinctions as well, influencing the rise of public education available to all.
	Monasteries, too, contributed to education by copying and keeping scrolls and books. We can also mention the rise of universities founded specifically on Christian values and ideals.
11. Christianity benefits philosophy (Premise)	What of the great ideas? Socrates, Plato, and Aristotle all lived before Christianity, so what could Christians possibly contribute to the realm of philosophy? A great deal, according to the historical record. Great thinkers such as Augustine and Aquinas have arisen from Christianity. Whether developing unique arguments for God, making a case for beneficial ethics, or exploring the great questions of life, Christian thinkers have not merely seen fit to stay within the walls of academia, but their ideas have moved Christians of all kinds to make positive differences in the world for Christ's sake.
12. Non-Christian beliefs can also benefit the world in these areas (Objection)	This is true, and Christians should not deny the underlying sentiments behind this point. Critics, however, can claim that since this is the case, then Christianity's supposed "benefits" aren't unique to it. If non-Christians have also benefited science, the arts, humanitarian efforts, literature, government, education, and philosophy, then Christianity isn't unique or "better" than other worldviews. One could even argue that Christianity, though it seemingly offers "benefits," is actually harmful (chapter 20).
13. Not all do; some are detrimental. The beneficial influence of Christianity in these areas far surpasses that of other worldviews (Rebuttal)	Although Christians grant that other worldviews may also benefit the world, in some instances this is not the case. One could argue, for instance, that worldviews and ideologies inspired by atheism have resulted in great harm by way of oppression, attempted genocide, and the deaths of countless millions in the twentieth century alone. Atheists are not known for founding orphanages, hospitals, universities, or humanitarian aid

organizations. This does not mean that atheists are immoral (quite the contrary, in most cases), but it does demonstrate the profound beneficial influence Christianity has had on the world, particularly compared to worldviews that deny the existence of God, transcendent objective values, and so forth.

14. Even if true, this does not mean Christianity is true (Objection)

Taken in isolation, this is correct. The truth of Christianity cannot be supported by the single pillar of its many benefits. A case for the beneficial qualities of Christianity is merely a part of the overall case for it. The fact that Christianity is indeed beneficial as a whole, if substantiated, cannot stand alone as a foolproof argument for the veracity of Christianity. We must also explore the truth claims, evaluate the offered evidence, and seek to arrive at the best explanation given the available evidence.

This does not mean, however, that demonstrating the benefits of Christianity can play no part in making the case for Christian truth. It is reasonable to conclude, for instance, that if God exists and if Christianity is true, then the results of such a faith would result in the many fruits (benefits) that we do indeed record throughout Christian history. If, on the other hand, Christianity were false, then at some point its "system" would seem likely to break down. Christians, however, believe God exists and that the Holy Spirit indwells and guides them, resulting in an elevation of human character via the pursuit of virtues such as humility and love in order to benefit others. Is such a worldview, properly followed, really harmful? It seems unlikely.

DISCUSSION QUESTIONS

1. How has Christianity benefited science?
2. What specifically has Christianity done to benefit communities?
3. Imagine if Christianity were removed from the realm of the fine arts. What would be lost?
4. How would you respond to the charge that Christianity is opposed to scientific investigation?
5. What benefits does atheism offer the world? And pantheism?

SUGGESTED ASSIGNMENTS

1. Select a topic addressed in Schmidt's *How Christianity Changed the World* and use it as a starting point to write a paper on the question. Examples include Christianity and science, art, music, literature, liberty, education, health care, or the sanctification of human life.

2. Research and write a paper on the best biblical approach to questions of faith and science. Consult such resources as *Christianity and the Nature of Science* by J. P. Moreland and *The Soul of Science* by Nancy Pearcey and Charles Thaxton.

3. Read and write a report on one of the following works: *What's So Great About Christianity?* by Dinesh D'Souza, *What If Jesus Had Never Been Born?* by D. James Kennedy and Jerry Newcombe, or *What Has Christianity Ever Done for Us?* by Jonathan Hill.

CHAPTER 10

Christ Rose from the Dead

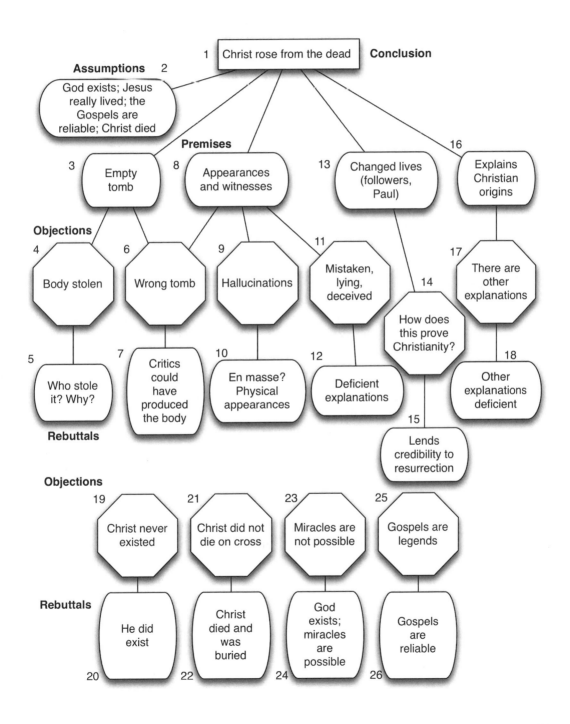

1. Christ rose from the dead (Conclusion)

The resurrection of Christ is central and foundational to Christianity. Without it, Christ was a great man but only a man. The early Christians recognized this fact; Paul the apostle wrote, "If Christ has not been raised, your faith is futile; you are still in your sins" (1 Cor. 15:17 NIV).

Some forms of liberal Christianity claim the ability to strip Christ of his miracles, including the resurrection, yet retain a powerful message for humanity. However, Christianity without a risen Christ can never be more than another ideological option among many, a sort of secular humanism. The conclusion in point 1, then, is critical to understanding and defending the faith: Christ rose from the dead.

A few points are in order. First, Christ rose from the dead literally, not figuratively. Second, he rose bodily, not as a mere spirit as some argue. Third, he rose in the same body that died, albeit in a glorified resurrection body.

2. God exists, Jesus really lived, Gospels reliable, Christ died (Assumptions)

In making this overall argument for the resurrection, Christians begin with certain assumptions and presuppositions (as does anyone making a viable case for an argument). God must exist in order to perform miracles and for Christ's claims to correspond with reality. If God does not exist, then miracles in a theistic sense are impossible. Assuming a purely naturalistic world, events such as the resurrection are impossible or highly improbable, depending on the approach taken by the materialist. This is why naturalistic explanations of the resurrection at times border on the absurd; nevertheless, any such explanation of the resurrection is preferred by naturalists over the Christian claims of the miraculous, which entail the existence of God.

The conclusion that Christ rose from the dead also entails a certain degree of reliability of the gospel records. If, for instance, the Gospels were written hundreds of years after the time of Christ, then the possibility of interpolations increases. Who, then, is to say whether or not Christ actually rose from the dead, claimed he would rise from the dead, or was seen after his death?

The conclusion also assumes that Christ really existed in history and consequently is not mere legend or myth.

3. Empty tomb (Premise)

The argument map shows four key premises supporting the conclusion that Christ rose from the dead (points 3, 8, 13, and 16). Other premises can be added, and some Christians will at times place more emphasis on some premises than others.

The empty tomb, however, is important as a premise supporting the resurrection. Even Christ's enemies acknowledged the empty tomb, as the Gospels record.

4. Body stolen (Objection)

Objections to the resurrection claims are many. Reasonable critics understand the centrality of the resurrection to Christianity. One popular objection to the empty tomb is that the body of Jesus was stolen. The body could have been stolen to perpetrate a hoax. The disciples may have done this in order to keep the movement going despite the death of the founder. Perhaps some elements within the disciples wanted to raise up a political or militant movement to overthrow Roman oppression.

6. Wrong tomb (Objection)

Although not implemented too often these days, this objection is sometimes still raised. Supposedly, the disciples simply went to the wrong tomb and, finding it empty, jumped to the conclusion that Christ must have risen.

Rebuttals 5, 7, 10, 12, 15, and 18

All the rebuttals to the primary objections to the resurrection are addressed here. In summary, critics offer no solid or convincing insights; in fact, the objections often make little sense.

Responding to point 4, point 5 wonders who would have stolen the body of Christ. The disciples were broken and defeated, having witnessed Christ's death. They had no motive to steal the body. There are many problems with this theory. What evidence exists to support it? It is true that this claim was circulated directly following the resurrection. But why would the disciples steal the body? They had nothing to gain from such actions except persecution and even death. Furthermore, if they stole the body, then there is no viable explanation for their transformation from weak, frightened followers to bold proclaimers of the gospel, many of whom would later die for what they purportedly knew to be a lie (the resurrection). Moreover, the stolen body theory does not explain the appearances of Christ to witnesses.

If followers of Christ had gone to the wrong tomb (point 6), then the authorities could easily have gone to the right tomb and produced the body. At some point, at any rate, someone would have said, "The tomb of Jesus is over there," and Christianity would never have gotten started.

Did the disciples hallucinate (point 9)? Not only are true hallucinations uncommon, but mass hallucinations stretch the bounds of believability. But the New Testament clearly records a number of appearances, such as in 1 Corinthians 15:6 where it is said Christ "appeared to more than five hundred brothers at one time, most of whom are still alive." Given that Paul wrote 1 Corinthians between A.D. 53 and 55, only about twenty years had passed since the time of Christ's death—hardly enough time to develop legends or myths. Besides, Paul notes that "most" of the five hundred individuals who saw the risen Christ "are still alive." This is compelling evidence for the veracity of the claims of Christians regarding appearances of the risen Christ.

Saying the disciples were mistaken, lying, or deceived (point 11) does not offer the best explanation of the events or the known facts. How could they have been so mistaken that they were willing to die for their faith? If they were deceived, then how were they deceived and who deceived them? If they were lying, then they knew they were lying and died for their faith anyway.

Moreover, the radically changed lives of the disciples lend credibility to their account of what happened (point 15).

Finally, all other explanations of the resurrection are deficient. Other non-miraculous explanations of the resurrection have been proposed, but none fit the facts better than the Christian explanation. For instance, one scholar claims that Christ had a twin brother who happened to appear on the scene just as Christ was executed and decided to impersonate the risen Jesus. This claim stretches the bounds of credulity. Not only is there no evidence for a twin brother, but this solution results in further difficulties, such as what happened to this alleged twin brother? Other naturalistic explanations are similarly flimsy, coming across as grasping at straws rather than offering credible explanations.[1]

8. Appearances and witnesses (Premise)

Another premise supporting the resurrection of Christ is the many reports of postcrucifixion appearances to many witnesses. Paul, for instance, records that at one time more than five hundred people witnessed the risen Christ at the same time (1 Cor. 15:6). These appearances took place over a period of forty days, according to Acts 1:3, and were accompanied by "many convincing proofs" (NIV; "infallible" or "certain" proofs in the Greek). That Christians claimed Christ rose bodily is

---

1. Lest some readers think the "twin theory" of Jesus is fabricated, apologist William Lane Craig has debated Robert Greg Cavin, who has defended the twin theory as an explanation of claims of resurrection. Craig vs. Cavin, "Dead or Alive? A Debate on the Resurrection of Jesus" (Anaheim, CA: Simon Greenleaf University, February 1995).

clear. Jesus encouraged Thomas to touch him as proof that he was flesh, not a spirit. Jesus also ate food with his followers after the resurrection.

9. Hallucinations (Objection)

Some critics have claimed that the postcrucifixion appearances may be explained away as mass hallucinations. Such an objection stretches the bounds of what is reasonable. Is it reasonable to explain the claimed appearance of Christ to more than five hundred people at once as a hallucination? Again, this is a bias on the part of the naturalistic critic who will not allow for miracles.

11. Mistaken, lying, deceived (Objection)

This trio of objections underscores other lines of objections to the resurrection surrounding the claims of witnesses and Christ's appearances (point 8). Were the disciples mistaken? If so, how could all of them have made such an incredible error?

Were they lying? If so, why? What did they have to gain? How were other lives they impacted existentially transformed? In other words, the Christian message claims to actually change lives, but if Christ never rose, then how are so many lives dramatically changed? How does one explain away Christ's physical appearances?

What about some sort of deception? Were the disciples deceived by others or self-deluded?

None of these objections are strong. Although the "self-deluded" objection may have some merit, it fails to adequately account for all of the viable premises supporting the conclusion that Christ rose from the dead.

13. Changed lives (followers, Paul) (Premise)

While not a convincing premise on its own, the fact that lives were radically changed as claims of resurrection followed Christ's crucifixion lends support to the Christian account of events. The followers of Christ suddenly and dramatically transformed from a scared band of disciples to a band of bold proclaimers of Christ and his resurrection. What did they have to gain? Certainly not power or riches or prestige. Many of them gained death for their troubles.

The conversion of Paul, too, is significant, as he was once openly hostile to Christians and their claims. His conversion demands explanation. How is it that such a vehement enemy of the cross dramatically changed sides? The best explanation of Paul's conversion is that he really encountered the risen Christ as the book of Acts records.

14. How does this prove Christianity? (Objection)

This objection is responding to the premise that the resurrection changed lives (see point 13). Again, point 13 is not a stand-alone argument for the resurrection; it works in conjunction with the other premises to build an overall cumulative case for the resurrection as the best explanation. Still, this does not mean that the changed-lives premise has no merit. While by itself it does not "prove" Christianity, it does lend support to the resurrection as well as presenting a puzzle to critics. If, as they claim, Christ did not rise, then why did so many people believe he did, and why did they change so dramatically?

16. Explains Christian origins (Premise)

This premise follows from the previous one (changed lives). Without dramatically transformed lives, it is highly improbable that Christianity would have grown or spread as it did. The first Christians were wholeheartedly committed to belief in the resurrected Christ. They knew Christ had died, they knew the tomb was later empty, they saw the risen Christ, and their lives were changed. Christian commitment to these truths resulted in the incredible origins of Christianity. A small band of Jews, somehow transformed, began a religion in a hostile climate, not only surviving but ultimately thriving.

17. There are other explanations (Objection)

As is true for any event, there are other explanations for how Christianity began. Perhaps a group of disgruntled Hebrews merely wished to start a movement to overthrow Roman power, or an astute Rabbi wished to spread his philosophy, a clever author or group of authors may have created a series of fictional stories in the hopes that others might believe them as true, or early Christians borrowed from pagan religions in order to try to improve upon Judaism.

But are any such alternative explanations reasonable? Are they the best explanations? In short, as point 18 rebuts, other explanations of the origins of Christianity are deficient.

19. Christ never existed (Objection)

If Christ never existed, then obviously the resurrection is not factual history but a legend, myth, or fairy tale. We may as well claim that the Easter Bunny rose from the dead. However, the view that Christ never existed is a minority view even among liberal scholars.

20. He did exist (Rebuttal)	The evidence for the historicity of Christ is overwhelming. Even the vast majority of liberal scholars accept that Jesus was a real, historical person.[2]
21. Christ did not die on the cross (Objection)	This objection is sometimes raised by Muslims, who believe that God would never allow a great prophet such as Christ to die by crucifixion. Muslims claim that God only made it appear as though Christ died on the cross, or that he substituted someone else in Christ's place, supposedly Judas, and made it look as though it was Christ.
22. Christ died and was buried (Rebuttal)	The evidence for Christ's death is extensive. He underwent beatings, blood loss, impalement by a spear, and more. Besides, the Romans were experts at execution by crucifixion and knew when someone had died. Also, if Christ did not die but only "swooned" on the cross, as some have suggested, then how, in his critically weakened state, did he manage to move the boulder from the tomb, get past the guards, and then somehow convince his disciples that he was the glorified, victorious, and risen Christ? Furthermore, what happened to him after his appearances? Did he leave the country? These explanations are, to say the least, farfetched.
23. Miracles are not possible (Objection)	Naturalistic critics deny miracles. Consequently, no supernatural explanation of any kind will convince them of the resurrection. The objection here may be firm in claiming that miracles are impossible, or less firm by claiming that an event such as a resurrection is highly improbable, going against the normative pattern of nature. Since people die all the time and stay dead, then it is highly improbable that Christ rose from the dead.
24. God exists, miracles are possible (Rebuttal)	The naturalistic approach that miracles are impossible or highly improbable presupposes that the theistic God does not exist. If this is the case on the part of the critic, then it may benefit the apologist to first make the case for the existence of God prior to arguing a detailed case for the resurrection of Christ. However, responses here will differ based on one's apologetic methodology. The author favors a cumulative case, classical apologetics approach, which would typically make the case for God's existence first. However, other approaches such as evidentialism may wish to argue for the resurrection based on

---

2. See, for instance, R. T. France, *The Evidence for Jesus*.

the overwhelming evidence for it and its centrality to Christianity rather than, at this juncture, making the case for a theistic but not explicitly Christian God.

25. Gospels are legends (Objection)

This objection dismisses the Gospels as merely legendary documents, thereby avoiding arguments about the resurrection altogether. After all, if the documents are legendary, then they can hardly be expected to present factual history.

26. Gospels are reliable (Rebuttal)

If the Gospels are truly legends and therefore not reliable history, then the critic is right to object to the conclusion that Christ rose from the dead. But if the Gospels can be demonstrated to be reliable historical documents, then claims that they are nothing more than legend are invalid and the resurrection demands a response.

DISCUSSION QUESTIONS

1. If Christ did not rise from the dead, would Christianity still retain value and meaning to life?
2. Explain why the following two objections to the resurrection are weak: (1) the body of Christ was stolen; (2) the disciples went to the wrong tomb.
3. Is there validity to the claim that the disciples who claimed to see the risen Christ were merely hallucinating?
4. How does the resurrection explain the origins of Christianity?
5. Which premise (point 3, 8, 13, or 16) in support of the resurrection resonates with you the most? Why?

SUGGESTED ASSIGNMENTS

1. Research and write a paper defending the historicity of Christ in light of claims that the Christ was a mythical figure. See, for instance, *The Evidence for Jesus* by R. T. France, *He Walked Among Us* by Josh McDowell and Bill Wilson, and *The Historical Jesus* by Gary Habermas.
2. Defend the possibility of miracles given the theistic worldview. See, for instance, *Miracles* by C. S. Lewis, *Miracles and the Modern Mind* by Norman Geisler, and *In Defense of Miracles* edited by R. Douglas Geivett and Gary Habermas.
3. Assess theologically the meaning and significance of Christ's resurrection to the Christian worldview. Consult such resources as *The Case for the Resurrection of Jesus* by Gary Habermas and Michael Licona and *The Case for the Resurrection* by Lee Strobel.

CHAPTER 11

Christ Is the Only Way of Salvation

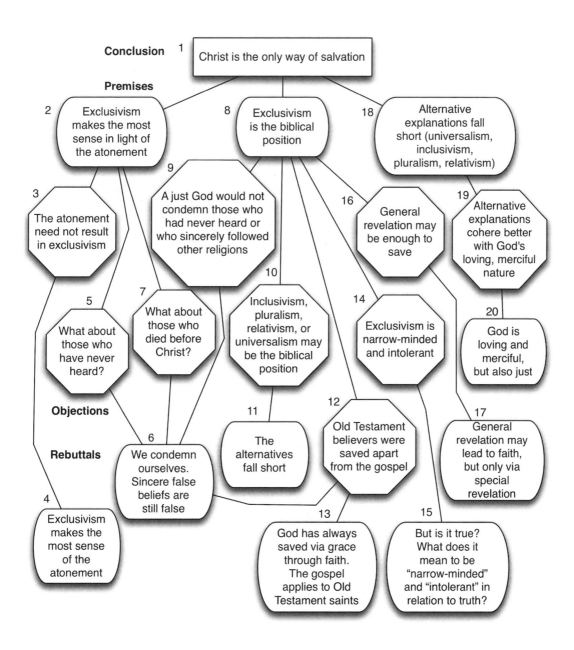

Conclusion 1 — Christ is the only way of salvation

Premises

2 — Exclusivism makes the most sense in light of the atonement

8 — Exclusivism is the biblical position

18 — Alternative explanations fall short (universalism, inclusivism, pluralism, relativism)

3 — The atonement need not result in exclusivism

9 — A just God would not condemn those who had never heard or who sincerely followed other religions

16 — General revelation may be enough to save

19 — Alternative explanations cohere better with God's loving, merciful nature

5 — What about those who have never heard?

7 — What about those who died before Christ?

10 — Inclusivism, pluralism, relativism, or universalism may be the biblical position

14 — Exclusivism is narrow-minded and intolerant

20 — God is loving and merciful, but also just

Objections

Rebuttals

4 — Exclusivism makes the most sense of the atonement

6 — We condemn ourselves. Sincere false beliefs are still false

11 — The alternatives fall short

12 — Old Testament believers were saved apart from the gospel

17 — General revelation may lead to faith, but only via special revelation

13 — God has always saved via grace through faith. The gospel applies to Old Testament saints

15 — But is it true? What does it mean to be "narrow-minded" and "intolerant" in relation to truth?

1. Christ is the only way of salvation (Conclusion)

Sometimes referred to as Christian exclusivism, particularism, or restrictivism, this conclusion holds that only through Christ can the lost be saved. Some forms of competing positions, such as inclusivism, also argue that Christ is ultimately the only way of salvation, but those involved in other religions may find this way, perhaps even inadvertently. That is not the conclusion of this diagram, however.[1] Rather, since Christ himself made claims of exclusivity, such as in John 14:6, and since his followers also made such claims, such as in Acts 4:12, then it follows that Christ is the only way of salvation.

2. Exclusivism makes the most sense in light of the atonement (Premise)

The atonement of Christ is a theological doctrine having to do with God's solution to the Fall, which resulted in human separation from God due to human sin. In some manner—there are numerous atonement theories—Christ's death provided for the restoration of the broken human relationship with God.

If individuals could be saved or spiritually liberated or enlightened in another manner apart from Christ, then that would appear to minimize if not entirely negate the purpose of Christ's atonement. Given the biblical, theological, and logical evidence, then, Christian exclusivism is the best explanation of salvation and its terms.

3. The atonement need not result in exclusivism (Objection)

This objection may be offered by both Christians and non-Christians. Non-Christians, for instance, may claim that all religions are essentially true (chapter 22), and consequently God, or whatever reality is behind the universe, will accept people from various, if not all, religious traditions and belief systems. In this view, Christ is only one way to spiritual liberation.

Some Christian inclusivists and even universalists would object by noting that exclusivism seems contrary to God's nature. God might make exceptions, for instance, for those who have never heard the gospel (points 5 and 7); or he may accept sincere worship even though it is mistakenly offered to false deities. Universalists may agree in a sense with the atonement of Christ, but argue that in the end God will somehow bring every soul into his heavenly kingdom because to do otherwise would demonstrate that God is less then all-powerful and all-loving.

---

1. On these matters see Morgan and Peterson, *Faith Comes by Hearing*.

4. Exclusivism makes the most sense of the atonement (Rebuttal)

5. What about those who have never heard? (Objection)

7. What about those who died before Christ? (Objection)

9. A just God would not condemn those who had never heard or who sincerely followed other religions (Objection)

6. We condemn ourselves. Sincere false beliefs are still false (Rebuttal)

We are really back to point 2 here, but we are not arguing in a circle. If the best explanation of the biblical evidence at hand is indeed exclusivism, then any alternative is by definition false.

Three objection points are combined here (5, 7, and 9) since they converge on the same rebuttal (point 6)

Another objection to point 2 is the common question about those who have never heard the gospel message of Christ (point 5). Isn't it unfair that God would condemn such people to death without even giving them an opportunity to hear the message of salvation through Christ?

The objection in point 5 claims that God would be unjust not to make exceptions or provide some way for those who have never heard to accept Christ and the salvation he offers. One response is to note that salvation is always by God's grace through faith. Old Testament saints, for example, were theists (response to point 7). Since they lived before Christ, we face something of a puzzle in relation to their salvation—or so it seems. But God transcends our understanding of time; hence, Christ's death over 2,000 years ago atones for our sins today even though we were not born in the first century. The same principle can extend the other direction in time, which explains how people in Old Testament times were saved.

Another possible option considers the passage in 1 Peter 3:19 about how Christ "went and made proclamation to the imprisoned spirits" (NIV). Perhaps, some argue, Christ presented the gospel message to those who died before his time on earth, thus granting them an opportunity to embrace his truth.

At any rate, the exclusivist can respond by noting that in reality we each condemn ourselves. Human depravity and sin is more than enough for God to condemn us. In fact, God being completely holy is perfectly within his rights, so to speak, to condemn everyone to hell. Moreover, sincerity that is sincerely wrong is still wrong. God has given us enough information to know that he exists (Ps. 19:1; Rom. 1:20) and enough evidence to accept the claims of Christ. Any rejection of that evidence and those claims is enough to condemn us.

As for the objection in point 9, again we must reiterate that we condemn ourselves and that our sincere beliefs, if false, are still false. God is indeed holy and just. Consequently, he would be justified in condemning all of humanity. By his grace he does not. In fact, he offers the way of salvation via Christ's atoning death and resurrection.

8. Exclusivism is the biblical position (Premise)	Exclusivists marshal an impressive array of biblical evidence in support of their claim. We have already noted John 14:6 and Acts 4:12. To this we may add Romans 10:17: "So faith comes from hearing, and hearing by the word of Christ" (NASB). In other words, those who respond to Christ's exclusive claims must do so through directly hearing his claims presented. Given the convergence of biblical evidence in support of exclusivism, alternatives such as religious pluralism (chapter 22), inclusivism, and universalism are to be rejected.
10. Inclusivism, pluralism, relativism, or universalism may be the biblical position (Objection)	Those who hold to one of these positions will offer evidence that appears to contradict exclusivist claims. New Age pantheists, for instance, may claim that Jesus came to show us "a way" of spiritual liberation, but certainly not the "only way." Perhaps he merely phrased it in such terms for the benefit of the simple people he was speaking to at the time. In reality, we can all share in the Christ consciousness. Christian inclusivists, on the other hand, do not deny verses such as John 14:6. Instead, they attempt to fit those verses within an inclusivist approach to salvation.
11. The alternatives fall short (Rebuttal)	The exclusivist rebuttal is, simply, that the alternative explanations fall short. The biblical evidence clearly supports exclusivism, which in turn makes the most sense in light of the atonement (point 2). Moreover, as the line of reasoning beginning with point 18 demonstrates, the alternative explanations simply do not measure up to the exclusivist position.
12. Old Testament believers were saved apart from the gospel (Objection)	This objection believes that there must have been a different standard of salvation in the Old Testament. Consequently, God may similarly establish a different way, or even ways, of salvation after Christ.
13. God has always saved via grace through faith. The gospel applies to Old Testament saints (Rebuttal)	See point 6 for a general response to the objection in point 12.
14. Exclusivism is narrow-minded and intolerant (Objection)	The claim is that by presenting itself as exclusive, Christianity demonstrates that it is a backwards religion that is not only narrow-minded but also intolerant.

15. But is it true? What does it mean to be "narrow-minded" and "intolerant" in relation to truth? (Rebuttal)	These objections are touched upon in chapter 20. It's not a matter of whether or not one is "narrow-minded" or "intolerant," but whether or not the claims in question are true or not. What really matters here is whether or not Christ's exclusive claims correspond to reality. If so, typically emotional responses, such as from those who claim Christianity is narrow-minded and intolerant, fail to defeat the truth of the claim. Besides, it is not Christ's followers who made up the claim, but Christ himself. Is Christ, then, narrow-minded and intolerant?
16. General revelation may be enough to save (Objection)	The objection here is that through nature and human conscience (general revelation), God may indeed reveal enough of himself to save the lost without need for special revelation.
17. General revelation may lead to faith, but only via special revelation (Rebuttal)	God has indeed provided general revelation to awaken human beings to his existence. Hence, Psalm 19:1 appeals to the wonders of creation, while Romans 1:20 also notes that God has clearly revealed himself through creation. In addition, Romans 2 demonstrates that everyone has God's laws written on their hearts. But even though these signs may point us to faith and belief in God, especially for those who accept the validity of natural theology, such general revelation is not sufficient. Otherwise, why would God have bothered sending Christ? Special revelation is required. Through Christ, God's specific plan of redemption for humanity via the atonement is made clear.
18. Alternative explanations fall short (universalism, inclusivism, pluralism, relativism) (Rebuttal)	The reasoning here is that of inference to the best explanation (abductive reasoning). If the convergence of various lines of evidence better supports the exclusivist position, then the alternatives are likely wrong.
19. Alternative explanations cohere better with God's loving, merciful nature (Objection)	Exclusivism is rejected not necessarily on the basis of biblical evidence alone, but on the basis that other explanations harmonize better with God's character attributes of love and mercy. A loving God would allow for salvation outside of the exclusive claims of Christ.
20. God is loving and merciful, but also just (Rebuttal)	The rebuttal underscores material addressed in point 6. God is indeed loving and merciful, but is also holy and he demands justice. Those who reject his way of salvation and attempt to restore and redeem their relationship with God in any other way contradict God's plan of salvation through Christ.

DISCUSSION QUESTIONS

1. How would you respond to the claim that Christian exclusivism is intolerant and narrow-minded?
2. What biblical evidence exists for the inclusivist position?
3. How can God's mercy be reconciled with the exclusivist position?
4. Is general revelation sufficient or insufficient when it comes to salvation?
5. Respond to the statement, "Wouldn't a truly loving God save everyone?"

SUGGESTED ASSIGNMENTS

1. Read *Faith Comes by Hearing*, edited by Christopher Morgan and Robert Peterson, and write a report assessing exclusivism and inclusivism.
2. Compare and contrast biblical exclusivism with inclusivism, pluralism, and universalism.
3. Research three different Christian systematic theologies on the question of salvation. Summarize their findings, noting anything they say about exclusivism, inclusivism, and related matters.
4. Write a report on the biblical view of God's holiness, justice, and mercy and how they come into play in relation to salvation. Consult such resources as *The Holiness of God* by R. C. Sproul and volume 2 of Norman Geisler's *Systematic Theology*, specifically chapters on the relevant attributes of God.

CHAPTER 12

The Argument from Desire

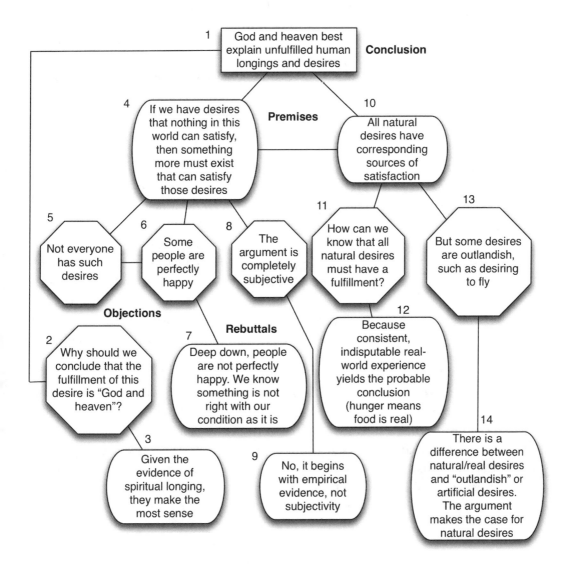

1 God and heaven best explain unfulfilled human longings and desires — **Conclusion**

Premises

4 If we have desires that nothing in this world can satisfy, then something more must exist that can satisfy those desires

10 All natural desires have corresponding sources of satisfaction

Objections

5 Not everyone has such desires

6 Some people are perfectly happy

8 The argument is completely subjective

11 How can we know that all natural desires must have a fulfillment?

13 But some desires are outlandish, such as desiring to fly

Rebuttals

2 Why should we conclude that the fulfillment of this desire is "God and heaven"?

7 Deep down, people are not perfectly happy. We know something is not right with our condition as it is

12 Because consistent, indisputable real-world experience yields the probable conclusion (hunger means food is real)

3 Given the evidence of spiritual longing, they make the most sense

9 No, it begins with empirical evidence, not subjectivity

14 There is a difference between natural/real desires and "outlandish" or artificial desires. The argument makes the case for natural desires

1. God and heaven best explain unfulfilled human longings and desires (Conclusion)

This argument has roots in Augustine and Pascal, but in more recent times it was popularized by C. S. Lewis, with further contemplations on it by Peter Kreeft.[1] The conclusion reasons that human desires (longings) that remain unfulfilled in this world demonstrate that we were probably made for another world (i.e., heaven).

2. Why should we conclude that the fulfillment of this desire is "God and heaven"? (Objection)

This is a major objection to the conclusion of the argument. Why, after all, should we conclude that "God and heaven" either must be or are probably the best explanations for this supposed desire? Couldn't we just be deluded or mistaken? Moreover, aren't some people truly happy without the need to appeal to God or heaven? (point 6)

3. Given the evidence of spiritual longing, they make the most sense (Rebuttal)

The argument from desire takes empirical evidence—unfulfilled human desires compared with desires that are truly fulfilled in nature—and observes that the natural world cannot satisfy deep human longings. Since nature cannot satisfy these desires, there must be something beyond nature that does (God) and a place where this fulfillment is attained (heaven).

Although this argument can only go so far on its own, it can be compelling when integrated into a larger case for Christianity. If God exists, for instance, then it follows that human fulfillment resides in our Maker, not in ourselves or anything in this world.

4. If we have desires that nothing in this world can satisfy, then something more must exist that can satisfy those desires (Premise)

The idea here is that we strive for fulfillment in this life, but it remains elusive no matter what. Material wealth, for instance, does not completely satisfy, as many wealthy individuals will attest. Relationships do not fully satisfy us. Something remains elusive—something that, the argument goes, God must have placed within us, and he is its only true fulfillment. These are not simple desires, but deep-seated desires of the human soul for spiritual meaning.

Those who have experienced such longings—everyone, according to the argument—feel these emotional pangs of want, of desire for something that is supposed to fill the void within us. Since we cannot find their ultimate fulfillment in this world, then isn't it probable that we were made for another world and for God?

---

1. See Kreeft and Tacelli, *Handbook of Christian Apologetics*, 78–81; and Kreeft, "C. S. Lewis's Argument from Desire," in *G. K. Chesterton and C. S. Lewis: The Riddle of Joy*, eds. Michael H. Macdonald and Andrew A. Tadie (Grand Rapids: Eerdmans, 1989).

5. Not everyone has such desires (Objection)

6. Some people are perfectly happy (Objection)

These objections claim that there are exceptions to the belief that everyone has these kinds of desires and that some people are perfectly happy and fulfilled. If exceptions exist to the claim that everyone has unfulfilled desires, then isn't the argument refuted by a simple counterexample? Again, if some people claim to be perfectly happy, feeling no need for further fulfillment, then isn't this yet another counterexample refuting the argument from desire? It would seem so.

7. Deep down, people are not perfectly happy. We know something is not right with our condition as it is (Rebuttal)

Those who claim they do not have such desires or are perfectly happy either do not understand the kind of longing and fulfillment the argument is presenting or are being dishonest with themselves and with others. They are denying a critical aspect of what makes them human. The history of human thinking is littered with vain attempts to solve the riddle of human meaning and unfulfilled desires. Only Christ offers the solution and the evidence to back up his claims (chapter 10).

8. The argument is completely subjective (Objection)

The objection claims the argument is completely subjective. How can anyone really know how others feel in relation to this supposed desire or longing?

9. No, it begins with empirical evidence, not subjectivity (Rebuttal)

See point 3. The argument observes empirically that in nature, desires are fulfilled (hunger is fulfilled by eating food, for instance). It then observes human behavior and the need for fulfillment, concluding that if nature cannot truly satisfy this human desire, then something beyond nature must exist that can in fact fulfill the desire.

10. All natural desires have corresponding sources of satisfaction (Premise)

We observe nature and we see that all natural desires find fulfillment in the natural world. Hunger is satisfied by food, for instance, and thirst by water. Consequently, we can infer that if a longing or desire dwells in us that we cannot satisfy in nature, its fulfillment is most probably found outside the natural world.

11. How can we know that all natural desires must have a fulfillment? (Objection)

Is it possible for us to know this beyond doubt? Doesn't it seem like we are begging the question, as though somehow we know ahead of time that all natural desires have a corresponding fulfillment?

12. Because consistent, indisputable real-world experience yields the probable conclusion (hunger means food is real) (Rebuttal)

Based on our observations of natural desires and their real, corresponding fulfillment in nature, we can conclude with high probability that desires do indeed find fulfillment. It is simply the way the universe is wired, so to speak. Theists believe it is wired by God; thus, any human desire that cannot find true fulfillment in this world must find its fulfillment beyond (in God and heaven). We can make justifiable inferences based on the available evidence.

13. But some desires are outlandish, such as desiring to fly (Objection)

Does the argument really mean that if someone desires to swim to the deepest depth of the ocean, then that desire must be fulfilled naturally somehow? Doesn't this kind of example reduce the argument from desire to absurdity? Don't people desire all kinds of outlandish things? Do their outlandish desires have real fulfillments?

14. There is a difference between natural/real desires and "outlandish" or artificial desires. The argument makes the case for natural desires (Rebuttal)

Peter Kreeft calls desires like wishing to fly "artificial" desires: "The existence of the artificial desires does not necessarily mean that the desired objects exist. Some do; some don't."[2] But, some may object, aren't we arbitrarily labeling some desires as natural and others as artificial simply to bolster our case for the argument from desire? What if the desire for fulfillment is itself artificial? As Kreeft and Ronald Tacelli explain,

> There are differences between these two kinds of desires. We do not, for example, for the most part, recognize corresponding states of deprivation for the second, the artificial, desires, as we do for the first [natural]. . . . The natural desires come from within, from our nature, while the artificial ones come from without, from society, or advertising or fiction. . . . The natural desires are found in all of us, but the artificial ones vary from person to person. The existence of artificial desires does not necessarily mean that the desired objects exist. . . . But the existence of natural desires does, in every discoverable case, mean that the objects desired exist. No one has ever found one case of an innate desire for a nonexistent object.[3]

Consequently, if we can substantiate the claim that a desire for fulfillment is natural and indeed central to human experience, then it is not an arbitrary decision to consider it a natural desire rather than an artificial one.

---

2. Kreeft and Tacelli, *Handbook of Christian Apologetics*, 78.
3. Ibid.

DISCUSSION QUESTIONS

1. If successful, what does the argument from desire accomplish?
2. What is one weakness of the argument from desire?
3. How would you respond to someone who claims to have no elusive desires and is, in fact, perfectly content?
4. Why does the reasoning behind the argument from desire not apply to the desire to fly?
5. Do you find the argument from desire compelling or not? Why or why not?

SUGGESTED ASSIGNMENTS

1. Read Peter Kreeft's essay on the argument from desire in *G. K. Chesterton and C. S. Lewis: The Riddle of Joy* and write a report evaluating Kreeft's approach.
2. Read C. S. Lewis's brief case for the argument from desire in *Mere Christianity*, book 3, chapter 10, then summarize and evaluate it in writing.
3. Read *The Apologetics of Joy* by Joe Puckett Jr., and write a report summarizing the approach taken to C. S. Lewis's argument from desire.

CHAPTER 13

Pascal's Anthropological Argument

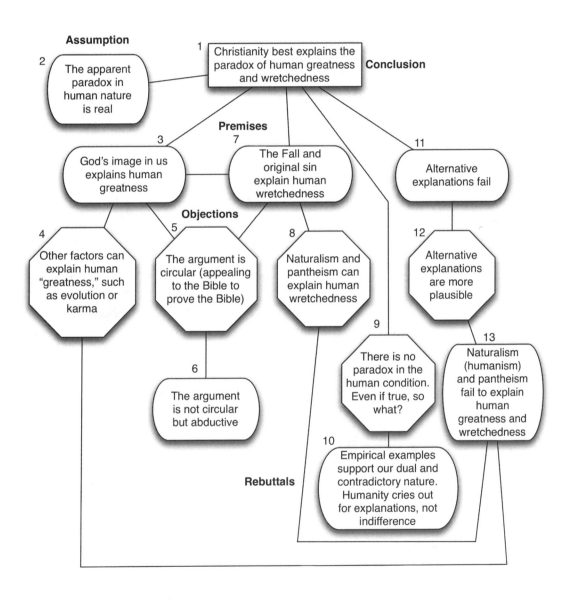

Assumption

2 The apparent paradox in human nature is real

1 Christianity best explains the paradox of human greatness and wretchedness **Conclusion**

Premises

3 God's image in us explains human greatness

7 The Fall and original sin explain human wretchedness

11 Alternative explanations fail

Objections

4 Other factors can explain human "greatness," such as evolution or karma

5 The argument is circular (appealing to the Bible to prove the Bible)

8 Naturalism and pantheism can explain human wretchedness

12 Alternative explanations are more plausible

9 There is no paradox in the human condition. Even if true, so what?

13 Naturalism (humanism) and pantheism fail to explain human greatness and wretchedness

6 The argument is not circular but abductive

Rebuttals

10 Empirical examples support our dual and contradictory nature. Humanity cries out for explanations, not indifference

1. Christianity best explains the paradox of human greatness and wretchedness (Conclusion)

This argument claims that there is a paradox inherent within human beings. We exhibit qualities of greatness, but also qualities of wretchedness. Blaise Pascal used abductive reasoning to demonstrate that Christianity best explains this reality.[1]

In order for this argument to succeed, it must be demonstrated that human greatness and human wretchedness are real and thus pose an existential problem. It must also be demonstrated that Christianity explains this apparent paradox better than alternative explanations. If Christianity indeed appears to furnish the best explanation of humanity's conflicted condition then that would lend credence to Christianity as a whole offering a better explanation of reality than competing worldviews.

2. The apparent paradox in human nature is real (Assumption)

The argument assumes that the apparent paradox of human nature is real. For evidence of this assumption, see point 10.

3. God's image in us explains human greatness (Premise)

Although we have already touched upon the image of God in us and its implications in chapter 3, we will reiterate and supplement those remarks here. Biblically speaking, human beings are made in God's image (Gen. 1:26–27). What does this mean? We are not identical with God, but we reflect aspects of his nature and being. For instance, as God is creative and imaginative, so too are humans to a lesser extent. As God is a rational being, so are we. In addition, we are moral creatures, aware of right and wrong despite our fallen nature. Obviously, we are also personal beings. God is not a wooden statue devoid of personality, but is a vibrant, living, personal being. We humans likewise exhibit personal qualities. Although corporeal, we are also spiritual in nature, and in this sense we are like God the Father, who is incorporeal.

Pascal's anthropological argument grants that human beings are capable of greatness—acts of altruism, for instance. Only because we are made in God's image can we do anything great. Consequently, people risk their lives to save others, go-

---

1. Abductive reasoning is sometimes accused of being circular or of committing the *post hoc* fallacy, which, in short, states that since one event followed another, it must have been caused by the other. Properly implemented, however, abductive reasoning appeals to evidence and the best explanation approach rather than being circular or *post hoc*. Pascal's anthropological argument, for example, appeals to the evidence for human greatness and wretchedness first, then seeks to find a worldview that best fits with these facts. See Robert Velarde, "Greatness and Wretchedness: The Usefulness of Pascal's Anthropological Argument in Apologetics," *Christian Research Journal* 27, no. 2 (2004).

ing against the instinct for self-preservation. We also create beautiful works of art, music, and other creative expressions because God's image in us drives us creatively.

4. Other factors can explain human "greatness," such as evolution or karma (Objection)

The objection turns to the possibility of alternative explanations for human "greatness." If other explanations are just as reasonable or better than the explanation in point 3, then the argument fails. Can evolution explain human greatness? The argument in its favor would seem to point to some evolutionary drive within humans that is tied to survival. As humans strive to survive in a hostile environment, they must exhibit what we refer to as "greatness" in order to evolve and adapt.

Another objection may point to karma as a solution. If we are part of a system that punishes our bad behavior but rewards our good behavior, then human greatness is a sign of our good behavior manifesting itself in reality.

Besides, in order to accept the Christian explanation of human greatness, much other apologetic work must be done. One must show that God exists, that the Bible is reliable, that Christianity is true, and so forth. It doesn't seem necessary to explain human greatness in such a convoluted way.

One may also deny the term "greatness" in reference to, say, moral acts and even creative acts. If God does not exist, then "greatness" is a false view of reality. There is nothing truly "great" or "beautiful" if God does not exist, but all such human thinking on ethical and aesthetic matters is relative and ungrounded in any transcendent source. If monistic pantheism is true, then good and evil are all part of the same impersonal force driving the universe. Consequently, there are no distinctions between greatness and wretchedness.

5. The argument is circular (appealing to the Bible to prove the Bible) (Objection)

Point 3 appears to appeal to the Bible in order to prove the Bible. In other words, it claims Christianity explains greatness and wretchedness because the doctrines that deal with humans made in God's image and with the Fall are true. How is this not circular?

6. The argument is not circular but abductive (Rebuttal)

Point 5 misunderstands the argument. Pascal is trying to reason to the best explanation, thus making logical inferences. This sort of reasoning is often applied in scientific thinking. Pascal is looking at the observable evidence, noting that humans exhibit seemingly paradoxical behavior (both greatness and wretchedness). He then seeks to find a solution to this problem. If being made in God's image and then distorted by the Fall best explains our condition of both greatness and wretchedness, then the argument is not circular but instead rests on evidence.

However, Pascal's argument alone is probably insufficient, serving rather to corroborate a cumulative apologetic case. One may need to argue further for the existence of God, the reliability of the Bible, and the truth of Christianity.

7. The Fall and original sin explain human wretchedness (Premise)

Human beings are not basically good, as some pop psychology suggests. If the history of humanity teaches us anything, it should teach us that human beings are constantly at war with themselves and with others. Acts of wretchedness abound in history and in our present world. Why?

If Christianity is true, then the Fall offers a plausible explanation. We have fallen from our once great place in the world, resulting in broken, depraved humanity with inclinations to sin.

8. Naturalism and pantheism can explain human wretchedness (Objection)

Why turn to biblical fairy tales for an explanation when other worldviews can better explain our wretchedness? Supposed acts of "wretchedness" within naturalism (atheism) can be attributed to evolutionary factors. Some people behave wretchedly in order to get ahead and survive. These are evolutionary instincts and need not be labeled "bad" or "wretched."

The naturalist may also explain "bad" examples of wretchedness, such as violence, rape, and so forth, as anomalies which evolution can weed out and eventually eliminate from humanity.

What of pantheism's explanation for so-called human wretchedness? We touched on this explanation in point 4 when we discussed the doctrine of karma.

9. There is no paradox in the human condition. Even if true, so what? (Objection)

This objection responds directly to the conclusion (point 1): There is no paradox in the human condition. Even if true, so what? Human beings are what they are. Some people exhibit greatness, some wretchedness, but this need not mean Christianity is true. Social conditions may have contributed to behavior, resulting in some just being lucky, achieving and exhibiting greatness, while others were not so lucky, resulting in wretched behavior.

One may even argue that the reality of wretched acts in the world does not argue for God but against him (see chapters 14 and 19 on the problem of evil and suffering). Besides, even if this supposed paradox of greatness and wretchedness exists, so what? Does it really matter or prove to be metaphysically meaningful?

10. Empirical examples support our dual and contradictory nature. Humanity cries out for explanations, not indifference (Rebuttal)

Much of the objection in point 9 is akin to nihilistic despair or at least indifference. Rather than shrug our shoulders and press on in a seemingly cruel world, Pascal calls us to examine the empirical examples that support our dual and contradictory nature. We exhibit greatness, but also wretchedness. Why is this the case? Humanity cries out for explanations, not indifference. If the best explanation points to a transcendent truth (God) and offers us a solution (Christ), then why should we shun or reject it?

Social conditions are insufficient explanations of human greatness and human wretchedness. One may argue, for instance, that the morals of a society have no basis in reality if they derive from non-Christian worldviews that deny an objective, transcendent source of morality.

Moreover, Pascal's observation of greatness and wretchedness in human beings spans human history and the entirety of the human experience. To attribute greatness and wretchedness merely to social conditions is farfetched in light of observational evidence. It's a possible explanation, but the Christian worldview as a whole better explains the human condition on the basis of the Fall and our likeness in God's image.

11. Alternative explanations fail (Premise)

The anthropological argument offers its explanation and argues that alternative explanations fail. Atheism cannot account for the paradox of human greatness and wretchedness since on atheistic terms there is no good reason for human beings to behave altruistically or in ways that are counterintuitive to their survival. Neither can pantheism explain human greatness and wretchedness, particularly since pantheism does away with such distinctions, viewing morality as relative. Pantheism therefore cannot rightly make moral distinctions between greatness or wretchedness, since it sees everything as divine.

12. Alternative explanations are more plausible (Objection)

The objection is that alternative explanations are more plausible; however, the objection may also be nuanced to say that other explanations are equally as plausible as the conclusion in point 1. If so, then we are at a standstill with no specific explanation being markedly superior to another. One may also argue that an alternative explanation, such as is offered by naturalism or monistic pantheism, is superior, in which case the Christian explanation fails.

13. Naturalism (humanism) and pantheism fail to explain human greatness and wretchedness (Rebuttal)

But as we have seen, alternative explanations fall short. We do have a dual nature of greatness and wretchedness; existential human needs require that it be explained; and the doctrines of the Fall and of human beings made in God's image offer the best explanatory power and scope. Pascal's argument not only diagnoses the human condition but also points to a solution in the person of Christ. In a sense, Pascal is calling all worldviews to the table of judgment via intellectual scrutiny. Can any one worldview plausibly explain human greatness and wretchedness?

DISCUSSION QUESTIONS

1. What is the paradox Pascal identifies within human beings? Why is it that he considers Christianity the best explanation of this seeming paradox?
2. Why is the anthropological argument not circular in its reasoning?
3. Respond to the objection that the human condition needs no explaining.
4. What empirical evidence supports the claims that human beings are both great and wretched?

SUGGESTED ASSIGNMENTS

1. Read the chapter on deposed royalty in *On Pascal* by Douglas Groothuis and write a report summarizing and evaluating the material.
2. Make a case for the biblical doctrines of the Fall and original sin, taking into account God's image in us and its relationship to Pascal's anthropological argument.
3. Research and write a short paper explaining the differences between inductive, deductive, and abductive reasoning, showing how Pascal's anthropological argument uses abductive reasoning. For definitions of these kinds of logic, see the glossary.

CHAPTER 14

Christianity Best Explains Evil

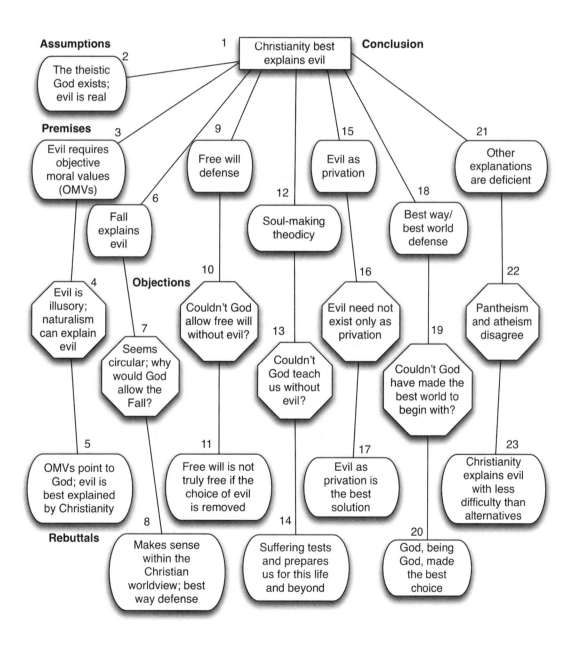

Assumptions

1 Christianity best explains evil

Conclusion

2 The theistic God exists; evil is real

Premises

3 Evil requires objective moral values (OMVs)

9 Free will defense

15 Evil as privation

21 Other explanations are deficient

6 Fall explains evil

12 Soul-making theodicy

18 Best way/ best world defense

4 Evil is illusory; naturalism can explain evil

Objections

10 Couldn't God allow free will without evil?

16 Evil need not exist only as privation

22 Pantheism and atheism disagree

7 Seems circular; why would God allow the Fall?

13 Couldn't God teach us without evil?

19 Couldn't God have made the best world to begin with?

5 OMVs point to God; evil is best explained by Christianity

11 Free will is not truly free if the choice of evil is removed

17 Evil as privation is the best solution

23 Christianity explains evil with less difficulty than alternatives

Rebuttals

8 Makes sense within the Christian worldview; best way defense

14 Suffering tests and prepares us for this life and beyond

20 God, being God, made the best choice

1. Christianity best explains evil (Conclusion)	The conclusion succinctly claims that Christianity best explains evil. Note that this does not mean that Christianity explains every aspect of evil to everyone's complete satisfaction, but rather, that in comparison to other explanations, Christian theism offers the *best* explanation for evil and suffering. Every worldview that grapples with the problem of evil faces challenges, but some worldviews address the problem more adequately than others.
2. The theistic God exists; evil is real (Assumptions)	Prior to concluding that Christianity best explains evil, it is assumed that the theistic God exists and evil is real. If the theistic God does not exist, then Christianity is false. If evil does not exist, then Christian explanations of it are unnecessary.
3. Evil requires objective moral values (Premise)	Because Christianity holds to belief in a transcendent moral lawgiver (God), it can rightly claim that good and evil exist. Without such a transcendent standard for good and evil, one cannot truly call anything good or evil. Consequently, evil requires objective moral values, which in turn require the existence of the theistic God as their source.
4. Evil is illusory; naturalism can explain evil (Objection)	This rebuttal takes the forms of absolute pantheism, such as Advaita Vedanta, in claiming that evil is illusory, as well as atheistic explanations, which hold that naturalism can explain evil without recourse to the supernatural. Absolute forms of pantheism claim that since all is one (monism) and all is divine (pantheism), then there are no real distinctions between what we call good and evil. Evil does not really exist but is an illusion, the product of our unenlightenment. Some atheists, on the other hand, will argue that naturalism is perfectly capable of explaining what we term evil without needing to appeal to God. Evil may, for instance, be a by-product of evolution, allowing the strong to survive and thrive while the weak perish.
5. OMVs point to God; evil is best explained by Christianity (Rebuttal)	The Christian may offer the rebuttal that objective moral values point to God, as noted earlier. Therefore, evil is best explained by Christianity. As for the explanations for evil given by pantheism and atheism, see points 21 through 23.

6. Fall explains evil (Premise)	Within the worldview of Christianity, the Fall explains evil, both moral and natural. According the Bible, the Fall influenced not only the spiritual and physical states of human beings, but also the creation as a whole (see Rom. 8:22, for instance, where the whole creation is said to be "groaning"). In other words, the Fall resulted not only in moral evil, but also in natural evil—earthquakes, diseases, and other natural disasters.
7. Seems circular; why would God allow the Fall? (Objection)	Two objections are given. First, to appeal to the Fall as an explanation for evil and suffering appears circular. In other words, one is appealing to Christianity to explain Christianity's explanation for evil.
	Additionally, why would God allow the Fall? The response to this objection is addressed in points 18 through 20.
8. Makes sense within the Christian worldview; best way defense (Rebuttal)	Given that the problem of evil is being explained within the Christian worldview, it makes perfect sense to appeal to key doctrines of that worldview. So it is not circular reasoning to appeal to the Fall in explaining evil. After all, if the Fall is an accurate account of reality, and if it touches on the problem of evil (which it does), then appealing to it is not circular but supremely relevant.
9. Free will defense (Premise)	The so-called free will defense is offered here as a supporting premise to the claim that Christianity best explains evil because it remains a popular evangelical response to the problem of evil and suffering. There is no evangelical or broadly Christian consensus on its efficacy; nevertheless, it helps to know about the free will defense.
	In short, the free will defense argues that God's granting of human freedom allowed the possibility of evil. For humans to be truly able to choose, they must be allowed to choose to do evil. This does not make God the author of evil. God made human freedom possible, but humans make individual choices that result in evil. Thus God made evil a potential, but he is not the author of evil. A world where free creatures could choose to love and follow God was worth the consequences of a world of potential, but not eternal, evil.
10. Couldn't God allow free will without evil? (Objection)	The objection wonders why God could not have allowed free will, but without the possibility of evil. At least theoretically, it seems that God could have done so.

11. Free will is not truly free if the choice of evil is removed (Rebuttal)

Would removing the option to choose evil have resulted in the best possible world? By its very nature, true freedom must allow the possibility for people to freely act in ways that are evil; otherwise true freedom would not exist. If the choice of evil is removed, then can it be said that the free will God has given us is truly free? See points 18, 19, and 20.

12. Soul-making theodicy (Premise)

The so-called soul-making theodicy attempts to reconcile God's goodness with the reality of evil and suffering by claiming that suffering gives humans the opportunity to develop virtuous character traits. Without suffering we could not become all that God wishes us to be. The purpose of evil and suffering, then, at least in part, is for the greater good of positively developing our character.

13. Couldn't God teach us without evil? (Objection)

The objection is straightforward. After all, given Christian theology, weren't angels created without lives of evil and suffering? If so, then why couldn't God teach us without allowing evil and suffering in our lives and in our world?

14. Suffering tests and prepares us for this life and beyond (Rebuttal)

If God is striving to move some of us along to the best possible world (see points 18, 19, and 20), and if allowing us to experience temporary evil and suffering furthers his objective, then the goal of the best possible world remains a worthy one.

Moreover, we are limited beings, especially in comparison to God. Who are we to question his motives and purposes when it comes to the reality that he created? We lack sufficient data as well as sufficient capacities to fully comprehend exactly how and why God makes the decisions he does. This is not an appeal to mystery or human ignorance; rather, it is just the truth that we are severely limited as human beings. If suffering prepares us to grow in moral character in this life, ultimately helping us to prepare for the life beyond, then the soul-making theodicy succeeds in answering at least part of the problem of evil and suffering.

The atheist, on the other hand, has no good reasons for explaining the reality of evil and suffering, much less infusing it with greater and lasting meaning. Neither can monistic pantheism offer satisfactory explanations (see points 21–23).

15. Evil as privation (Premise)	Evil is not a thing or a substance. Rather, it is a privation. When good that should be present is missing, there is evil. Evil is, as C. S. Lewis has suggested, a parasite; it is, "good spoiled." If this is so, then God is not the author of evil because evil itself is not a thing or substance, but a lack of good. Augustine argued along these lines.
16. Evil need not exist only as a privation (Objection)	The "privation" solution seems contrived and weak. To the typical atheist, evil and suffering are real. They impact lives in tangible ways. How, then, can evil be merely an absence of good or a privation? To the monistic pantheist, on the other hand, evil is merely an illusion and therefore needs no real explanation.
17. Evil as privation is the best solution (Rebuttal)	Viewing evil as a privation has solid historical precedent, particularly in thinkers such as Augustine and Aquinas. The view that the effects of evil and the suffering it produces in the world are real, but it denies that evil is an actual "thing" or "substance." Since an all-loving and good God cannot make evil, per se, viewing evil as a privation is an acceptable form of responding to the problem of evil. It may not be a flawless approach, but in the end the Christian explanation of evil and suffering still surpasses the alternatives.
18. Best way/best world defense (Premise)	This Augustinian approach to solving the problem of evil and suffering admits to the reality of evil, but it claims that although evil now exists, one day it will be completely, finally, and definitely defeated. However, to reach this point God must first allow a time of evil and suffering. In short, while this is not the best world at this time, it is ultimately the best way to the best world.
19. Couldn't God have made the best world to begin with? (Objection)	This is a valid and common objection to the best way defense. In other words, why couldn't God have skipped over all the messy business of evil and suffering and created a world that already was the best possible world? Why the interlude of suffering?
20. God, being God, made the best choice (Rebuttal)	As we suggested earlier, we lack sufficient data. God, being God, does not. Therefore, if all the qualities that Christian theism attributes to God are correct, we can surmise that God has allowed evil and suffering for a variety of greater purposes such as free will, soul-making, and others.

21. Other explanations are deficient (Premise)

The problem of evil and suffering is not just a problem for Christian theism. Atheism and pantheism, too, must grapple with explaining evil and suffering.

Monistic pantheism, which views evil as an illusion, must explain why this illusion has seemed so real to so many throughout so many years of human history. If all is one and all is divine, then where did we ever get such a strong idea and sense of evil and suffering? To claim that evil is just an illusion offers no real intellectual or emotional solution to the problem of evil and suffering.

Atheism, on the other hand, typically acknowledges the reality of evil and suffering, but it has no solid foundation for making moral distinctions between good or evil. If no deity exists and we are merely the products of an undirected, impersonal process that happened to form thinking human beings, how on earth can we even explain moral distinctions such as good and evil without appealing to a transcendent source?

22. Pantheism and atheism disagree (Objection)

Neither atheists nor pantheists consider their perspectives deficient. Consequently, they disagree that Christianity best explains evil. As we've noted, monistic pantheism appeals to evil as illusion, while atheism accepts the reality of evil and suffering but has no real foundation to make such moral distinctions. In short, both these worldviews lack explanatory power and scope when it comes to explaining evil and suffering. Still, this objection must be noted. Obviously, atheists do not consider their explanations for evil as being deficient. While most atheists acknowledge the reality of evil and suffering, using its reality as an argument against the existence of God, this does not mean that they believe their explanation is inferior to other explanations. Within atheism, evil and suffering may simply be part of the makeup of an evolutionary reality—survival of the fittest in a neutral or even harsh universe. One need not appeal to God to explain evil, as we need only to appeal to the fact that human beings have a long history of committing evil against one another.

Monistic pantheists deny the reality of evil. If all is one and all is divine, then there really are no distinctions between good or evil. All we need to do to realize this is to achieve enlightenment.

23. Christianity explains evil with less difficulty than alternatives (Rebuttal)

How does Christianity best explain evil, as point 1 concludes that it does? It does not do so perfectly, with no flaws whatsoever, but in comparison with other worldview explanations of evil and suffering, Christianity explains evil with less difficulty.

Given a theistic universe, the Christian explanations for evil and suffering offer the best solution to a challenging set of problems. Christianity can explain moral, human evils, as well as so-called natural evils. Where an atheist may see gratuitous evil, a Christian who believes in God's attributes can understand that our viewpoint and data as humans are limited. Thus we cannot say with any certainty whether any evil is truly "gratuitous" or unwarranted. If God is who he claims to be, then no evil is unjustified but serves greater purposes. Suffering can, in fact, grant others the opportunity to show love, care, and mercy, thus contributing to our soul-making—helping us grow in moral virtue.

DISCUSSION QUESTIONS

1. Do you agree that evil is a privation? Why or why not?
2. Do you think the free will defense is sufficient to answer all aspects of the problem of evil?
3. Is the best way defense reasonable to you? Explain your answer.
4. What are some differences between the intellectual and emotional problem of evil?
5. Are there any merits to atheist or pantheist explanations of evil?
6. In explaining the problem of evil, do theists and atheists have any common ground? If so, what?
7. What do you find appealing or unappealing about the soul-making theodicy?
8. How would you respond to the claim that God is the author of evil?

SUGGESTED ASSIGNMENTS

1. Read *The Roots of Evil* by Norman Geisler. Write a short paper listing points you agree with and disagree with as presented in the book, being careful to list your reasons for your agreement and disagreement.
2. Assume the role of an atheist critical of Christianity in relation to the problem of evil. Write a paper listing your main arguments against the Christian explanations for evil and suffering. On the final page of your paper list the best theistic responses to the atheist criticisms you wrote about.
3. Meet with a pastor in order to better understand how to address the pastoral, often emotional aspects of evil and suffering. Consider requesting to accompany a pastor

on hospital visits to gain a better understanding of the compassion required to address emotional problems of evil.

4. Study a newer religious movement that adheres to some form of pantheism (e.g., Christian Science or various so-called New Age beliefs). Research your topic and document the view that the group takes on evil and suffering. Note areas of agreement and disagreement with the Christian view.

CHAPTER 15

Hell Is Justifiable

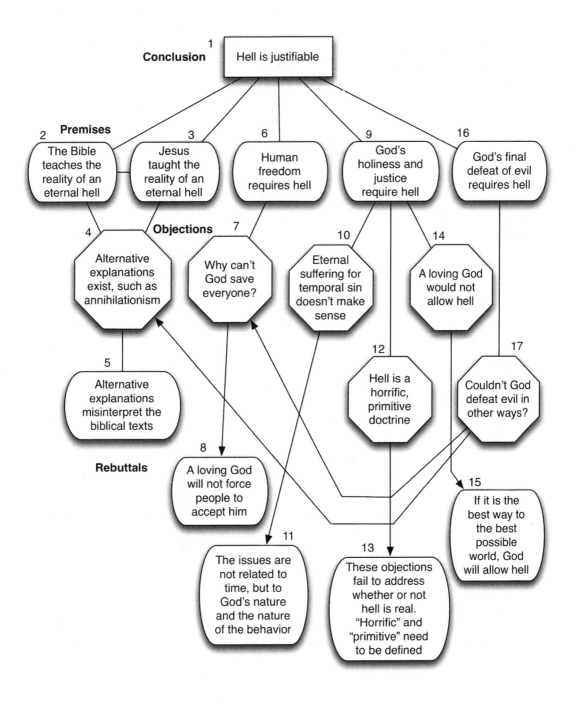

Conclusion

1 Hell is justifiable

Premises

2 The Bible teaches the reality of an eternal hell

3 Jesus taught the reality of an eternal hell

6 Human freedom requires hell

9 God's holiness and justice require hell

16 God's final defeat of evil requires hell

Objections

4 Alternative explanations exist, such as annihilationism

7 Why can't God save everyone?

10 Eternal suffering for temporal sin doesn't make sense

14 A loving God would not allow hell

5 Alternative explanations misinterpret the biblical texts

12 Hell is a horrific, primitive doctrine

17 Couldn't God defeat evil in other ways?

Rebuttals

8 A loving God will not force people to accept him

15 If it is the best way to the best possible world, God will allow hell

11 The issues are not related to time, but to God's nature and the nature of the behavior

13 These objections fail to address whether or not hell is real. "Horrific" and "primitive" need to be defined

1. Hell is justifiable (Conclusion)	The orthodox Christian teaching on hell is that it is both real and justifiable. Hell is eternal punishment for those who reject Christ. The traditional biblical position on hell rejects various alternatives such as universalism and annihilationism. A significant, common criticism of Christianity involves the doctrine of hell, which detractors claim is barbaric and unjustified.
2. The Bible teaches the reality of an eternal hell (Premise)	Despite criticisms of the doctrine of hell, the Bible clearly teaches it. Given that the Bible teaches the doctrine, and given that the theistic God exists and has revealed himself in the Bible, we are left with the conclusion that a holy and just God must have valid reasons for justifying the reality of hell. Exceptions to this conclusion can only arise if we are somehow misinterpreting the biblical record or if Christianity is in error.
3. Jesus taught the reality of an eternal hell (Premise)	In addition to the Bible's overall teaching regarding the doctrine of hell, we also have an extensive record of Jesus' teachings on hell. If we deny these teachings, then either our interpretation of such passages is in error or the reliability of Christ is in question. Given substantial evidence in support of the reliability of the biblical record as well as ample evidence demonstrating the existence of God, the conclusion is that the biblical record is correct.
4. Alternative explanations exist, such as annihilationism (Objection)	One theistic solution that has been offered is known as annihilationism. In this system, those who reject God are not sent to suffer eternally in hell, but instead are annihilated (that is, destroyed). How this is supposedly better than the reality of hell is certainly questionable and does little to help God's reputation, so to speak. Nevertheless, annihilationists offer a variety of arguments in support of their interpretation of Scripture. For instance, they claim that eternal suffering in hell for temporal sins does not make sense. They also interpret the biblical evidence in ways that avoid an eternal hell in favor of annihilationism—for instance, by denying that the word "eternal" in references to hell really means forever.
5. Alternative explanations misinterpret the biblical texts (Rebuttal)	Alternative explanations not only misinterpret the biblical texts but also fail to comprehend the reasons for hell from a sound theological position. Part of what is at stake here is God's eternal holiness, which demands just punishment for sin. Christians who hold to libertarian views of human free-

dom (point 6), for instance, can argue that hell must exist in order to accommodate those who willingly and freely reject God. Others may argue that hell is necessary in light of the egregious extent and magnitude of sin in the face of a holy God.

6. Human freedom requires hell (Premise)

Christians who accept libertarian freedom can argue on the basis of the free will defense that hell is necessary for those who freely choose to reject God. What can God do with such people? He cannot force them to believe, since this would impinge on human free choice. Instead, God chooses to quarantine such rebels in hell, eternally. But is it possible that those in hell could at some point repent? If so, then can't God let them into heaven later? This view misunderstands the extent and nature of sin. Those who are in hell have no interest in leaving so long as leaving is on God's terms.

7. Why can't God save everyone? (Objection)

The objection here can point to God's omnipotence. If God is indeed all-powerful, then why can't he see to it that the world he created results in the salvation of everyone (universalism)? Did God somehow fail? Does God want some people to suffer eternally? If so, then isn't he less than loving? Couldn't he have done something?

8. A loving God will not force people to accept him (Rebuttal)

For those who hold to libertarian freedom, a loving God will not force people to accept him. Moreover, God has done something gracious, which is what Christianity at its root is all about. God sent his son, Jesus Christ, to suffer and die for human sins so that whoever believes can be saved. The incarnation is in this sense the most remarkable religious act ever conceived or recorded in the pages of human thought. God became man and suffered so that human beings might escape the condemnation of a justifiable hell.

9. God's holiness and justice require hell (Premise)

God is not a friendly grandfather in heaven, to allude to a passage in the writings of C. S. Lewis. People wish God to be this way, but he is otherwise. Though loving, he is also holy and just. His holiness and justice require hell because a holy and just God cannot allow evil to go unpunished. We must not lose sight of the magnitude of human depravity and the many manifestations of sin which are an egregious affront to the holy God.

10. Eternal suffering for temporal sin doesn't make sense (Objection)

But why would God punish and torture people eternally for temporal sins? It doesn't seem to make sense. Suppose a woman lives a life of seventy or eighty years, should her punishment for rejecting God for that finite period of time really result in an eternity of torment? Isn't God overreacting? Why not punish people for a set number of years, then let them into heaven?

11. The issues are not related to time, but to God's nature and the nature of the behavior (Rebuttal)

The issues are not temporal but eternal. Those who reject God have demonstrated a pattern of attitudinal behavior that is against God and his holiness. No amount of time can heal this attitude. If there were a way, God would find it, but the biblical record leaves no room for such a loophole. We must also question the use of the word "torture" in point 10. God never tortures anyone.

12. Hell is a horrific, primitive doctrine (Objection)

Surely religion has advanced beyond such barbarism as the doctrine of hell. Any religion that would teach such an offensive view must be rejected.

13. These objections fail to address whether or not hell is real. "Horrific" and "primitive" need to be defined (Rebuttal)

The issue is not whether or not we find the doctrine of hell abhorrent but whether or not the doctrine is true. If it is true, as the biblical record substantiates, and if God is the kind of God the Bible reveals him to be, then a loving, holy God can be reconciled with the reality of hell.

14. A loving God would not allow hell (Objection)

But why would a loving God allow hell? He would not. Hence, our interpretations of the biblical record must be incorrect or else Christianity is merely a deficient worldview not worthy of our attention.

15. If it is the best way to the best possible world, God will allow hell (Rebuttal)

If we grant that this world is not the best possible world, but instead is the best way to the best possible world, then hell is a necessary reality where those who reject God are kept.

16. God's final defeat of evil requires hell (Premise)

According to the Bible, God will ultimately and utterly defeat evil, resulting in the eternal joys of heaven in God's presence. Those who reject God and continue to sin can no longer be allowed to cause mischief in God's kingdom. Such souls are condemned to hell eternally.

17. Couldn't God defeat evil in other ways? (Objection)

But couldn't God have found another way to defeat evil? Isn't annihilationism better? Isn't universalism better? If we as humans are so bothered by the doctrine of hell, why doesn't God seem bothered about it to our extent? And if he is not, then perhaps such a God does not exist or he is not as good or loving as we suspect. See points 5 and 8.

In brief, the biblical evidence for hell is clear. In addition, God's holy and just nature requires the reality of hell. God, moreover, is not a twisted tormentor, enjoying the fact that some of his creations will end up in hell (see, for instance, Lam. 3:33).

DISCUSSION QUESTIONS

1. Why is the doctrine of eternal hell a difficult obstacle for some to overcome?
2. How does eternal suffering for temporal sin make sense?
3. Where did Jesus speak about the reality of eternal hell?
4. Why wouldn't God simply annihilate those who won't believe?
5. What do God's justice and holiness have to do with hell?

SUGGESTED ASSIGNMENTS

1. Compile a list of biblical passages addressing the topic of hell and formulate a cohesive systematic theology about the doctrine. Be sure to include key aspects of God's nature as they relate to the doctrine.
2. Research the viewpoint of Christian annihilationists and prepare a list of their key arguments, evaluating each one logically and biblically.
3. Research the viewpoint of universalism and prepare a list of its key arguments, evaluating each one logically and biblically.

PART 3

Arguments Against God and Christianity

CHAPTER 16

God Does Not Exist (Atheism)

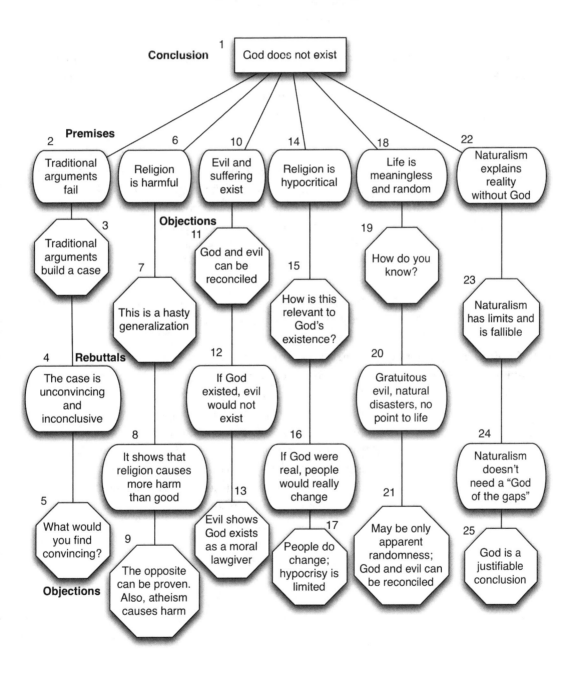

Conclusion 1 — God does not exist

Premises

2 — Traditional arguments fail

6 — Religion is harmful

10 — Evil and suffering exist

14 — Religion is hypocritical

18 — Life is meaningless and random

22 — Naturalism explains reality without God

3 — Traditional arguments build a case

Objections

11 — God and evil can be reconciled

19 — How do you know?

23 — Naturalism has limits and is fallible

7 — This is a hasty generalization

15 — How is this relevant to God's existence?

Rebuttals

4 — The case is unconvincing and inconclusive

12 — If God existed, evil would not exist

20 — Gratuitous evil, natural disasters, no point to life

24 — Naturalism doesn't need a "God of the gaps"

8 — It shows that religion causes more harm than good

16 — If God were real, people would really change

5 — What would you find convincing?

13 — Evil shows God exists as a moral lawgiver

17 — People do change; hypocrisy is limited

21 — May be only apparent randomness; God and evil can be reconciled

25 — God is a justifiable conclusion

Objections

9 — The opposite can be proven. Also, atheism causes harm

125

1. God does not exist (Conclusion)	This is the conclusion of atheism, based on the premises listed in points 2, 6, 10, 14, 18, and 22. Note that with the possible exception of the premise in point 22, all of these arguments are negative, meaning that they are arguments against the existence of God as opposed to positive arguments in favor of atheism. Many of these premises, moreover, are addressed in other chapters, as noted, but this argument map serves as a bird's-eye perspective on the overall case against Christianity as commonly presented by atheists.
2. Traditional arguments fail (Premise)	Atheists find fault with all traditional arguments for the existence of God, such as cosmological arguments, design arguments, moral arguments, and ontological arguments.
	Note the plural form in the listing of these arguments. There are variations of each of these "families" of arguments. In some cases, atheists may be familiar with only one version of a moral argument, or they may in fact be arguing against a poor representation of the argument. If so, then it benefits the theist to present the arguments accurately as well as offer variations of them. In addition, some people will resonate more with one family of arguments for God while others will not. As apologists, one of our tasks is to determine what line of reasoning will suit a particular individual best. For a presentation and brief defense of some traditional arguments for God's existence, see chapter 6.
3. Traditional arguments build a case (Objection)	Atheists sometimes believe that if they have refuted one particular argument for God's existence, they therefore have defeated all arguments for God's existence. Of course this is not the case. An atheist may, for example, believe an argument for morality has been defeated, but he may neglect to address a design or cosmological argument. If, however, an atheist firmly argues that all traditional arguments for God fail, then the apologist must learn more about what the atheist knows about the different arguments and their forms. Moreover, the theist must emphasize that arguments for God's existence build a cumulative case for it, sometimes emphasizing different attributes of God more than others in the process. For instance, cosmological arguments tend to emphasize God's omnipotence as the Creator of the cosmos.
	Taken together, these traditional arguments based on natural theology make a strong case for the existence of a theistic

God. This in itself does not make a direct case for Christianity, but if it convinces the atheist of the possibility of a theistic God, then that is a significant step which the apologist may use to make a direct case for Christianity. Traditional arguments for God are valuable and can help the apologist create a "haunted universe" for the atheist, to note a phrase used by Dallas Willard.[1]

4. The case is unconvincing and inconclusive (Rebuttal)

The atheist may rebut that the case for God remains unconvincing and inconclusive. Various reasons may be offered, such as dissatisfaction with certain aspects of the arguments as well as the objection that the conclusion is not certain but leaves too much room for doubt regarding God's existence. For instance, atheists may explain elements of design as only being "apparent" design. They may deny objective moral values. Or they may claim that there are alternative explanations for the origins of life and the universe that need not appeal to God.

5. What would you find convincing? (Objection)

After determining whether or not the atheist's objections mentioned above in point 4 are valid (for perhaps they are not), the theist may ask what the atheist *would* find convincing evidence of God's existence. An atheist may be so firmly entrenched in her worldview that she does not leave any room for even the possibility of a God. One may then argue that the atheist's worldview is unfalsifiable, since she claims that nothing would sway her in favor of God.

Some atheists may contend that God should immediately reveal himself to them. Then they would believe. In other words, they argue that God hides himself. Why not reveal himself directly and overtly? If this is the case, the theist must be prepared to respond intelligently. We are not in a position to demand that God appear to us as proof of his existence. God has given us general revelation, via creation and moral conscience (Rom. 1:20; 2:14–16), as well as special revelation via the person of Christ and the Bible. We have more than enough evidence available to us to know that God indeed does exist.

---

1. Dallas Willard, "Language, Being, God, and the Three Stages of Theistic Evidence," in *Does God Exist? The Great Debate*, by J. P. Moreland and Kai Nielsen (Nashville: Thomas Nelson, 1990). Also available at http://www.dwillard.org/articles/artview.asp?artID=42.

6. Religion is harmful (Premise)	The objection that religion is harmful is not so much a direct argument against God but an indirect one. The claim is that wherever one finds religion, one also finds trouble of some sort—violence, religious wars, persecution, and so forth. If a good, loving God exists, as theists claim, then why does religion cause so much harm?
7. This is a hasty generalization (Objection)	Is *all* religion harmful at *all* times and in *all* ways? The atheist seems to assume this, but if it is not true, then the atheist has made a hasty generalization. For more in response to point 6, see chapter 9, which describes all the good that Christianity does. For more on the atheist case against Christianity on the basis of its being harmful, see chapter 20.
8. It shows that religion causes more harm than good (Rebuttal)	See chapters 9 and 20.
9. The opposite can be proven. Also, atheism causes harm (Objection)	In other words, religion is demonstrably beneficial, and in the case of Christianity, extensively beneficial as shown by the historical record (chapter 9).

While the latter part of this point may seem somewhat childish in its response, it is nevertheless true that atheism has caused significant historical harm through atheistic worldviews such as communism. If, then, both religious and nonreligious worldviews are shown to cause some amount of harm, then the "harmful" test seems deficient as an overall method of evaluating whether or not any worldview is true or false (though the tangible benefits a worldview offers the world may play a role in a cumulative case for it). |
| **10. Evil and suffering exist (Premise)** | This is a common atheist argument against Christianity and is addressed in further detail in chapters 14 and 19. In short, the atheist believes that the existence of a theistic God cannot be reconciled with the reality of evil and suffering in the world. At some point, atheists argue, God's theistic attributes fail or are misunderstood, assuming God exists. For instance, if God is omnipotent, then he has the power to do away with evil. If God is omniscient, then he should know how to do away with evil. If God is omnibenevolent, then he would not have allowed evil to proliferate at all. Since evil does exist, the atheist concludes that either God does not exist or else God is not all-powerful or omnibenevolent. |

11. God and evil can be reconciled (Objection)	See chapter 14, wherein it is explained that there are various ways Christian theism reconciles the realities of evil and God, such as by appealing to the Fall, the free will defense, soul-making theodicy, evil as a privation, the best way/best world defense, and more.
12. If God existed, evil would not exist (Rebuttal)	See chapters 14 and 19. On the monistic pantheist view of evil, see chapter 23.
13. Evil shows God exists as a moral lawgiver (Objection)	See chapter 8. In short, for the atheist to have any moral grounds on which to claim something is good or evil, the atheist must appeal to some moral standard that can arbitrate between what is good or evil. If the atheist believes evil exists, then he must believe there is a standard of good by which one may deem certain things, such as moral behavior, to be good or evil. But where does this standard come from? The best explanation is that it has its roots in an objective moral lawgiver—that is, God.
14. Religion is hypocritical (Premise)	Some atheists claim that the rampant hypocrisy among theists, especially Christians, demonstrates that God does not really exist. If God did exist and really indwelt followers, as Christians claim, then there would not be such blatant hypocrisy among Christians. The question of religious hypocrisy is taken up in more detail in chapter 24.
15. How is this relevant to God's existence? (Objection)	Religious hypocrisy is an irrelevant thesis fallacy when it comes to arguing for God's existence. In other words, the hypocrisy charge does nothing to argue against traditional arguments for God's existence (chapter 6) or to argue against the compelling case for Christianity (chapter 5). Moreover, what if one finds hypocritical atheists? Should we conclude that their worldview has no merit either? While it is true that hypocrisy is not beneficial to one's cause, it cannot be taken in isolation with respect to other arguments for the worldview in question.
16. If God were real, people would really change (Rebuttal)	Since there are religious hypocrites, and since theistic worldviews like Christianity claim they can change lives for the better, but lives are not changed for the better but for the worse, then God must not exist.

17. People do change; hypocrisy is limited (Objection)	Christianity does change lives for the better. Those who are hypocrites within Christianity may not truly be Christians or may simply be Christians demonstrating their human depravity as a result of their fallen nature. Granted, such Christians do nothing to help the cause of Christ, but they do at least demonstrate the reality of sin in human nature, in which case we are back to the question of how the atheist can claim anything is truly good or evil. In addition, Christian hypocrisy is limited and should not cancel out all the good that Christianity has done for the world (chapter 9) or other sound arguments for God's existence (chapter 6).
18. Life is meaningless and random (Premise)	If God exists, then one would expect meaning and purpose to life. But based on the available evidence, our universe is merely a product of an undirected process, completely the result of non-intelligence. Ultimately our world will end, as will the universe, leading to nothing of true eternal value or purpose. The best we can do is try to enjoy our lives during the short time that we have before we all cease to exist.
19. How do you know? (Objection)	The Socratic method inquires, "How do you know?" How does one know that life is meaningless and random? Furthermore, on what basis does one deem something meaningless or meaningful? Again we have the problem of atheism lacking a firm foundation to make such moral claims.
20. Gratuitous evil, natural disasters, no point to life (Rebuttal)	The atheist may once again turn to the problem of evil to aid its case. On these objections see chapters 14 and 19.
21. May be only apparent randomness; God and evil can be reconciled (Objection)	What the atheist deems random may be only apparent randomness. If God exists, then God has a plan and a purpose for his creation, at least within the framework of Christian theism. See chapter 14.
22. Naturalism explains reality without God (Premise)	If naturalism can explain reality without God and do so in a more compelling way, then God need not exist. See chapter 17.
23. Naturalism has limits and is fallible (Objection)	See chapter 17. The short answer is that naturalism is not omnipotent or omniscient. Additionally, even if it could explain all reality scientifically, this does not mean it can meaningfully answer any metaphysical questions about reality.

24. Naturalism doesn't need a "God of the gaps" (Rebuttal)	Naturalism need not rely on the crutch of Christianity or the existence of a supposed deity to explain reality. Science can explain reality quite nicely without appealing to a deity.
25. God is a justifiable conclusion (Objection)	Given the arguments for God's existence and their superiority in comparison to arguments for competing worldviews, belief in God is justifiable. Christianity does not seek a "God of the gaps" to fill in missing scientific knowledge.[2] Even if science were capable of explaining all the scientific workings of the universe, philosophical and metaphysical questions about ultimate reality would still remain. Christians need not point to God to explain what they don't understand; they point to God as the ultimate answer to the big questions of life, meaning, and reality. God, in short, should not be used as an excuse to remain ignorant.

DISCUSSION QUESTIONS

1. Of the six premises in the diagram (2, 6, 10, 14, 18, 22), which one do you find the most challenging to the existence of God? Why?
2. What is fallacious about the claim, "All religion is harmful"?
3. Do any of the premises offer positive arguments against the existence of God?
4. If you were to continue the line of reasoning in the diagram by adding at least three rebuttals to the final objections (5, 9, 13, 17, 21, and 25) what would they be?

SUGGESTED ASSIGNMENTS

1. Research a contemporary atheist and his or her objections to Christianity. Note any parallels to the premises listed in the diagram as well as any additional evidence or premises for the position that God does not exist. See, for instance, works by popular atheists such as Sam Harris, Christopher Hitchens, or Richard Dawkins.
2. Respond via a research paper to the claim that since life is meaningless and random, God must not exist.
3. Compare the case for atheism in this diagram with the positive case for God offered in chapter 6. Summarize the case for and against God's existence, noting strengths and weaknesses of the arguments.

---

2. "God of the Gaps" is a term that claims that as a substitute for real knowledge or scientific truth, theists often simply turn to God as the explanation. It is at times used by Christians to point out that gaps in human knowledge support the reality of God.

CHAPTER 17

Nontheistic Evolution Is True (God Is Unnecessary)

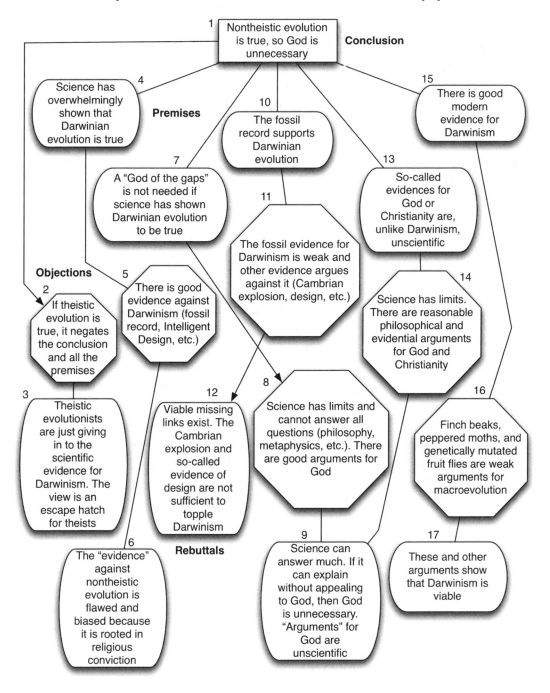

1 Nontheistic evolution is true, so God is unnecessary — **Conclusion**

4 Science has overwhelmingly shown that Darwinian evolution is true

Premises

10 The fossil record supports Darwinian evolution

15 There is good modern evidence for Darwinism

7 A "God of the gaps" is not needed if science has shown Darwinian evolution to be true

13 So-called evidences for God or Christianity are, unlike Darwinism, unscientific

11 The fossil evidence for Darwinism is weak and other evidence argues against it (Cambrian explosion, design, etc.)

14 Science has limits. There are reasonable philosophical and evidential arguments for God and Christianity

Objections

2 If theistic evolution is true, it negates the conclusion and all the premises

5 There is good evidence against Darwinism (fossil record, Intelligent Design, etc.)

3 Theistic evolutionists are just giving in to the scientific evidence for Darwinism. The view is an escape hatch for theists

12 Viable missing links exist. The Cambrian explosion and so-called evidence of design are not sufficient to topple Darwinism

8 Science has limits and cannot answer all questions (philosophy, metaphysics, etc.). There are good arguments for God

16 Finch beaks, peppered moths, and genetically mutated fruit flies are weak arguments for macroevolution

6 The "evidence" against nontheistic evolution is flawed and biased because it is rooted in religious conviction

Rebuttals

9 Science can answer much. If it can explain without appealing to God, then God is unnecessary. "Arguments" for God are unscientific

17 These and other arguments show that Darwinism is viable

1. Nontheistic evolution is true, so God is unnecessary (Conclusion)

The conclusion sees God as unnecessary in light of the naturalistic explanation for human origins (i.e., Darwinian evolution, macroevolution). If human life arose as a result of purely natural, undirected causes, then there is no need to posit the existence of a supernatural deity. The whole show, so to speak, is explained by natural causes.

2. If theistic evolution is true, it negates the conclusion and all the premises (Objection)

Theistic evolutionists believe in the reality of a personal, transcendent God, but they accept the essential process of Darwinian evolution with the exception that they claim God is involved in it. This does not so much "negate" the premises offered by nontheistic evolutionists as accept them, but within a theistic evolutionary framework. Hence, theistic evolutionists do see scientific evidence of macroevolution, including the fossil record.

3. Theistic evolutionists are just giving in to the scientific evidence for Darwinism. The view is an escape hatch for theists (Rebuttal)

Some who oppose Darwinism (such as Intelligent Design proponents) do so because they think the evidence for evolution is insufficient and the evidence against evolution is massive. This rebuttal claims that rather than acknowledging serious difficulties with Darwinism, theistic evolutionists are compromising their faith in order to accommodate Darwinism. After all, Darwinism was offered as a naturalistic solution to the origins of life, making God unnecessary.

Besides the lack of convincing evidence for Darwinism, critics of theistic evolution point to difficulties in associating Darwinism with an all-powerful creator God. If, for instance, God is involved in evolution, then is he actively involved, allowing genetic mutations, for example, to advance the evolutionary process, as well as eliminating species in order to further evolutionary ends? Or did God merely initiate the process of evolution and is no longer involved?

In any event, critics of theistic evolution are not willing to give up and accept Darwinism, as they see too many serious faults in it and see better evidence for an intelligent designer. It should be noted that naturalists reject theistic evolution not only on the grounds that it appeals to a deity, but also because it ignores the naturalistic evidence for evolution—a system that need not incorporate any supernaturalism at all. In other words, from the point of view of the naturalist, adding a deity to the evidence for Darwinism unnecessarily complicates an already adequate explanation. It also violates Occam's razor—the view that the simplest explanation is most probably correct and there is not need to multiply assumptions more than necessary. Theists who deny theistic evolution, on the other hand, do not believe the evidence for theistic evolution is compelling. For instance, why would God work through deficiencies such as genetic mutations in order to progress humanity along an evolutionary path?

4. Science has overwhelmingly shown that Darwinian evolution is true (Premise)

The broad scientific establishment accepts Darwinian evolution as the best explanation of life, including human origins. Only a small number of vocal opponents question the theory, many of whom are not scientists, and their objections are flimsy and religiously motivated.

5. There is good evidence against Darwinism (fossil record, Intelligent Design, etc.) (Objection)

Those who object to Darwinism note that there is good evidence against it. For example, the fossil record has significant gaps that contemporary science has yet to satisfactorily fill. This lack of so-called transitional forms is troubling for Darwinism, as much more abundant evidence of these transitional forms should be available but isn't (see points 10 and 11).

Moreover, microbiology has uncovered evidences of design via what Intelligent Design proponents call *specified complexity* or *irreducible complexity*. Analogously, just as a mouse trap requires all of its parts to function, so too do certain microbiological systems require all of their parts to function. If only one part is removed, both the mouse trap and the systems will not operate properly. How, then, could such microbiological "machines" have evolved? It makes more sense to admit that certain aspects of nature show evidence of Intelligent Design.

6. The "evidence" against nontheistic evolution is flawed and biased because it is rooted in religious conviction (Rebuttal)

Those who disagree accept the evidence for Darwinism as credible. Moreover, objections are rooted in religious conviction, not scientific truth. Theists, it is claimed, are biased and, therefore, cannot look at the evidence objectively. They are unwilling to give up their theistic worldview and, as a result, will stretch or interpret the evidence as they see fit in order to maintain their beliefs. Consequently, no matter what evidence is offered for nontheistic evolution, theists will reject it or find a way around it. Theistic arguments are driven by emotional religious conviction, not scientific facts.

7. A "God of the gaps" is not needed if science has shown Darwinian evolution to be true (Premise)

A "God of the gaps" is an appeal to a supernatural deity to explain a phenomenon for which people are too ignorant to know the real explanation, such as thunder or lightning in ages past. As science progressed, it was able to explain human origins without appealing to a supernatural being or creation myths. Therefore, God is no longer needed as an explanation of reality. Science is the answer, not religious myths.

8. Science has limits and cannot answer all questions (philosophy, metaphysics, etc.). There are good arguments for God (Objection)

Some questions are beyond the realm of science, even though at times science appears to wander into these other realms of thought. Even if science were to offer explanations for all the natural occurrences in the universe, it cannot answer basic questions of human philosophy and meaning such as, "Why is there something rather than nothing?" "Why am I here?" or "What is the meaning of ultimate reality?" Science needs to know its limits. Besides, there are good, reasonable arguments in support of the existence of God (chapter 6).

9. Science can answer much. If it can explain without appealing to God, then God is unnecessary. "Arguments" for God are unscientific (Rebuttal)

The rebuttal says that science can answer much, including questions of human origins. If such explanations are compelling, then why appeal to God at all? God becomes superfluous. Moreover, arguments for God are unscientific.

While a further objection is not offered in the diagram, the theist will obviously have further objections. For instance, one could press the matter until it is admitted that science has limits. One could also make a case for the existence of God on the basis of reasonable argumentation.

10. The fossil record supports Darwinian evolution (Premise)

Critics of the fossil record are ignorant of the advances made in this area. There are viable intermediary (transitional) fossils that demonstrate that Darwinism is true. It is true that we do not have a complete fossil record and we never will due to the nature of how fossils are preserved. This does not mean, however, that we can dismiss the missing links that we have found. They offer convincing evidence of the truth of Darwinism. Examples of missing links include archaeopteryx or, more recently, IDA, a primate fossil found in Germany.

11. The fossil evidence for Darwinism is weak and other evidence argues against it (Cambrian explosion, design, etc.) (Objection)

Scientists who tout missing links as evidence of Darwinism read too much into such findings. They see evidence of Darwinism in such fossils only because they presuppose that Darwinism is true. They are tainted by their presuppositions and will do whatever it takes to support their assumptions rather than honestly evaluate the evidence at hand. Moreover, events such as the Cambrian explosion, wherein a variety of life forms appeared suddenly and fully formed in the fossil record, are evidence against evolution.

12. Viable missing links exist. The Cambrian explosion and so-called evidence of design are not sufficient to topple Darwinism (Rebuttal)

Darwinists maintain that viable missing links exist. Interpreting the evidence on the basis of a scientific theory is not biased or based on presuppositions, but is honestly looking at the evidence at hand and making viable conclusions.

13. So-called evidences for God or Christianity are, unlike Darwinism, unscientific (Premise)

The claim is made that science is the only real way of arriving at truth, while religious considerations are dismissed as being "unscientific." In other words, the scientific method is superior to other forms of inquiry and therefore has more credence than alternative explanations.

14. Science has limits. There are reasonable philosophical and evidential arguments for God and Christianity (Objection)

The objection reminds us that science has limits and cannot answer everything about reality. In addition, there are reasonable arguments for God and Christianity that cover a variety of areas of inquiry including science, history, archaeology, philosophy, and so forth. See also point 9.

15. There is good modern evidence for Darwinism (Premise)

Darwinists argue that there is modern evidence in support of Darwinism, such as variations in finch beak sizes, peppered moths, genetically mutated fruit flies, and more. If we can see evidence of evolutionary change, even on a small scale, then we can extrapolate that it occurs on a broad scale, albeit over lengthy periods of time that we cannot directly observe.

16. Finch beaks, peppered moths, and genetically mutated fruit flies are weak arguments for macroevolution (Objection)

Finch beak size variations are a far cry from proving macroevolution—that drastic, extensive evolutionary changes occurred, for instance, to transform a land mammal into a sea creature. Microevolution is a reality. We know there are different kinds of cats and dogs, for instance, but finches with varying beak sizes remained finches. They have not evolved into any new radically different creature, which is what Darwinism purports can occur in nature via an undirected process.[1]

17. These and other arguments show that Darwinism is viable (Rebuttal)

Unmoved by such objections, Darwinists maintain that these and other arguments show that Darwinism is viable. It is the best explanation we have, given scientific inquiry and empirical evidence. There is no need to appeal to a God or supernatural source, though one may do so. It must be remembered,

---

1. On many of these supposed evidences of Darwinism see Jonathan Wells, *Icons of Evolution*.

however, that religious belief is essentially unscientific, while Darwinism is grounded in scientific reality. Alternative theories have yet to offer any compelling reason to abandon the central unifying explanation of biological reality. Darwinism remains our best option.

DISCUSSION QUESTIONS

1. Can Darwinian evolution and theistic evolution be reconciled with the biblical record? How so?
2. Does the Genesis account of creation rule out theistic evolution?
3. Given the same evidence available to proponents of nontheistic evolution and creationists, why do you think they disagree on so many key points?
4. Why is the fossil record important in relation to questions about macroevolution?
5. What questions is contemporary science suited to answer? What questions are beyond its abilities to resolve?
6. What do Christian young earth creationists, old earth creationists, and theistic evolutionists agree on when it comes to God and creation?

SUGGESTED ASSIGNMENTS

1. Research the case for nontheistic evolution and the case offered by proponents of Intelligent Design and write a paper on your findings. On Intelligent Design, see authors such as William Dembski and Phillip E. Johnson. On nontheistic evolution see authors such as Richard Dawkins.
2. Evaluate the fossil record and so-called missing links, offering an evaluation of your findings. See, for instance, *The Fossil Record* by John Morris and Frank Sherwin, as well as *Evolution: The Challenge of the Fossil Record* by Duane Gish.
3. Read the case for theistic evolution offered by a contemporary proponent of the perspective. Whether or not you agree with the position, write a paper delineating the key arguments in favor of it as well as any biblical insights on the matter. See, for instance, works by Francis Collins as well as the chapter in *What's So Great About Christianity* by Dinesh D'Souza in support of theistic evolution.

CHAPTER 18

Belief in God/Christianity
Is Delusional

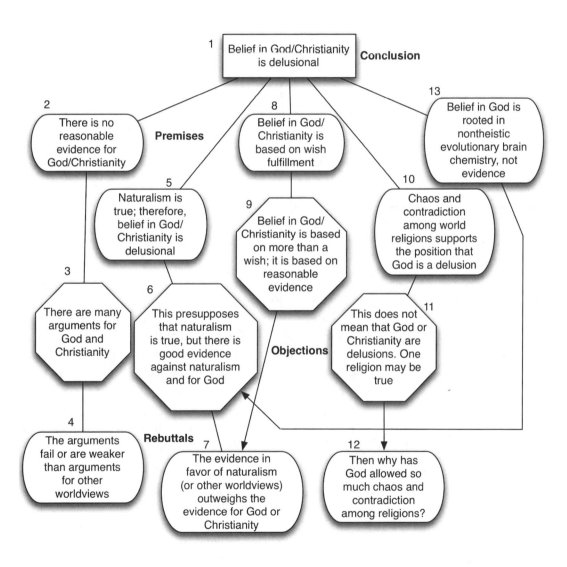

1. Belief in God/ Christianity is delusional (Conclusion)

A delusion is a belief that is held to firmly even though it is unfounded, going against established reality and reason. Some critics of theism and Christianity claim that those who believe are essentially struggling with a mental disorder (a delusion) rather than facing the facts of the universe. If true, then those who believe in God must abandon this belief, while those who also believe in Christianity must likewise abandon their Christian beliefs in light of the evidence reality offers against God and Christianity.

The Christian theist may immediately recoil at the thought of being accused of being delusional, but remember that we are seeking to determine what is true—what corresponds to reality (chapter 7). Consequently, we must desire to investigate any viable claims against our worldview, even if their potential truth may result in the collapse of our own worldview. If God exists and if Christianity is true, then these beliefs have nothing to hide from intellectual inquiry, properly executed.

2. There is no reasonable evidence for God/ Christianity (Premise)

The critic of theism and Christianity may take a variety of approaches in seeking to demonstrate that God does not exist and that Christianity is not true. Showing that God does not exist, or that it is highly probable that God does not exist (chapter 16), is enough to cast serious doubt on Christianity if not defeat it entirely.

This premise claims there is no "reasonable evidence" for God or Christianity. It may be that the skeptic has vigorously sought for such evidence (chapter 6) and yet, despite theistic claims to the contrary, has found evidence for God lacking. It may also be that the critic has not thoroughly investigated the evidence for God and Christianity, has misunderstood it, or has other motives for rejecting the evidence (but here we enter into the realm of psychology and psychoanalysis, which is beyond our scope).

3. There are many arguments for God and Christianity (Objection)

The theist and Christian theist may counter that there are many arguments for God and Christianity (see all of part 2). Far from being based on blind faith and/or poor reasoning, belief in God and Christianity is substantiated by a number of lines of reasoning and evidences. Christians are no intellectual bumpkins, but have substantial reasons for believing in God and in the truth claims of Christianity.

4. The arguments fail or are weaker than arguments for other worldviews (Rebuttal)

The critic's rebuttal counters that the arguments for God and Christianity are weaker than arguments for atheism, pantheism, and other competing worldviews. Here we enter into questions regarding testing truth claims.

Given the evidence, are Christians weighing it fairly? If we are, and if the critic remains skeptical of the existence of God and the truth of Christianity, then what? We may be at an intellectual impasse, meaning that we can no longer progress in a direction of meaningful dialogue that can further our pursuit of truth.

Here the Christian must keep in mind that not everyone will respond to the gospel or to our best efforts to share and defend the faith. Gentleness and respect must continue on our part, as well as prayer and a willingness to continue to dialogue so long as we deem it fruitful. Nevertheless, there are times when dialogue must end, particularly if the person we are interacting with is belligerent, psychologically abusive, or has demonstrated a pattern of intellectual behavior that demonstrates not only a contrary attitude, but a hardened mind and heart. We do not abandon such people, but unless God's Spirit calls us to continue in our apologetic, it may be time to conclude our efforts.

5. Naturalism is true; therefore, belief in God/Christianity is delusional (Premise)

Those who hold this position may have good reasons from their perspective for doing so, such as being convinced of materialism or believing that Darwinism makes theism unnecessary (chapter 17). Naturalism and theism cannot both be true. If naturalism is true, as the naturalist assumes in this premise, then she is correct in deeming theism and Christianity false and delusional.

6. This presupposes that naturalism is true, but there is good evidence against naturalism and for God (Objection)

We may add that there is also good evidence for Christianity, but for our purposes and approach (classical apologetics), we would do well to first demonstrate that God exists before moving ahead to demonstrating that Christianity is true.

In the case of the naturalist, we must show as best we can that there is (1) good evidence in support of supernaturalism, and (2) good evidence against naturalism. The first approach leads us into positive apologetics, wherein we offer positive evidences in support of our position. The second approach leads us into negative apologetics, wherein we offer criticisms of the opposing viewpoint—in this case, naturalism. If we can demonstrate that the naturalist worldview has serious weaknesses while also showing sound reasons for belief in supernaturalism (God), then we can begin to move forward with making a case for Christianity.

As for the question of brain chemistry issues and religious belief (point 13), this, too, presupposes that naturalism is true. Again, abundant evidence shows that belief in God and Christianity is no mere matter of brain chemistry and certainly is neither unfounded nor delusional.

7. The evidence in favor of naturalism (or other worldviews) outweighs the evidence for God or Christianity (Rebuttal)

See point 4. Naturalism looks at the facts of science and impartially evaluates the evidence without allowing emotions or preconceptions to cloud judgment. If God did exist there would not be so much evil and suffering in the world, there would not be so much evidence of suboptimal design, and there wouldn't be so many contradictory religious beliefs. Darwinism, too, argues in favor of naturalism and against any form of religious belief.

8. Belief in God/ Christianity is based on wish fulfillment (Premise)

Freud essentially held to this objection, believing religion as a whole to be founded on delusional wish fulfillment—we strongly desire or wish for religion to be true, but in reality it is not. Ludwig Feuerbach also held to this wish-fulfillment theory. The universe, experience demonstrates, is a scary place. Therefore, neurologically we wish for some sort of safety. Hence, God.

9. Belief in God/ Christianity is based on more than a wish; it is based on reasonable evidence (Objection)

The Christian theist may counter that belief is not based merely on some unsubstantiated wish or desire but on reasonable evidence. Well-grounded Christian thinkers do not base their beliefs on unsubstantiated absurdities with no basis in reality; to do so would indeed be delusional wish fulfillment. Instead, we believe Christianity is "true and reasonable" (Acts 26:25) because of the evidences in its favor.

Now, if belief in God and Christianity had no more to go on than a "feeling" or a wish or an unfounded desire (as opposed to a desire based on reason, as in chapter 12), then the premise in point 8 has value, but the majority of thinking theists and Christians do not hold to this position (there are, of course, some exceptions, such as fideists).

10. Chaos and contradiction among world religions supports the position that God is a delusion (Premise)

If God were real, then he would not allow the extent of chaos and contradiction among the world religions. Since there is intellectual chaos and contradiction among the world's religions, it follows that God is a delusion. Otherwise, why would we end up with so many contradictory and competing metaphysical perspectives?

11. This does not mean that God or Christianity are delusions. One religion may be true (Objection)

Contradiction and diversity among metaphysical and philosophical beliefs does not logically mean that God is a delusion, or that he does not exist, or that Christianity is false. Given the Christian position, human depravity is more than enough of an explanation for the proliferation of many false worldviews. Their existence does not invalidate or dismiss the evidences in favor of the existence of God and the truth claims of Christianity.

12. Then why has God allowed so much chaos and contradiction among religions? (Rebuttal)

Why would God allow so much chaos and contradiction among religions? After all, according to Christian theism God wants all people to repent and come to him. If he does, why make things so muddled and difficult for humans? Why not simply and forthrightly make his truth clear? If God is so aloof, no wonder that human beings have come up with so many contradictory beliefs. Doesn't it make more sense to simply admit that God does not exist, which would explain our metaphysical predicament and confusion better than if he did?

13. Belief in God is rooted in nontheistic evolutionary brain chemistry, not evidence (Premise)

The claim is that the existence of religion has a naturalistic explanation: evolutionary brain chemistry. If this is so, then perhaps religious belief was needed for a period of time in evolutionary progress, but now that we have advanced scientifically, we can see belief in God or the gods for what it truly was—a delusion.

DISCUSSION QUESTIONS

1. Discuss the claim that belief in God and/or Christianity may be delusional. What do you think of the evidence for and against this claim?
2. What is the wish-fulfillment argument?
3. If God exists, then why is there so much chaos and contradiction among world religions?

4. If you were to extend the argument diagram and offer objections to the rebuttals in points 4, 7, and 12, what would your objections be? How might the opposing perspective respond to your new objections?

SUGGESTED ASSIGNMENTS

1. Read *The God Delusion* by Richard Dawkins and at least one theistic response to it (e.g., *God Is Great, God Is Good*), then write a paper evaluating both resources, your findings, and the case made by each.
2. Research claims that belief in God is rooted in brain chemistry, as well as responses to this perspective, then write a paper about the topic.
3. Take an informal poll of Christians or other religious adherents and ask them what evidence they point to in support of the reality of God or their religious perspective.

CHAPTER 19

Evil Exists, So God Does Not Exist

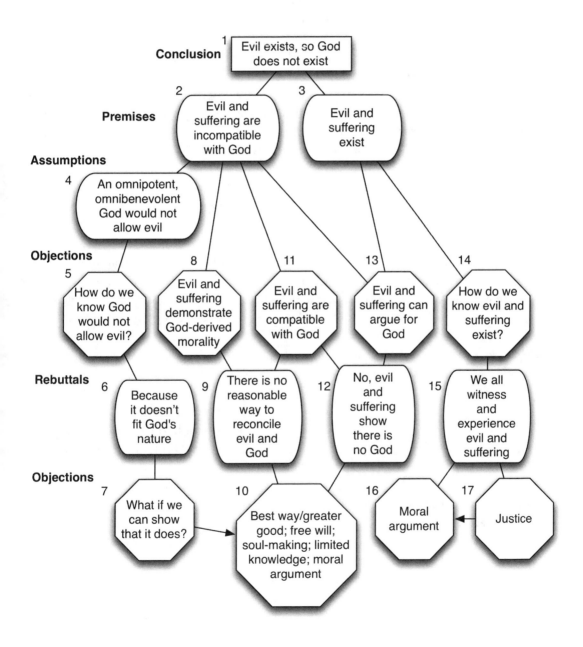

Conclusion — 1 Evil exists, so God does not exist

Premises — 2 Evil and suffering are incompatible with God — 3 Evil and suffering exist

Assumptions — 4 An omnipotent, omnibenevolent God would not allow evil

Objections — 5 How do we know God would not allow evil? — 8 Evil and suffering demonstrate God-derived morality — 11 Evil and suffering are compatible with God — 13 Evil and suffering can argue for God — 14 How do we know evil and suffering exist?

Rebuttals — 6 Because it doesn't fit God's nature — 9 There is no reasonable way to reconcile evil and God — 12 No, evil and suffering show there is no God — 15 We all witness and experience evil and suffering

Objections — 7 What if we can show that it does? — 10 Best way/greater good; free will; soul-making; limited knowledge; moral argument — 16 Moral argument — 17 Justice

1. Evil exists, so God does not exist (Conclusion)

Some atheists may state the conclusion "God does not exist" differently—for example, "God probably does not exist." On a popular level, the objection still arises that "God does not exist" due to the problem of evil; however, academically, most atheists have set aside this form of the conclusion. They opt instead to argue that, based on the evidence, it is unlikely or improbable that God exists. In either case, the remainder of the argument map will shed light on the nature of the argument and how to respond to it.

2. Evil and suffering are incompatible with God (Premise)

3. Evil and suffering exist (Premise)

Beginning with point 2, atheists present the premises for their conclusion. Recall that premises support conclusions (or at least, they should). In this case, the premise is, "Evil and suffering are incompatible with God." It and point 3 appear to work together to support the conclusion that God does not exist. The atheist generally argues, "Evil and suffering exist." This may seem obvious, yet as we have seen in studies of pantheism, some worldviews deny the reality of evil and suffering. In this sense, then, atheism and Christianity agree: evil and suffering are real.

4. An omnipotent, omnibenevolent God would not allow evil (Assumption)

The atheist assumption is that an all-powerful (omnipotent), all-loving (omnibenevolent) God would find a way to create a world where no form of evil exists. (See chapter 8 regarding possible worlds God could or could not have created.)

5. How do we know God would not allow evil? (Objection)

This brings up a point we will revisit in this chapter, namely, that human beings possess limited knowledge of God and his plans. As point 10 will point out, there are a number of reasons why God may permit evil, at least for a limited period of time. The objection in point 5 places the burden of proof on the atheist to demonstrate that an omnipotent, omnibenevolent God would not allow evil.

6. Because it doesn't fit God's nature (Rebuttal)

Points 6, 9, 12, and 15 offer possible rebuttals atheists may offer to theistic objections in points 5, 8, 11, 13, and 14. Of course, every reasonable rebuttal cannot be anticipated or diagrammed, which is why Christians must seek to equip themselves in a general sense to defend the faith and think critically in the process. In the case of point 6, the atheist rebuts the question, "How do we know God would not allow evil?" (point 5). In this rebuttal, the atheist claims, "Because it doesn't fit God's nature." The person who holds this position does not see how an all-powerful, all-loving God can be reconciled with evil, since, in the atheist's view, if God existed and did indeed have these attributes, then evil would not exist. This brings us back to the assumption (point 4): "An omnipotent, omnibenevolent God would not allow evil." In other words, the atheist is claiming the premise in point 2: "Evil and suffering are incompatible with God."

7. What if we can show that it does? (Objection)

Beginning with point 6, the theist proposes to demonstrate that evil and God are in fact reconcilable, referencing point 9 and its various solutions to the problem of evil.

8. Evil and suffering demonstrate God-derived morality (Objection)

11. Evil and suffering are compatible with God (Objection)

Objections 8, 11, and 13 directly respond to premise 2, which maintains that evil and suffering are incompatible with God. Points 8 and 11 work together in responding to this contention. Point 8 turns the problem of evil around, so to speak, and claims that evil and suffering demonstrate God-derived morality. If this is so, then evil and suffering are compatible with God (point 10). For a full discussion on how evil and suffering relate to God-derived morality, see points 10, 16, and 17 on moral arguments for the existence of God.

9. There is no reasonable way to reconcile evil and God (Rebuttal)

The relevant word in point 9 is "reasonable," which is open to debate. As point 10 will demonstrate, theists have responded to the problem of evil and suffering in a variety of ways. The fact that not all atheists are satisfied by the multitude of responses does not mean God does not exist.

Some theists may also choose a mystery response, meaning that ultimately it may be a mystery how the reality of God and the reality of evil can coexist (see "limited knowledge" under point 10). Astute theists may place this supposed mystery on one side of a scale, while on the other side placing a variety of positive evidence for the existence of God. If, in their view, the evidence for the existence of God outweighs some elements of mystery in relation to the reality of evil, then God exists despite our human limitations in understanding the reality of evil. In other words, the atheist may not view various theistic answers to the problem of evil as "reasonable," but this should not discount other evidence for the existence of God.

(Point 10 is addressed below in combination with points 16 and 17.)

12. No, evil and suffering show there is no God (Rebuttal)

Point 12 is tied to objections 11 and 13. It is not so much a formal rebuttal as a commitment to premise 2—that evil and suffering are incompatible with God.

13. Evil and suffering can argue for God (Objection)

Point 13 responds to both premises (2 and 3) by claiming, "Evil and suffering can argue for God." In other words, it makes the claim that evil and suffering are compatible with God (contra point 2) and, while acknowledging that evil and suffering exists, disagrees with point 12.

14. How do we know evil and suffering exist? (Objection)

Similar to the approach taken with the objection in point 5, point 14 asks, "How do we know evil and suffering exist?" The burden of proof is again placed on the atheist who, in this case, must offer evidence for the reality of evil and suffering. It is not that the theist disagrees with the atheist about the reality of evil, but acknowledging the reality of evil is not the same as offering evidence in support of its reality.

The underlying goal here is to move the atheist in the direction of trying to establish grounds for morality apart from the existence of God. There are a variety of approaches atheists may take in this regard, but the goal is to eventually make the case that true morality, and therefore true claims about good and evil, cannot be supported apart from the existence of a theistic God.

15. We all witness and experience evil and suffering (Rebuttal)

This atheist rebuttal is in direct response to point 14, which asks how we know that evil and suffering exist. The response is to the point, stressing the existential reality of evil and suffering: "We all witness and experience evil and suffering." In other words, premise 3 is true because evil and suffering are realities of life that we observe firsthand. Again, the theist is not denying the existential reality of evil but is merely seeking to have the atheist substantiate his or her claims that evil is real and on what basis it exists.

10. Best way/greater good; free will; soul-making; limited knowledge; moral argument (Objection)

16. Moral argument (Objection)

17. Justice (Objection)

Points 10, 16, and 17 tie together and so are treated together here. Note that all three objections contain references to a moral argument for the existence of God. The topic of justice relates to the moral argument and, as such, is pointing to it (17 to 16).

See chapters 8 and 15 for additional detail regarding moral arguments for the existence of God, including the topic of justice.

The rebuttal in point 15 offers evidence for the reality of evil and suffering, something theists do not refute. However, the fact that evil and suffering are existential realities can drive us to justice as a valid way of making moral claims about good and evil. If no standard of moral justice existed, we could not rightly or justly condemn anything as being evil. Inherently, we seek justice to right wrongs. But only the existence of God can adequately explain our desire for justice. Hence, the reality of evil and suffering combined with a sense of justice point to a moral argument for God.

Point 10 is more complex. Although the options listed are by no means exhaustive, they do represent general trends in theistic responses to reconciling evil and God. A version of the moral argument for God is listed, offering positive reasons for accepting the reality of God and the reality of evil.

Notable options omitted include the argument that God is not truly omnipotent and so cannot completely control evil. In other words, this option imposes limits on God in order to explain evil. (An example of this approach is found in *When Bad Things Happen to Good People* by Harold Kushner.) It is a deficient theistic response since it compromises God's essential attribute of omnipotence.

Also omitted is the explanation offered by some forms of pantheism that evil is an illusion (see chapter 23).

Still another explanation that has been omitted is the claim that God is punishing or judging humanity, and that therefore no one can avoid evil and suffering. The punishment response, however, has too many deficiencies to adequately explain the reality of evil and suffering, not to mention its pervasive scope. (See chapter 15 regarding God's judgment and punishment.)

We are left with four broad responses to the claims that evil and suffering exist; that they are incompatible with God; and that they therefore demonstrate conclusively that God does not exist or that his existence is highly unlikely.

The best way/greater good response to these claims is

broadly Augustinian. It acknowledges the reality of evil and suffering, affirming that the world as it is now is not the best possible world. But it reasons that the way things are must be the best way to the best possible world. Evil will ultimately be overcome, but for now it is necessary in order to achieve a greater good. However, the best way approach is not utilitarian (see chapter 14). Instead, it is based on God and his nature, accepting that even though we may not understand all aspects of evil and suffering (see the limited knowledge response below), ultimately the way things are will result in the best possible solution to evil and suffering.

The free will defense in response to the problem of evil emphasizes human choices. Indeed, much evil in the world is the result of human behavior. To an extent, this response helps address questions of moral evil, but it has a harder time explaining natural evil. After all, humans do not choose so-called natural disasters such as earthquakes or floods. Explaining them on the basis of the free will defense is still possible, but it requires an appeal to the Christian worldview. If, for instance, human choice resulted in the Fall of humanity, and if this Fall also resulted in the decay of the natural order of reality, then the free will defense may indeed apply to natural disasters. Briefly, although humans do not directly choose them, such disasters are the by-product of a fallen world in need of restoration.

The soul-making response is an interesting one and is usually tied to John Hick, known for his championing of religious pluralism (see chapters 11 and 22). At this juncture we must be careful in condemning a theory developed by Hick simply because we may disagree with his overall approach to other issues. In other words, to condemn the soul-making response on the basis of its origins would be to commit a genetic fallacy (see glossary). The soul-making theodicy attempts to explain the reality of evil and suffering by claiming that God permits evil in order to help build virtuous character in people. In a sense, then, it has some affinities with the best way/greater good approach in that by permitting evil and suffering, God has in mind a greater good: the positive development of human moral character. But even if this response is true, atheists may claim that it fails to address questions of gratuitous evil.

The limited knowledge response is, as the phrase suggests, ultimately an appeal to mystery, at least regarding some aspects of evil and suffering. Based on the fact that our understanding of why God permits evil and suffering is limited, this approach claims we simply do not have enough information to make a fully formed response to the problem of evil. While not an entirely satisfying response to evil and suffering, it is an epistemological reality, at least to those who hold the perspective. In some ways it echoes the approach to the problem of evil taken in the Old Testament book of Job.

Bear in mind that responses to the problem of evil and suffering may be multifaceted, incorporating various elements of different responses depending on the particular challenge raised by an atheist, skeptic, or even a theist seeking to understand how God and evil can be reconciled. Also consider the context of the discussion about evil. There are differences between addressing purely intellectual objections as opposed to existential objections. The former usually involves detached analytical discussion about a problem, while the latter is more of a pastoral or ministerial concern.

Remember as well that a robust theodicy may incorporate various aspects of different responses to the problem of evil, so long as those different responses are not contradictory in nature. In other words, some apologists view the problem of evil really as the *problems* of evil, meaning that there may be different responses that work together in order to respond to different elements and challenges that the problems of evil present.

We must also keep in mind that differing theistic theological traditions may emphasize certain responses to evil and suffering over others.

The argument map concludes (point 1) that God does not exist, based on the premises that evil and suffering are incompatible with God (point 2) and that evil and suffering exist (point 3). Is the argument as a whole compelling? Are the parts compelling? As discussed in chapter 2, it's important to accurately understand the components of an argument prior to evaluating it. Also recall from chapter 2 the concepts of strength and weakness in relation to arguments. Look, too, for assumed and/or faulty premises. In addition, ask if the premises do indeed support the conclusion. Moreover, recall that an argument form may be correct but its conclusions wrong.

In this case, the argument may appear strong initially, but many objections (5, 8, 11, 13, 14, 7, 10, 16, and 17) may be offered in opposition to its premises (2, 3) and conclusion (1), thus resulting in a weaker argument against the existence of God.

DISCUSSION QUESTIONS

1. How is it possible for evil and suffering to be compatible with God?
2. What is the soul-making theodicy?
3. How can the reality of evil and suffering argue in favor of God's existence rather than against it?
4. What is the best way defense?

SUGGESTED ASSIGNMENTS

1. Continue the diagram's line of reasoning by providing rebuttals to the objections in points 7, 10, 16, and 17.
2. Read a book on evil and suffering (e.g., *Making Sense Out of Suffering* by Peter Kreeft or *The Problem of Pain* by C. S. Lewis). Write a report on the solutions offered and evaluate them.

CHAPTER 20

Christianity Is Harmful

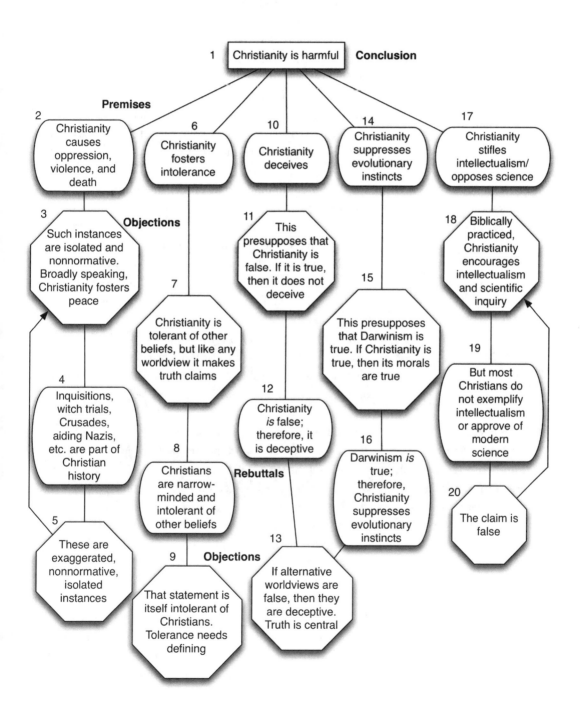

1 Christianity is harmful   **Conclusion**

Premises

2 Christianity causes oppression, violence, and death

6 Christianity fosters intolerance

10 Christianity deceives

14 Christianity suppresses evolutionary instincts

17 Christianity stifles intellectualism/opposes science

Objections

3 Such instances are isolated and nonnormative. Broadly speaking, Christianity fosters peace

7 Christianity is tolerant of other beliefs, but like any worldview it makes truth claims

11 This presupposes that Christianity is false. If it is true, then it does not deceive

15 This presupposes that Darwinism is true. If Christianity is true, then its morals are true

18 Biblically practiced, Christianity encourages intellectualism and scientific inquiry

19 But most Christians do not exemplify intellectualism or approve of modern science

4 Inquisitions, witch trials, Crusades, aiding Nazis, etc. are part of Christian history

8 Christians are narrow-minded and intolerant of other beliefs

12 Christianity *is* false; therefore, it is deceptive

16 Darwinism *is* true; therefore, Christianity suppresses evolutionary instincts

20 The claim is false

Rebuttals

5 These are exaggerated, nonnormative, isolated instances

9 That statement is itself intolerant of Christians. Tolerance needs defining

Objections

13 If alternative worldviews are false, then they are deceptive. Truth is central

1. Christianity is harmful (Conclusion)

This conclusion echoes the warning of many contemporary atheists. Whether Christianity is viewed as a poison, virus, or other such blight on the world, the conclusion is that religion in general and Christianity in particular are harmful, not beneficial (see chapter 9). Christianity is portrayed as harmful on a large scale, such as through the behavior of adherents involved in religious wars, persecution of non-Christians, the Inquisition, the Crusades, the Salem witch trials, aid given to the Nazi regime, intolerance in general, and so forth. Christianity is also sometimes portrayed as harmful to individuals via encouraging anti-intellectualism, psychological abuse, or delusional beliefs. Some critics even argue that Christian parents are harming their children in a number of ways, thus equating Christian child rearing with abuse.

2. Christianity causes oppression, violence, and death (Premise)

This premise can manifest itself in numerous ways, and therefore we cannot anticipate every sort of argument that will arise from it. However, we can present briefly some commonly held examples of Christianity causing harm. Some usual accusations include religiously motivated wars, alleged Christian oppression against non-Christians, violence resulting from the Crusades, the Inquisition, and so forth. It is claimed that such actions by Christians throughout history are evidence that Christianity is harmful and consequently should not be touted as a cure or benefit to the world. Instead, at best it needs to be curtailed and controlled or at worst eliminated from society lest it continue to foment strife or worse.

3. Such instances are isolated and nonnormative. Broadly speaking, Christianity fosters peace (Objection)

The Christian may reply by taking the stance that such instances are isolated and nonnormative. Moreover, broadly speaking, Christianity fosters peace, not harm. One approach in making this case is to demonstrate Christian principles from the New Testament record, particularly the admonitions of Christ to love God, love neighbor, care for others, avoid hypocritical judgments, and so on. In addition, other New Testament examples beyond the four gospels can be cited in support of Christian ethics as positive and beneficial. In sum, Christianity nowhere teaches its followers to perpetuate any kind of holy war, abuse on either an individual or a collective scale, oppression, violent intolerance, or the execution of those who would ideologically oppose the Christian faith. In fact, quite the opposite is true if Christianity is followed in the way it was meant to be followed.

Why, then, the critic may object, are so many Christians involved in such harmful behavior? There are many answers to this question. First, not all professing Christians are true Christians; sometimes a person who claims to be a Christian really isn't one. Second, if the Christian belief in sin and human depravity is true, then negative human behavior is inevitable. This never excuses such behavior, but it does explain it (see, for instance, chapter 8), whereas opposing worldviews such as atheism and monistic pantheism fail to ground their values meaningfully. Third, opposing worldviews are also littered with episodes of oppression, violence, and death. Atheistic communism, for example, is responsible for the deaths of multiple millions in the twentieth century alone, while militant Islam is also responsible for many deaths, from its inception to the present day. Should we therefore immediately conclude that atheism, for example, is false because its ideology is responsible for millions and millions of deaths? Again, this last argument does not absolve any worldview of wrongdoing, but it does demonstrate that the supposed "harmfulness" of a worldview is an insufficient test of its truth.

4. Inquisitions, witch trials, Crusades, aiding Nazis, etc. are part of Christian history (Rebuttal)

The rebuttal here brings up specific examples where the critic believes Christianity has indeed done serious harm. It is no small matter to torture individuals simply because they hold to nontraditional Christian beliefs, to try and execute individuals supposedly involved in witchcraft, to violently invade other territories in the name of Christianity (and against Islam), and to either assist Nazis or do nothing to stop them. If Christianity is true, the critic avers, then why are these terrible episodes even associated with Christianity? Isn't the best explanation simply that Christianity is probably false?

5. These are exaggerated, nonnormative, isolated instances (Objection)

Is this Christian response sufficient? A historical investigation demonstrates that the dire manner in which critics of Christianity portray these instances is often exaggerated. For instance, not many individuals were tried and executed for witchcraft. Moreover, while some Christian citizens were complacent in the face of Nazi Germany, and some professing Christians may indeed have supported the Nazi government, the fact remains that many committed Christians risked their lives to speak out against the regime, undermine it, and let others know of the plight of their nation. The pastor and Christian thinker Dietrich Bonhoeffer is a foremost example.

Besides, do we really want to play the comparison game regarding the harm any particular worldview has done? If so, atheism clearly loses, as does monistic pantheism. The former has caused millions of deaths while the latter neglects humanitarian aid and compassion toward the suffering and needy for fear of interfering with their karma (chapter 21).

Christians must grant that in *some* cases at *some* times and in *some* places, professing Christians have done harm. However, we must underscore the fact that neither Christ nor the New Testament teachings ever condone Christian oppression, violence, or death as a means to spread or defend the Christian message. Instead, Christians are called to defend the faith with "gentleness and respect" (1 Peter 3:15). The goal is to persuade others intellectually, not force anyone to believe on pain of death.

6. Christianity fosters intolerance (Premise)

Isn't Christianity just another example of an intolerant religion that is incapable of getting along peacefully with the rest of the world and the beliefs of others? Can't Christians just respect non-Christian beliefs? What sort of children are Christians raising if they are teaching them intolerance? These and related claims form another premise supporting the critical conclusion that Christianity is harmful.

7. Christianity is tolerant of other beliefs, but like any worldview it makes truth claims (Objection)

The issue here, at least in part, is a matter of understanding what is meant by tolerance and intolerance. Should we, for instance, tolerate pedophiles? Should we tolerate theft? Murder? Are we intolerant if we disagree with the mathematical solution to two plus two?

We must understand the differences between truth and tolerance. Being tolerant, for example, is more than acceptable when it comes to matters of taste.

When it comes to respecting the beliefs of others, true Christianity is indeed tolerant. As we've noted before, Christians should seek to gently persuade others, reasonably, not force others to believe, which is intolerant and unreasonable.

8. Christians are narrow-minded and intolerant of other beliefs (Rebuttal)

Can't Christians see that they are being foolish by being so narrow-minded and intolerant? What about other sincere people who believe that God is everything or that God does not exist? Why should they be marginalized, or worse, oppressed simply because they hold different views?

9. That statement is itself intolerant of Christians. Tolerance needs defining (Objection)

Those who vehemently claim that another belief system is intolerant typically demonstrate the very intolerance they claim to oppose. Is truth narrow-minded simply for adhering to what is true? If so, then it is narrow-minded to hold that there is only one true answer to a simple math problem.

Is a surgeon being narrow-minded by adhering to the truth of a particular surgical procedure? We don't claim a doctor is intolerant of other beliefs when he tells a patient that her appendix requires removal. We don't claim aeronautical engineers are being intolerant by adhering to truths about aircraft design and the physics of flight. Yet for some reason, we think religious truth claims are in a different category. Are they?

Either God exists or he does not. We may use differing means to determine whether the answer to the question is true or not, but in the end it is a truth question.

Every meaningful worldview makes truth claims (chapter 7). Truth claims are either true or false. Atheism, for instance, claims that God does not exist. If this were true, then every belief system that believes in God would necessarily be false. Is atheism therefore "intolerant" in asserting its belief? Is pantheism "intolerant" of those who deny God or who claim that God is personal and transcendent?

At some point, every worldview is intolerant of what it views as wrong answers to questions of ultimate truth. This does not make such intolerance harmful, nor does it mean that intolerance should lead to physical or emotional abuse of any kind.

But again, whether Christianity is intolerant is a matter of definition. If by "intolerant" one means a worldview that uses coercive means—including physical, legal, or financial intimidation, imprisonment, violence, and death—to repress all competing ideologies, then Christianity is absolutely not intolerant. But if one means a worldview that upholds definitive views of truth and considers other views erroneous, then by that definition, Christianity is intolerant. But then, so is every worldview and every person who ever lived and held a conviction or an opinion.

10. Christianity deceives (Premise)

This premise claims that by perpetuating Christianity as true, Christians deceive not only themselves, which is a form of self-harm, but also others, such as children in their own families or non-Christians who are being influenced by Christians. Deception is wrong. Consequently, Christians who perpetuate deception, which is all of them if Christianity is false, inflict harm.

11. This presupposes that Christianity *is* false. If it is true, then it does not deceive (Objection)	We are back to the truth question here, as well as to the danger of assuming that our presuppositions are true. If opposing worldviews are true, such as pantheism or atheism, then Christians are indeed deceived (chapter 18) and are going about deceiving others, even if they are sincere and their deceit is unintentional.

Of course, that principle works both ways. The critic is assuming (presupposing) that Christianity is false. What if good evidence can be marshaled to demonstrate Christianity is true? Then Christianity is not deceitful but is encouraging truth. |
| **12. Christianity *is* false; therefore, it is deceptive (Rebuttal)** | But that's the point, rebuts the critic. Christianity *is* false and therefore deceptive.

Perhaps this critic has made the case for his worldview as well as against Christianity. Is he, then, justified in his conclusion that Christianity is harmful? After all, the worldview stakes are high for all involved. |
| **13. If alternative worldviews are false, then they are deceptive. Truth is central (Objection)** | We seem to be arguing in circles with one another, or at the very least talking past one another. We must step back and carefully evaluate the most significant claims of viable worldviews, examine the evidence carefully, and seek to understand what is most probably the best explanation of reality. We do not do this arbitrarily or in a vacuum or on the basis of our own worldview presuppositions. Instead, we test claims via helpful standards that reasonably apply to any search for truth.[1] What matters is truth and seeking it honestly. |
| **14. Christianity suppresses evolutionary instincts (Premise)** | Christianity is harmful because it suppresses our evolutionary instincts. We are products of an undirected process intended to perpetuate our improvement and survival, not to become deluded or led astray by false religious beliefs that are no longer useful in our evolutionary survival. Some potential examples brought up by the critic may include Christianity's support of monogamous marriage relationships, the family unit, false belief in a future heaven in order to motivate people by false hope, or intolerance of nontraditional relationships. |

---

1. Abductive reasoning, for instance, is a scientific approach which infers to the best explanation. Some tests along these lines for determining truth are found in *A World of Difference* by Kenneth Samples (chapter 2) and *Christian Apologetics* by Douglas Groothuis (chapter 3). Examples of these tests or criteria for testing worldviews, drawn from Samples and Groothuis, include the coherence test (logical consistency within a worldview); the verification test (whether or not the claims of a worldview can be verified); and the requirement that a worldview and its central claims must be "existentially viable."

15. This presupposes that Darwinism is true. If Christianity is true, then its morals are true (Objection)	See chapter 17 for more on the Darwinism argument against Christianity. In short, point 14 assumes that nontheistic evolution is true. But if Christianity is true, then its morality is also rooted in truth. Moreover, this morality would be rooted in a transcendent source (God), giving it significant weight. If this is the case, then Christian morality is not working against Darwinian instincts, but is instead trying to get humanity to function properly within God's moral standards; otherwise we will ruin ourselves.
16. Darwinism *is* true; therefore, Christianity suppresses evolutionary instincts (Rebuttal)	This rebuttal is insistent in its belief that Darwinism (nontheistic evolution) is true. Consequently, Christianity suppresses evolutionary instincts.
17. Christianity stifles intellectualism/opposes science (Premise)	The premise is that Christianity is in part harmful because of the way it stifles intellectualism and opposes science. If only Christians would move beyond their primitive outlook, abandon their blind faith, and use reason to arrive at truth, then we could have a constructive dialogue.
18. Biblically practiced, Christianity encourages intellectualism and scientific inquiry (Objection)	*Some* Christians may indeed stifle intellectualism and oppose science, but not all do. In fact, biblically speaking, the life of the intellect is highly regarded (chapter 3), and when properly integrated with the Christian worldview, scientific inquiry is encouraged (chapter 9). Many respected Christians are intellectuals and scientists who see no conflict whatsoever between having faith and using their minds and engaging in scientific inquiry.
19. But most Christians do not exemplify intellectualism or approve of modern science (Rebuttal)	Aren't most Christians anti-intellectual, highly focused on their emotional experiences of God instead of living in reality and reason? Aren't most Christians opposed to science by holding to creationism or Intelligent Design instead of facing the modern scientific facts? If so, they are burying their heads in the sand rather than seeking to apprehend truth.
20. The claim is false (Objection)	Not only are the claims in point 19 false, but they are misleading in a number of ways. What evidence does the critic offer to support the claim that "most Christians" hold to what the critics claim they hold to? We have established that Christianity encourages the use of the intellect to arrive at truth (chapter 3), that reason is important in the Christian life (chapter 4),

and also that Christianity was largely responsible for the rise of modern science (chapter 9). To say otherwise is to create a straw man by caricaturing Christianity; and it is to make hasty generalizations about all Christians that do not reflect reality.

DISCUSSION QUESTIONS

1. How do arguments that demonstrate Christianity's harmful influence fit into an overall case against the Christian worldview?
2. What value is there in pursuing a line of reasoning that assesses the benefits and detriments of any worldview?
3. Does Christianity stifle intellectualism and oppose science? Why or why not?
4. Do historical examples of events such as the Inquisition or the Crusades help or harm the cause of Christianity? How would you respond to someone who brought up these or similar examples as evidence against Christianity?

SUGGESTED ASSIGNMENTS

1. Read the book *God Is Not Great* by Christopher Hitchens, and evaluate the arguments it presents. Write a report on your findings.
2. Read *What's So Great About Christianity?* by Dinesh D'Souza and write a report on specific ways in which it makes a case in favor of the Christian worldview and responds to criticisms.
3. Read the section on Christianity and science in *For the Glory of God* by Rodney Stark and use your reading as the basis for a paper about the role of science and faith in relation to Christianity.

CHAPTER 21

Monistic Pantheism Is True

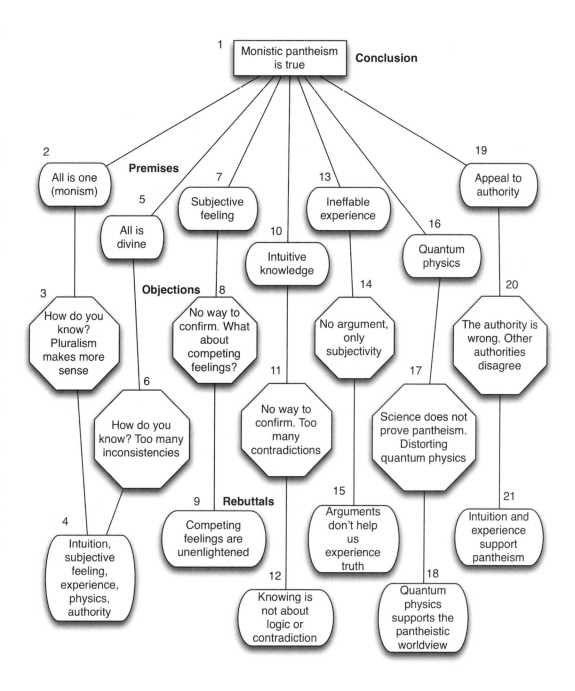

1 Monistic pantheism is true — **Conclusion**

Premises

2 All is one (monism)

5 All is divine

7 Subjective feeling

10 Intuitive knowledge

13 Ineffable experience

16 Quantum physics

19 Appeal to authority

Objections

3 How do you know? Pluralism makes more sense

6 How do you know? Too many inconsistencies

8 No way to confirm. What about competing feelings?

11 No way to confirm. Too many contradictions

14 No argument, only subjectivity

17 Science does not prove pantheism. Distorting quantum physics

20 The authority is wrong. Other authorities disagree

Rebuttals

4 Intuition, subjective feeling, experience, physics, authority

9 Competing feelings are unenlightened

12 Knowing is not about logic or contradiction

15 Arguments don't help us experience truth

18 Quantum physics supports the pantheistic worldview

21 Intuition and experience support pantheism

1. Monistic pantheism is true (Conclusion)

What is the case for monistic pantheism? This diagram offers seven premises in support of its conclusion. Keep in mind that monistic pantheism, such as Advaita Vedanta, is but one form of pantheism. It is addressed here because of its popularity in the West. In short, monistic pantheism believes that all is one and all is divine. Divine, however, within monistic pantheism is quite unlike divinity within theistic worldviews such as Christianity. Rather than holding to the existence of a personal, transcendent being, monistic pantheists believe in an impersonal divine force or power that permeates all reality.

2. All is one (monism) (Premise)

This metaphysical premise holds that all reality is one—a unified whole without distinctions between, for instance, a creator God and created beings or any creation whatsoever. By its very nature, then, monism is non-dualistic and non-pluralistic. Monism opposes any pluralistic view of reality such as Christian theism.[1]

3. How do you know? Pluralism makes more sense (Objection)

This objection questions how the monist comes to know that all reality is one. As other premises will reveal (points 7 and 10, for instance), the monist often appeals to subjective feeling and intuitive knowledge of monism rather than offering any philosophical arguments or justifiable logical reasons for holding to their view.

But does pluralism make more sense? There are good reasons why it does. Morally speaking, for instance, pluralistic views of reality are preferred, such as Christian theism, since they maintain a moral foundation for distinguishing between good and evil. Monism, on the other hand, cannot make such distinctions. If all is truly one, then there really is no good or evil.

We can also discern differences in being, such as between a creator God and his creation, which includes human beings. Thus, different kinds of beings exist. If this is so, then reality is more than just one (monism); it is at least two (dualistic): God and creation. Pluralism, consequently, is more robust both ethically and philosophically.

---

1. Pluralism can refer to religious pluralism—the idea that all religions are basically the same, as addressed in chapter 22. The term pluralism may also refer to a view of reality that sees it not as one (monism) but as plural (such as God and other beings).

4. Intuition, subjective feeling, experience, physics, authority (Rebuttal)	This rebuttal makes its case by referring to other premises, namely, points 7, 10, 13, 16, and 19 in support of monism.
5. All is divine (Premise)	This premise upholds the essential worldview of pantheism (all is god). Note that divinity from the point of view of pantheism is not personal or transcendent, as is the Christian God. Pantheism, then, denies the reality of a personal creator God who exists apart from the reality of the universe. In other words, within pantheism the divine and the universe are one and the same, albeit with the divine being an impersonal force.
6. How do you know? Too many inconsistencies (Objection)	What is the evidence in support of the pantheistic position? There appear to be numerous inconsistencies if pantheism is accepted as the best explanation of reality. For instance, we lose distinctions between good and evil. Monistic pantheists, as a result, may view evil and suffering as illusions, which flies against our existential and experiential perceptions of the reality of evil and suffering (chapters 14, 19, and 23). We also know there are distinctions between us and other beings, hence supporting pluralism over monism (point 3). Moreover, the evidence in support of the existence of the theistic God is far superior to any evidence in support of pantheistic worldviews (chapter 6).
7. Subjective feeling (Premise)	Monistic pantheists, particularly of the popular Western variety, often appeal to subjective feeling as the evidence for monistic pantheism. Adherents claim to somehow "just know" subjectively that monistic pantheism is true.
8. No way to confirm. What about competing feelings? (Objection)	Subjectivism, however, is insufficient evidence to support any worldview on its own. Besides, there are competing feelings that, if true, would contradict monistic pantheism. If other evidence in favor of monistic pantheism were compelling, then perhaps the worldview could contend as being a better explanation of reality than other alternatives such as theism. As it stands, monistic pantheism hardly distinguishes itself as a viable worldview, especially when it comes to its lack of real ethics and weak response to the problem of evil and suffering. This is not to say that feelings or experience may play no part in contributing to an overall case for a worldview (see chapter 25), but monistic pantheism fails worldview tests again and again.

9. Competing feelings are unenlightened (Rebuttal)	The monistic pantheist may play the enlightenment card, claiming that competing feelings are merely unenlightened. If others would achieve enlightenment or some sort of spiritual liberation or heightened state of awareness, then they, too, would accept monistic pantheism as subjectively and intuitively true.
10. Intuitive knowledge (Premise)	Monistic pantheists will at times also appeal to intuitive knowledge as substantiating their view of reality. Similar to subjective feeling (point 7), intuitive knowledge is an innate sense that their view is correct.
11. No way to confirm. Too many contradictions (Objection)	As with responses to the subjective feeling premise, there is no way to confirm or test whether or not claimed intuitive knowledge, in and of itself, is true or not. In fact, given the many inherent contradictions within the monistic pantheism worldview, intuitive knowledge claims do nothing to bolster the monistic pantheism view.
12. Knowing is not about logic or contradiction (Rebuttal)	Monistic pantheists may, at this point, demonstrate their opposition to logic in relation to knowing and to intellectualism as a whole. They may claim that logic is merely a Western invention, but that other kinds of knowing, such as intuitive knowledge, are superior, . This line of reasoning, however, will not help monistic pantheists, since in the process of responding to criticisms, they too must employ logic and appeal to reason.
13. Ineffable experience (Premise)	Some monistic pantheists will appeal to ineffable experience in support of their worldview. An ineffable experience is one that cannot be described or clearly communicated due to the severe limitations we have in the face of ultimate reality.
14. No argument, only subjectivity (Objection)	There is really no argument in point 13, only subjectivity and perhaps more claims of intuitive knowledge. And yet monistic pantheists have in many cases gone to great lengths to explain what they believe is unexplainable and ineffable.
	Moreover, if the theistic God exists, and if he chooses to reveal himself to us and communicate with us, then he is far from ineffable. He is capable of providing us with information about himself via such means as his creation, moral conscience, and special revelation (i.e., the biblical record). Such a God defines and describes himself to us in numerous ways.

15. Arguments don't help us experience truth (Rebuttal)	This rebuttal claims that arguments don't help us experience truth.[2] Only experience matters. Once we understand that we are all part of the infinite, impersonal divine force, we will reach a state of enlightenment that will lead us to understanding of the truth. No Western logic can help us.
16. Quantum physics (Premise)	Some monistic pantheists appeal to quantum physics in support of their views. For instance, they may claim that quantum physics substantiates the monistic pantheism view of reality as all being an impersonal energy or force that permeates everything. Science, they claim, substantiates monistic pantheism.
17. Science does not prove pantheism. Distorting quantum physics (Objection)	Point 16 is hardly evidence of the central claims of a monistic pantheism worldview.[3] Pantheistic adherents who cite quantum physics sources in support of pantheism distort the sources to fit their worldview. As Victor Stenger has written, "Quantum mechanics . . . is misinterpreted as implying that the human mind controls reality and that the universe is one connected whole that cannot be understood by the usual reduction to parts [tenets of monistic pantheism]. However, no compelling argument or evidence requires that quantum mechanics plays a central role in human consciousness or provides instantaneous, holistic connections across the universe. Modern physics, including quantum mechanics, remains completely materialistic and reductionistic while being consistent with all scientific observations."[4]
18. Quantum physics supports the pantheistic worldview (Rebuttal)	Some monistic pantheists may dogmatically cling to quantum physics in support of their worldview. Indeed, such an appeal is often their only appeal to some sort of evidential support for monistic pantheism, though, as we have noted (point 17), such an approach is misguided at best.
19. Appeal to authority (Premise)	Monistic pantheists may at times appeal to an authority figure or other source or sources in support of their view of reality. This appeal can vary greatly, involving everything from ascended masters, to ethereal records such as the Akashic

---

2. Arguments are helpful in assessing various truth claims and can indeed help us weigh evidence and come to conclusions that are more probable than other conclusions.
3. See, for instance, Reisser, Mabe, and Velarde, *Examining Alternative Medicine*, 182–87; and Victor Stenger, "Quantum Quackery," in *Skeptical Inquirer* 21, no. 1 (January/February 1997), http://www.csicop.org.
4. Stenger, "Quantum Quackery."

Records, to beings who claim to have reached enlightenment and therefore know that all reality is one and divine, and more.

20. **The authority is wrong. Other authorities disagree (Objection)**

There are valid reasons why certain appeals to authority are considered to be logically fallacious. The authority may be simply wrong, for instance. Or authorities may disagree with one another. It is true that appeals to authority are in certain instances quite valid, but not if the authority is highly suspect (such as ethereal records), lacks credibility, or holds to views that clearly go against established knowledge of reality.

21. **Intuition and experience support pantheism (Rebuttal)**

The appeal may once again be made to intuition and experience in support of pantheism (see points 7 and 10 and responses to those premises).

DISCUSSION QUESTIONS

1. What is monistic pantheism?
2. What are the differences between a monistic view of the world and a dualistic or pluralistic view?
3. Does quantum physics support the monistic pantheist worldview?
4. How do subjective feelings and intuitive knowledge support the monistic pantheist view?
5. What are key differences between the Christian view of God and the pantheistic view of reality?

SUGGESTED ASSIGNMENTS

1. Read *Unmasking the New Age* by Douglas Groothuis or *Apologetics in the New Age* by David Clark and Norman Geisler, and write a paper evaluating the arguments presented in the resource you have selected.
2. Research and write a paper on how proponents of monistic pantheism, or other forms of pantheism, have utilized quantum physics in support of their position and evaluate their arguments biblically and logically. See, for instance, works by Deepak Chopra such as *Ageless Body, Timeless Mind* and Christian critiques of these positions such as chapter 9 of *Examining Alternative Medicine* by Paul Reisser, Dale Mabe, and Robert Velarde.

CHAPTER 22

All Religions Are Essentially True (Christianity Is Not Unique)

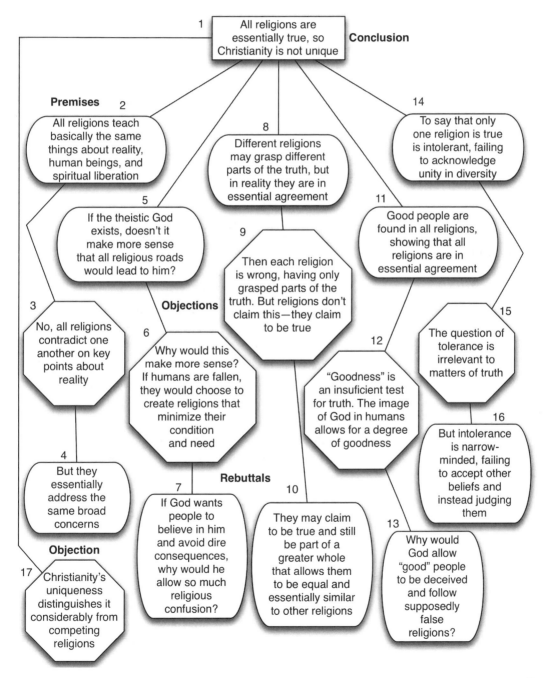

1 All religions are essentially true, so Christianity is not unique
Conclusion

Premises

2 All religions teach basically the same things about reality, human beings, and spiritual liberation

8 Different religions may grasp different parts of the truth, but in reality they are in essential agreement

14 To say that only one religion is true is intolerant, failing to acknowledge unity in diversity

5 If the theistic God exists, doesn't it make more sense that all religious roads would lead to him?

9 Then each religion is wrong, having only grasped parts of the truth. But religions don't claim this—they claim to be true

11 Good people are found in all religions, showing that all religions are in essential agreement

3 No, all religions contradict one another on key points about reality

Objections

6 Why would this make more sense? If humans are fallen, they would choose to create religions that minimize their condition and need

12 "Goodness" is an insuficient test for truth. The image of God in humans allows for a degree of goodness

15 The question of tolerance is irrelevant to matters of truth

16 But intolerance is narrow-minded, failing to accept other beliefs and instead judging them

4 But they essentially address the same broad concerns

Rebuttals

7 If God wants people to believe in him and avoid dire consequences, why would he allow so much religious confusion?

10 They may claim to be true and still be part of a greater whole that allows them to be equal and essentially similar to other religions

13 Why would God allow "good" people to be deceived and follow supposedly false religions?

Objection

17 Christianity's uniqueness distinguishes it considerably from competing religions

1. All religions are essentially true, so Christianity is not unique (Conclusion)

This conclusion may be offered by a New Age monistic pantheist or someone with an affinity for such teachings. An atheist may also offer the variant argument that all religions are essentially the same. The underlying suggestion behind the New Age version of this conclusion is that Christianity is really no different from other religions and therefore is not unique. All paths lead to ultimate reality and spiritual liberation of some sort. Therefore, Christian exclusivism is unfounded and intolerant (see chapter 11).

2. All religions teach basically the same things about reality, human beings, and spiritual liberation (Premise)

All religions identify things that are wrong with the universe as it now is. Further, all religions note that human beings are not currently in their optimal state, but require some sort of spiritual liberation, enlightenment, or salvation. So in reality all religions are essentially true in their common observations about reality, the human predicament, and how to solve the problem. While there may be variations between different religious worldviews, in the end they are all essentially the same and true.

3. No, all religions contradict one another on key points about reality (Objection)

This objection notes that there are key, significant differences between religious views. Consequently, they can't all be true. One of them may be true, or perhaps they are all false. For example, Christians are Trinitarian monotheists, meaning that they believe in one God who reveals himself as Father, Son, and Holy Spirit. The three are coequal and coeternal but one in nature. But other religious beliefs hold to polytheism, such as forms of Hinduism, meaning that they believe in multiple deities. Monistic pantheists, moreover, believe that there is an impersonal force permeating all of reality, meaning that everything is divine (see chapter 21). The basic point here is that these three religious views are contradictory and consequently cannot all be true. There cannot be one personal God, many gods, and an impersonal divine force at the same time and in the same way.

Also, the means of spiritual liberation vary greatly from religion to religion. Christianity teaches salvation by grace through faith, not by works, while many Eastern religions emphasize that human ignorance must be overcome via meditative enlightenment through an emptying of the mind. These two views are contradictory. Christian repentance, moreover, emphasizes the reality of human sin, guilt, and the need for atonement via Christ's sacrificial death. Such a view has nothing in common with New Age views that human beings are perfect as they are; they are merely unenlightened or in need of achieving Christ-consciousness of some sort.[1]

The point is, there are vast differences in the core teachings of different religions, and therefore they are not all teaching the same things about reality.

4. But they essentially address the same broad concerns (Rebuttal)

The rebuttal may note that even though there are differences among religions, at bottom they essentially address the same broad concerns. While it is true that religions may deal with the same sorts of questions—such as the nature of ultimate reality, the nature of the human condition, and the nature of salvation—they answer such questions in markedly different and contradictory ways.[2]

5. If the theistic God exists, doesn't it make more sense that all religious roads would lead to him? (Premise)

Aren't all religions just describing the same thing in different ways like the blind men who touched different parts of the elephant and came to very different conclusions about its nature? If God really exists, it makes sense that all religious roads would lead to him, just as many different roads can lead to the top of the same mountain. God wants to see our sincerity in seeking him, but he doesn't care about the manner or religion we choose to find him.

6. Why would this make more sense? If humans are fallen, they would choose to create religions that minimize their condition and need (Objection)

There are many things wrong with point 5. If, for instance, one takes the "blind men and the elephant" analogy to its logical conclusions, then there was a truth to be grasped (the elephant) that all the blind men got wrong. Besides, those who claim all religions are essentially true put themselves in the unenviable position of saying, in essence, that religious adherents are wrong to believe that their worldview may be the only one that is essentially true. How can all religions be essentially true and yet wrong in claiming exclusivity? Shouldn't we ask the experts of those particular religions what they think of the solution that all religions are essentially true, so no religion is unique?

---

1. "Christ-consciousness" is a New Age term referring to the belief that all human beings can become enlightened and thus achieve an elevated spiritual status, essentially coming to the realization that they are perfect and divine.
2. See Harold Netland's *Encountering Religious Pluralism*, chapter 6.

While different paths may indeed lead to the top of the same mountain, what if someone is climbing the wrong mountain? For the Christian, the claim that all roads lead to God is true only in the sense that upon death we will all face God's judgment (Heb. 9:27).

God wants more than our sincerity, as one can be sincerely wrong. Christianity claims that God has given us enough revelation, both general and special, to arrive at the truth about Christ.

Since human beings are fallen, we create beliefs that minimize our fallen condition and God's solution for it.

7. If God wants people to believe in him and avoid dire consequences, why would he allow so much religious confusion? (Rebuttal)

This rebuttal argues that God would not allow so much religious confusion to proliferate if so much was at stake regarding our eternal human destinies. The Christian response is that human sin and depravity are responsible for the proliferation of false worldviews and beliefs. We want to seek our own way rather than God's way.

8. Different religions may grasp different parts of the truth, but in reality they are in essential agreement (Premise)

The blind man and the elephant analogy is often used in support of this premise, as is the story of all paths leading to the top of the mountain. See point 6.

9. Then each religion is wrong, having only grasped parts of the truth. But religions don't claim this—they claim to be true (Objection)

See point 6.

10. They may claim to be true and still be part of a greater whole that allows them to be equal and essentially similar to other religions (Rebuttal)

Like puzzle pieces that may look very different, various religious views may in the end all fit together to form a complete puzzle. Just because differences exist between religions does not mean those differences must outweigh the significance of the similarities.

11. Good people are found in all religions, showing that all religions are in essential agreement (Premise)	Aren't there good people in all religions? If so, then this minimizes the uniqueness or significance of any one religion. If good people can be found to represent every meaningful religious worldview, then what's so special about Christianity?
12. "Goodness" is an insufficient test for truth. The image of God in humans allows for a degree of goodness (Objection)	"Goodness" first of all requires a standard by which we can even make the claim that something is "good." Christian theism best provides this standard (chapter 8). Moreover, by itself goodness is not enough to test whether or not a worldview is true in all of its essential points and claims. "Good" people are found in various religious and even nonreligious worldviews because God's image in us includes a moral conscience.
13. Why would God allow "good" people to be deceived and follow supposedly false religions? (Rebuttal)	Doesn't God want everyone to know him? Isn't he all-loving? If so, why would he allow "good" people to be deceived and follow supposedly false religions?[3]
14. To say that only one religion is true is intolerant, failing to acknowledge unity in diversity (Premise)	Intolerance is unacceptable, and any religion that perpetuates intolerance, such as Christianity, fails to acknowledge the unity in diversity among religious views.
15. The question of tolerance is irrelevant to matters of truth (Objection)	Point 14 seems quite intolerant of Christianity. The response in point 15 is that we have confused questions of intolerance and truth.

Everyone can point to things they do not tolerate. Some things are quite frankly intolerable; for instance, we do not tolerate pedophiles.

But getting at the truth is not a matter of tolerance. There is a great diversity among religious beliefs, but disagreeing with one another in a civil manner, without forcing others to give up their beliefs, can result in healthy dialogue and further human understanding.

Every worldview is intolerant on some points; that is what makes every worldview unique. But this kind of intolerance (if |

---

3. God does not deceive anyone; we deceive ourselves out of our own sinful, rebellious natures. God has provided more than enough evidence via nature, human conscience, and the Bible to convict and convince us of the truth.

that is what it can even be called) should not cause confusion as we seek to determine what is true—that is, what corresponds to reality versus what does not (chapter 7).

16. But intolerance is narrow-minded, failing to accept other beliefs and instead judging them (Rebuttal)

Doesn't this make religions like Christianity narrow-minded and judgmental? Can't they just accept differing views without bothering adherents of other religions?

This rebuttal once again confuses tolerance and truth. No one would object that the correct solution to a simple math problem is intolerant because it excludes other answers. If an answer corresponds to reality, whether it involves mathematics or the great issues of life, then it is not narrow-minded. It is simply true (see chapter 11).

17. Christianity's uniqueness distinguishes it considerably from competing religions (Objection)

This is a general response to the overall conclusion of the argument in point 1. While every religion is unique in its own ways, Christianity is unique in ways that distinguish it as being a more compelling and viable worldview. For instance, it is unique in the compelling person of Christ—his life, his claims, and his miracles, especially the resurrection. No other worldview has made such monumental claims that have their root in real historical events and associated evidences.[4]

DISCUSSION QUESTIONS

1. Given what you know of various religions, is it true that all religions are essentially the same? Why or why not?
2. How would you respond to the story of the blind men and the elephant who each grasped a different understanding of the same reality?
3. What does the Bible say about the path to salvation?
4. Is the question of "goodness" sufficient evidence to demonstrate that all religions are in essential agreement?

SUGGESTED ASSIGNMENTS

1. Read the booklet *Are All Religions One?* by Douglas Groothuis and prepare a written assessment of the arguments and conclusions in the booklet.
2. Write a summary critique of the book *Encountering Religious Pluralism* by Harold Netland, noting key arguments offered.

---

4. See Josh McDowell, *The New Evidence That Demands a Verdict*, ch. 1 and part 2: "The Case for Jesus."

CHAPTER 23

Evil Is an Illusion

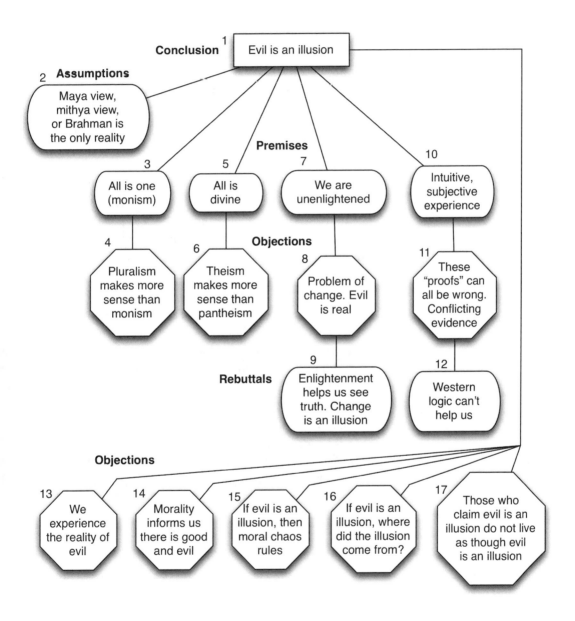

Conclusion ¹ Evil is an illusion

² **Assumptions**
Maya view, mithya view, or Brahman is the only reality

Premises

3 — All is one (monism)

5 — All is divine

7 — We are unenlightened

10 — Intuitive, subjective experience

Objections

4 — Pluralism makes more sense than monism

6 — Theism makes more sense than pantheism

8 — Problem of change. Evil is real

11 — These "proofs" can all be wrong. Conflicting evidence

Rebuttals

9 — Enlightenment helps us see truth. Change is an illusion

12 — Western logic can't help us

Objections

13 — We experience the reality of evil

14 — Morality informs us there is good and evil

15 — If evil is an illusion, then moral chaos rules

16 — If evil is an illusion, where did the illusion come from?

17 — Those who claim evil is an illusion do not live as though evil is an illusion

1. Evil is an illusion (Conclusion)	The monistic pantheism worldview of the New Age claims that evil is an illusion. If so, then alternative interpretations of evil and suffering are false, including the Christian view of the reality of evil, as well as forms of atheism that acknowledge evil and suffering. If evil is an illusion, then false views of reality are in need of correction.
2. Maya view, mithya view, or Brahman is the only reality (Assumption)	Monistic pantheism holds various assumptions in relation to the claim that evil is an illusion. These assumptions include *maya*, the view that the world as we experience it is illusory; *mithya*, the view that pluralism, too, is an illusion; and belief that Brahman is the only reality, meaning that the self is the same as ultimate reality (Brahman), thus supporting monism over pluralism.
3. All is one (monism) (Premise)	Monism is the view that all reality is one, thus ruling out pluralism—the view that many beings exist (e.g., God and his creatures). This view of reality, known as *pluralism*, is not to be confused with *religious pluralism*, which believes that all religious views are basically the same and lead to the same truths (chapter 22).
	If all is one, as monism claims, then there are no distinctions between good and evil since reality is one. If monism is true, then evil is an illusion. One argument in favor of monism was offered by Parmenides: "There cannot be more than one thing (absolute monism), for if there were two things, they would have to differ. For things to differ, they must differ either by being or by nonbeing. But since being is that which makes them identical, they cannot differ by being. Nor, on the other hand, can they differ by nonbeing, for nonbeing is nothing, and to differ by nothing is not to differ at all. Hence, there cannot be a plurality of beings but only one single indivisible being—a rigid monism."[1]
4. Pluralism makes more sense than monism (Objection)	In order to defeat the monistic worldview and its associated view that evil is an illusion, one may argue in favor of alternatives to monism. Although a few other alternatives to monism exist, our goal here is to argue for a pluralistic view of reality, which aligns best with the Christian worldview.[2]

---

1. Parmenides's viewpoint, as summarized by Geisler, *Systematic Theology*, 21–22.
2. For insights into the alternatives to monism noted here see Geisler, *Systematic Theology*, chapter 2. Note again that we are using the term pluralism here in contrast to monism, not as is used in reference to religious pluralism.

5. All is divine (Premise)

Another premise of the monistic pantheist in support of evil as illusory is the view that all is divine. After all, if everything is part of the divine force that permeates all reality, then what we perceive as good and evil are simply a part of this divine force. Since all is one (point 3) and all is divine, then it follows that our understanding of good and evil must be confused, since good and evil are illusory.

6. Theism makes more sense than pantheism (Objection)

Just as pluralism makes more sense than monism, so too does theism make more sense than pantheism (chapters 5 and 6; chapter 21). If a personal, transcendent creator God exists, then reality is not all one or all divine because God and other beings exist (pluralism) and God is separate from creation. If theism is true, then the monistic pantheism explanation of evil is wrong. In short, pantheism fails to explain the problem of evil and suffering, instead arguing that all is relative and, consequently, claiming that there really is no good or evil. Pantheism also fails to explain human personality. If, as pantheism claims, all is an impersonal, divine force, then why do we clearly notice the existence of human personalities?

7. We are unenlightened (Premise)

Since we are unenlightened to the reality that evil is an illusion, we misperceive reality and think that evil and suffering are real. If, however, we can become enlightened, then we will see that all reality is one (monism, point 3), that all is divine (pantheism, point 5), and that, therefore, evil is really an illusion.

8. Problem of change. Evil is real (Objection)

Absolute forms of monistic pantheism claim that once a person reaches spiritual enlightenment, he will realize that he, too, is divine and part of the impersonal force, the one reality. "But God is the changeless Absolute," as Norman Geisler states, adding that "humanity goes through a process of change called enlightenment because he [a person] has this awareness. So how could people be God when people change but God does not?"[3]

A greater problem for monistic pantheism as a whole is the fact that evil is real (chapter 14, chapter 19). See, for instance, points 13 and 14.

---

3. Geisler, "Pantheism," *Baker Encyclopedia of Christian Apologetics*, 581.

9. Enlightenment helps us see truth. Change is an illusion (Rebuttal)	But the enlightened will understand that evil is an illusion. Once we grasp this truth we will know that change, too, is an illusion.
10. Intuitive, subjective experience (Premise)	Our innate, intuitive, and subjective inner experience informs us that evil is an illusion. If we would just attune ourselves to this subjective understanding, we would know that evil is an illusion. If we place an unhealthy emphasis on reason, thinking through matters carefully and analyzing everything logically, we will stifle our intuitive experience and feelings which already know that evil is an illusion.
11. These "proofs" can all be wrong. Conflicting evidence (Objection)	These "proofs," being subjective, can all be wrong. Moreover, what of conflicting evidence that is derived from subjective experience? There are far better ways to determine truth, such as reasoning abductively to the best explanation of reality. If two subjective experiences contradict one another, then how are we to decide which view is true, if any? We must acknowledge the inherent laws of logic, including the law of noncontradiction. Moreover, if monistic pantheists wish to adhere to intuitive, subjective experience in their defense, they still must use logical reasoning to state their position and why it differs or disagrees with alternative explanations. In short, there is no escaping logic, even for those who would claim that subjective experience trumps all.
12. Western logic can't help us (Rebuttal)	But such thinking is a Western invention and can't help us truly comprehend reality. We must instead get in touch with our feelings and seek enlightenment to know truth.
13–17	This next cluster of objections argues overall against the claim that evil is an illusion.
13. We experience the reality of evil (Objection)	If evil is an illusion, then why did we ever get the idea that evil was not an illusion, but reality? Why has the history of humanity shown that, for the most part, worldviews all acknowledge some form of evil and suffering as real and ever present? Moreover, everyone experiences at some level the existential reality of evil and suffering. To insist that such experiences are not real but only illusory is to deny all the prima facie evidence we have in relation to the human experience of evil and suffering.

14. Morality informs us there is good and evil (Objection)	See chapter 8. In brief, the existence of objective moral values tells us that some things are good and some things are evil and that a transcendent source informs us of such moral laws.
15. If evil is an illusion, then moral chaos rules (Objection)	If evil is an illusion, then all morality reduces to relativism and there is no reason to call anything good or evil. We can neither condemn any "evil" actions, such as pedophilia, nor praise seemingly "good" or altruistic actions. If all is one, all is divine, and evil is an illusion, then nothing matters, morally speaking.
16. If evil is an illusion, where did the illusion come from? (Objection)	What is the source of the massive influence on humanity that has caused it to lose sight of the apparent fact that evil is an illusion? In other words, on what basis can monistic pantheism explain the origin of the human condition wherein most people at most times in history have acknowledged the reality of evil and suffering despite the proposition that evil is an illusion?
17. Those who claim evil is an illusion do not live as though evil is an illusion (Objection)	Many of those who claim that evil is an illusion do not always live as though that were the case. In short, the view that evil is merely illusory is an unlivable worldview. At heart, we know that something is wrong with reality as it is, and not only so, but also that something is wrong with us individually. Claiming that evil is an illusion does not solve the human predicament or condition; it only compounds our confusion and by denying what we know is true: that evil and suffering do indeed exist.

DISCUSSION QUESTIONS

1. What arguments would you offer against the conclusion that evil is an illusion?
2. Why do adherents of this view of evil believe evil is an illusion?
3. If evil is an illusion, then how are we supposed to deal with the seeming reality of evil and suffering?
4. What does the view that evil is an illusion do to issues regarding morality? If evil is an illusion, is there such a thing as right and wrong, good or evil?

SUGGESTED ASSIGNMENTS

1. Research and write a paper on Eastern views of evil as an illusion and how those views suggest overcoming our misperceptions of reality.
2. Research and write a paper on views of evil as an illusion as they appear in popularized Western spiritual teachings such as the New Age or nineteenth-century metaphysical religions such as Christian Science.

CHAPTER 24

Christian Hypocrisy Shows That Christianity Is False

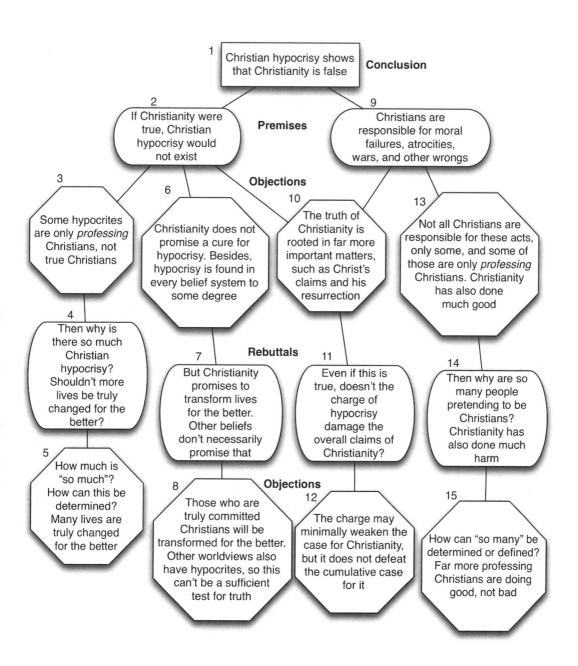

1 Christian hypocrisy shows that Christianity is false — **Conclusion**

Premises

2 If Christianity were true, Christian hypocrisy would not exist

9 Christians are responsible for moral failures, atrocities, wars, and other wrongs

Objections

3 Some hypocrites are only *professing* Christians, not true Christians

6 Christianity does not promise a cure for hypocrisy. Besides, hypocrisy is found in every belief system to some degree

10 The truth of Christianity is rooted in far more important matters, such as Christ's claims and his resurrection

13 Not all Christians are responsible for these acts, only some, and some of those are only *professing* Christians. Christianity has also done much good

4 Then why is there so much Christian hypocrisy? Shouldn't more lives be truly changed for the better?

Rebuttals

7 But Christianity promises to transform lives for the better. Other beliefs don't necessarily promise that

11 Even if this is true, doesn't the charge of hypocrisy damage the overall claims of Christianity?

14 Then why are so many people pretending to be Christians? Christianity has also done much harm

5 How much is "so much"? How can this be determined? Many lives are truly changed for the better

Objections

8 Those who are truly committed Christians will be transformed for the better. Other worldviews also have hypocrites, so this can't be a sufficient test for truth

12 The charge may minimally weaken the case for Christianity, but it does not defeat the cumulative case for it

15 How can "so many" be determined or defined? Far more professing Christians are doing good, not bad

1. Christian hypocrisy shows that Christianity is false (Conclusion)

Given the extent of hypocrisy demonstrated by professing Christians, why should anyone believe the claims of Christianity? Doesn't religious hypocrisy invalidate Christian claims? This conclusion observes the behavior of professing Christians, both in reference to individuals and to the church as a whole, and concludes that hypocritical examples within the church are enough to show that Christianity is false. After all, if Christianity were true, then lives would really be changed for the better, not for the worse.

2. If Christianity were true, Christian hypocrisy would not exist (Premise)

Given the claims of Christianity, such as the power to transform lives morally for the better, then if Christianity were true, Christian hypocrisy would not exist. Since Christian hypocrisy does exist, both within individual Christians and within the church as a whole, we can conclude that Christianity is false, or at least probably not true.

3. Some hypocrites are only *professing* Christians, not true Christians (Objection)

The Christian may object by pointing out the fact that some of the examples of observable hypocrisy on behalf of Christians are only perpetrated by *professing* Christians, not true Christians. In other words, not everyone who claims to be a Christian really is a Christian. Consequently, some examples of Christian hypocrisy are not perpetrated by Christians at all, but by non-Christians claiming to be Christians. We must acknowledge that some Christians do behave hypocritically, but not all of them.

4. Then why is there so much Christian hypocrisy? Shouldn't more lives be truly changed for the better? (Rebuttal)

But it appears to be the case that there is much Christian hypocrisy evidenced throughout history. If Christianity were true, shouldn't more lives be truly changed for the better? After all, Christianity claims to be a benefit to the world (chapter 9), but it seems that hypocrisy often leads Christians to cause harm (chapter 20). If more lives were truly transformed by Christ, then wouldn't we see more people like Mother Teresa changing the world? Instead, we see far more hypocrisy from the church.

5. How much is "so much"? How can this be determined? Many lives are truly changed for the better (Objection)

How can the critic objectively measure hypocrisy levels within the church? Such a task seems impossible. Of course, it's possible to point out specific examples, but given the extent of people claiming to be Christian (more than two billion), don't these instances of public hypocrisy in reality only represent a very small percentage of the overall Christian church? Even when considering smaller, nonpublic examples of alleged Christian hypocrisy, aren't these, by comparison to all professing Christians, relatively small instances or parts of the whole? Even granting more hypocrisy than is probably warranted by the claims of the critic, many lives are truly changed for the better, as Christians live and do their best to imitate the love of Christ and have a positive influence on the world. Couldn't we say that the many Christian acts of sincere love and compassion show that Christianity is true, or that such acts at least support its case?

6. Christianity does not promise a cure for hypocrisy. Besides, hypocrisy is found in every belief system to some degree (Objection)

Christianity does not promise a complete earthly cure for human hypocrisy. It does promise that those truly regenerated by Christ will show evidences of improvement in their character, but this does not mean they will never have lapses. Also, we must remember that not all professing Christians really are Christians and hence are not truly regenerated (point 3).

7. But Christianity promises to transform lives for the better. Other beliefs don't necessarily promise that (Rebuttal)

Christianity makes the unique claim that the power of Christ and the Holy Spirit will transform lives for the better, helping Christians live better lives. Other worldviews don't always make such promises, so hypocrisy can be expected from them at times.

8. Those who are truly committed Christians will be transformed for the better. Other worldviews also have hypocrites, so this can't be a sufficient test for truth (Objection)

Real Christians who rely on Christ truly are transformed for the better. Even if such people have hypocritical lapses, this can be attributed to human sin, explainable within the Christian worldview. Moreover, hypocrisy is found in every belief system to some degree. If atheist hypocrites and pantheist hypocrites exist, does this automatically mean that those worldviews are also false?

There must be more criteria to go on when evaluating worldviews than the question of hypocrisy. This is not to minimize hypocrisy; it does not help the cause of Christianity. Nevertheless, hypocrisy in itself is an insufficient test for the truth or falsity of any worldview.

9. Christians are responsible for moral failures, atrocities, wars, and other wrongs (Premise)

The Christian church as a whole is historically responsible for much more than mere personal "lapses" in behavior. Hypocrisy on a larger level has loomed throughout the history of the church, resulting in Christianity doing more harm than good (chapter 20). Much of this harm is the direct result of hypocritical behavior on the part of Christians.

10. The truth of Christianity is rooted in far more important matters, such as Christ's claims and his resurrection (Objection)

This is not to dismiss the criticism that some Christians are hypocrites, but to point out that whether or not Christianity is true is rooted in far more important matters, such as in Christ's claims (chapter 5) and in his resurrection (chapter 10).

Christ spoke out against hypocrisy (Matt. 23) and exhibited no signs of it himself, remaining true to his claims and moral ideals. While some of his followers may be hypocrites, not all of them are, and isolated hypocritical behavior does not negate the evidence for Christ's resurrection.

11. Even if this is true, doesn't the charge of hypocrisy damage the overall claims of Christianity? (Rebuttal)

Still, even if the truth claims of Christianity are rooted in more important issues, doesn't the charge of hypocrisy damage the overall claims of Christianity? After all, truly transformed lives would not behave hypocritically, causing more harm than good.

12. The charge may minimally weaken the case for Christianity, but it does not defeat the cumulative case for it (Objection)

True, hypocrisy on the part of Christians does nothing to enhance its case, but it does not defeat the cumulative case for Christianity. That case does not depend solely on whether or not some Christians or professing Christians behave hypocritically, since abundant positive evidence points to Christianity as the best explanation of reality (chapter 5). We should therefore not single out one criticism and give it such weight that it negates the far more compelling overall case for Christianity.

13. Not all Christians are responsible for these acts, only some, and some of those are only *professing* Christians. Christianity has also done much good (Objection)

As we noted in point 3, some Christian hypocrites are only professing Christians and may not represent Christianity accurately. Historically, it is true that some Christians have behaved hypocritically, but we must also note that Christianity has also done much good (chapter 9).

14. Then why are so many people pretending to be Christians? Christianity has also done much harm (Rebuttal)	The harm Christianity has done is also well documented (chapter 20). If Christianity were true, such instances of hypocritical harm on the part of Christians would not be so rampant throughout history.
15. How can "so many" be determined or defined? Far more professing Christians are doing good, not bad (Objection)	Again we have the problem of being unable to quantify the claims of the critic (point 5). We also return to the matter of hypocrisy being an insufficient test of the truth or falsity of any worldview. It may contribute to a negative case for such a worldview, but hypocrisy cannot be viewed in isolation. It must be considered along with other evidence in favor of the worldview in question.

DISCUSSION QUESTIONS

1. How does the charge that Christians are hypocrites argue against the truth of the Christian worldview?
2. Share how you would respond to the claim that Christians are responsible for moral failures, atrocities, wars, and other wrongs.
3. Is it possible for genuine examples of Christian hypocrisy to actually argue in favor of the Christian worldview? How so?
4. Does the fact that hypocrisy is also found in other belief systems absolve Christians of having to answer charges of hypocrisy? Does it help the Christian case at all?

SUGGESTED ASSIGNMENTS

1. Research criticisms of Christianity in relation to hypocrisy and prepare a list of the key points made against Christian theism on the basis of hypocrisy. Respond to the points.
2. Christ had much to say about hypocrisy (see, for instance, Matt. 23). Write a paper evaluating Christ's comments on hypocrisy and apply your findings to the question of Christian hypocrisy.

CHAPTER 25

Religious Experience Is Subjective and Cannot Be Tested

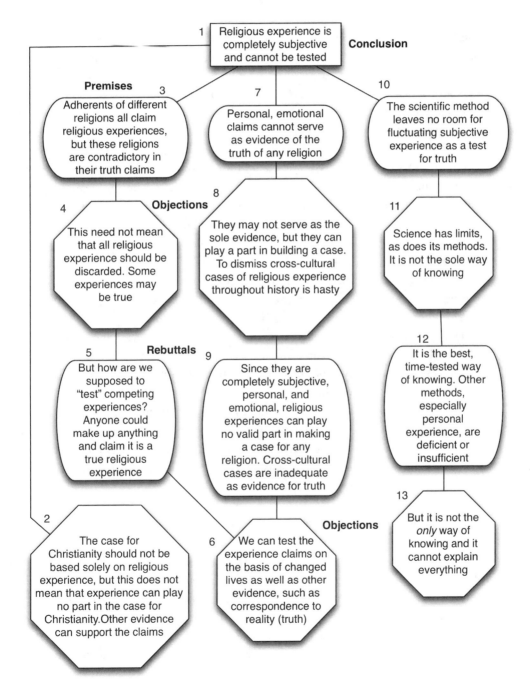

1 Religious experience is completely subjective and cannot be tested — **Conclusion**

Premises

3 Adherents of different religions all claim religious experiences, but these religions are contradictory in their truth claims

7 Personal, emotional claims cannot serve as evidence of the truth of any religion

10 The scientific method leaves no room for fluctuating subjective experience as a test for truth

Objections

4 This need not mean that all religious experience should be discarded. Some experiences may be true

8 They may not serve as the sole evidence, but they can play a part in building a case. To dismiss cross-cultural cases of religious experience throughout history is hasty

11 Science has limits, as does its methods. It is not the sole way of knowing

12 It is the best, time-tested way of knowing. Other methods, especially personal experience, are deficient or insufficient

Rebuttals

5 But how are we supposed to "test" competing experiences? Anyone could make up anything and claim it is a true religious experience

9 Since they are completely subjective, personal, and emotional, religious experiences can play no valid part in making a case for any religion. Cross-cultural cases are inadequate as evidence for truth

13 But it is not the *only* way of knowing and it cannot explain everything

2 The case for Christianity should not be based solely on religious experience, but this does not mean that experience can play no part in the case for Christianity. Other evidence can support the claims

Objections

6 We can test the experience claims on the basis of changed lives as well as other evidence, such as correspondence to reality (truth)

1. Religious experience is completely subjective and cannot be tested (Conclusion)

The essential criticism of religious experience as an aspect of making the case of religious beliefs such as theism is that experience is completely subjective. It therefore cannot be tested (or, in more technical terms, religious experience arguments lack veridicality). If religious experiences have no correspondence with reality, or at least no way to test such correspondence, then they can play no intellectual or effective part in making the case for any religious worldview.

2. The case for Christianity should not be based solely on religious experience, but this does not mean that experience can play no part in the case for Christianity. Other evidence can support the claims (Objection)

This major objection to the conclusion makes two important observations. First, the entire case for Christianity should not be based solely on religious experience. Second, recognizing the limits of religious experience in making a case for Christianity does not mean that experience should play no part at all.

In taking an integrated, cumulative case approach, it is more than feasible to bring in various arguments to support our position. Religious experience can certainly play a role in building our case. Christians should by no means shy away from communicating the power of their personal religious experience in strengthening their life and faith.

3. Adherents of different religions all claim religious experiences, but these religions are contradictory in their truth claims (Premise)

In support of point 1, it may be argued that since adherents of different religions claim religious experiences, but these experiences are contradictory, then logically, religious experiences prove nothing when it comes to verifying truth claims. They essentially cancel each other out, since anyone from any religion can claim a religious experience that in effect contradicts that of another religion. One person may claim that she experienced the personal, transcendent God of Christianity, but another may claim that he reached enlightenment and became one with the impersonal force of reality. Since both claims can't be true, we see that religious experience arguments offer little intellectual assistance in determining whether a worldview is true.

4. This need not mean that all religious experience should be discarded. Some experiences may be true (Objection)

While religious experience poses some problems, it does not necessarily follow that all religious experience should be discarded. After all, some experiences may be true. Is the critic being too hasty in dismissing all religious experience claims as invalid or irrelevant when it comes to making a case for a religious worldview? Moreover, some thinkers have made a strong case for believing in religious experience claims; they argue for accepting such testimonies on the basis of what is called the principle of credulity. This involves giving the person claiming a religious experience the benefit of the doubt, allowing her testimony to stand, so to speak, as innocent until proven guilty. To do otherwise is to immediately impugn the motives and character of the person making the claim of a religious experience.

Furthermore, some people who claim religious experiences "are intelligent, self-examining, rational people not prone to emotionalism."[1] In such cases, their claims appear to have some intellectual weight behind them, since such individuals are not generally known for making such claims without foundation.

Yet we must be careful not to accept any and all religious claims. Some are clearly outlandish and unsubstantiated, while others claim experiences that, upon investigation, break down in relation to the robustness of the associated worldview. For example, a monistic pantheist claims an experience with an impersonal force, thus seeking to substantiate the overall worldview behind the experience; but it can be demonstrated that the monistic pantheism worldview as a whole is severely flawed (chapter 21). Therefore, there must be another and better explanation for the claimed religious experience of the adherent (e.g., perhaps spiritual deception, self-delusion, or a misunderstanding of the experience).

5. But how are we supposed to "test" competing experiences? Anyone could make up anything and claim it is a true religious experience (Rebuttal)

Even granting the objections in point 4 to a point, this still does not mean that we should accept religious experience claims. After all, there appears to be no way to test such competing experiences. Anyone could make up anything and claim it was a true religious experience.

Besides, there is no way to repeat and test such experiences. Since by their very nature they are unique experiences, they cannot be reproduced in a clinical setting. They therefore must be dismissed as invalid evidence.

6. We can test the experience claims on the basis of changed lives as well as other evidence, such as correspondence to reality (truth) (Objection)

Those who make the objections typified in point 5 usually presuppose the atheistic worldview and thereby exclude the possibility of religious experience simply because they presuppose that naturalism is true and supernaturalism is false. But suppose naturalism is false and theism is true. If so, does it not allow the very real possibility of a theistic being revealing himself at times via religious experiences?

Moreover, various thinkers have suggested methods for

---

1. Moreland, *Scaling the Secular City*, 238.

testing religious experience claims. As Douglas Groothuis explains, "First, there is a long tradition of religious experience within Christianity, starting with the religious experiences recorded in the Bible itself. We may test our experience or the claims of others against that basic tradition, realizing that there are variations within it. Second, for any religious experience we may ask if there might have been factors present that render the experience unbelievable."[2]

J. P. Moreland, citing Evans's *Philosophy of Religion*, offers seven tests for evaluating "true from false perceptions of God."[3]

> First, if the experience is about an internally contradictory object (such as a Being who is both personal and impersonal) or if the experience is somehow self-refuting . . . then the object does not exist. . . .
>
> Second, do the experiences show similarities with those of mystics who are considered to be exemplars of numinous apprehension? . . .
>
> Third, if an experience of God is veridical, one would expect certain other experiences to usually follow. . . .
>
> Fourth, the consequences of such experiences should be good for the mystic in the long run (such as edifying his outlook on life, unifying to his personality, empowering to his devotion to God an others).
>
> Fifth, the consequences of such experiences should be good for others. . . .
>
> Sixth, the depth, profundity, the "sweetness" of the experience counts as evidence for its genuineness. . . .[4]
>
> Seventh, does the experience conform to an objective body of revelation, Holy Scripture, which can in turn be validated by means other than numinous claims . . . to keep from arguing in a circle?

In short, it is false to claim that there are no ways to test religious experience claims.

---

2. Groothuis, *Christian Apologetics*, 378.
3. Moreland, *Scaling the Secular City*, 239–40.
4. Ibid.

7. Personal, emotional claims cannot serve as evidence of the truth of any religion (Premise)

This premise relegates all religious experience to the realm of complete subjectivity and emotionality, thus claiming that such experiences cannot serve as evidence of the truth of any religion. The assumption is that rational, scientific "proof" is superior to all other means of knowledge (assuming other means even exist) and that religious experience claims are simply the fancies of overly emotional adherents who feel far more than they think.

8. They may not serve as the sole evidence, but they can play a part in building a case. To dismiss cross-cultural cases of religious experience throughout history is hasty (Objection)

Again we return to the apologetic approach that seeks to build an integrated case for Christian theism, allowing various lines of evidence and argumentation to work together to demonstrate that Christianity is the best explanation of reality (chapter 5). In such an approach, religious experience is not isolated but is part of a broader case for truth. If it can be demonstrated that a theistic God exists (chapter 6), then it follows that such a God can choose to reveal himself in various means, which may include religious experience.

In addition, dismissing cross-cultural and historical cases of religious experience throughout history is far too hasty. Doesn't the fact that religious experience claims exist throughout history as well as today offer some degree of evidence in favor of the religious worldview as a whole over the nonreligious worldview? One might add that belief in God via religious experience may even be properly basic—that is, these experiences "are part of the foundation of a person's system of beliefs."[5]

If a number of people throughout history have claimed Christian religious experiences and demonstrated their firm belief in such experiences by their transformed lives, and if the Christian worldview as a whole is robust enough to withstand other criticisms and make a positive case for itself, then it is hasty to dismiss so many claims of religious experience as mere delusions (chapter 18) or inadmissible as evidence in favor of God. Even non-Christian religious truth claims can contribute to the case for the view that religiously oriented worldviews as a whole are more reasonable than nonreligious worldviews.

---

5. Craig and Sinnott-Armstrong, *God?*, 26.

9. Since they are completely subjective, personal, and emotional, religious experiences can play no valid part in making a case for any religion. Cross-cultural cases are inadequate as evidence for truth (Rebuttal)

This response is expected from the naturalistic worldview, which values the empirical scientific method, including repeated testing, over any alternatives such as subjective experiences. Cross-cultural and historical cases of religious experience may be of interest to anthropologists, psychologists, or even sociologists, but such occurrences are merely religious artifacts of some interest in certain fields. They can play no real role in helping us understand reality.

The rebuttal to point 9 directs the reader to point 6 (see above). We may also add that once again there is an overreliance on the extent of what science can accomplish. (See chapter 17 for some responses and insights on the limits of science as well as thinking in points 10 through 13.)

10. The scientific method leaves no room for fluctuating subjective experience as a test for truth (Premise)

Because religious experiences cannot be tested scientifically, there is no room for such fluctuating subjective experiences as a test for truth.

Besides, such experiences may be explained by human brain chemistry, neurology, psychology, and other scientifically grounded explanations that don't require a supernatural being as their source.

11. Science has limits, as does its methods. It is not the sole way of knowing (Objection)

The limitations of science must be underscored in relation to metaphysical or philosophical matters. In short, the scientific method is not the sole or always superior method of knowing reality. Moreover, since the contemporary application of the scientific method presupposes naturalism, it is hardly fair in its assessment of religious experiences which, by their very nature, are beyond the testing methods of traditional science. This fact, however, does not mean that religious experiences cannot be tested, as noted in point 4.

12. It is the best, time-tested way of knowing. Other methods, especially personal experience, are deficient or insufficient (Rebuttal)

This approach does not acknowledge other means of knowing, instead favoring scientific approaches as far superior if not exclusively the means of true knowledge.

13. But it is not the *only* way of knowing and it cannot explain everything (Objection)

Again, science has limitations, especially when it comes to philosophical matters. If a reasonable case can be made for God being the best explanation of reality (chapter 6), then it follows that God can choose to reveal himself via religious experiences.

DISCUSSION QUESTIONS

1. Consider your personal religious experience as a Christian. How do you see it fitting into a larger case for the Christian worldview?
2. Why is the scientific method insufficient when it comes to testing metaphysical truth claims?
3. How can religious experience serve as part of a cumulative case for the truth of Christianity?
4. "Other people also claim religious experiences which contradict Christianity; therefore, religious experience is of no value in assessing truth." How would you respond to this statement?

SUGGESTED ASSIGNMENTS

1. Read chapter 16 of *Christian Apologetics* by Douglas Groothuis and write a paper assessing the arguments in support of religious experience as well as evaluating objections to the value of religious experience.
2. Read the case for and against religious experience in the book *God? A Debate Between a Christian and an Atheist* by William Lane Craig and Walter Sinnott-Armstrong, and write a paper assessing the pros and cons of religious experience as part of the case for Christianity.

Conclusion

Life is more than arguments and diagrams. It is one thing to review and consider reasons for and against Christianity within the controlled context of a book; it is quite another to successfully and practically apply ideas in daily life. Readers should therefore not see the argument maps in the previous pages as conclusive or definitive examples of how arguments will precisely flow in the course of a conversation. Instead, consider the diagrams as templates offering examples of the kind of back-and-forth dialogue that often occurs when two opposing viewpoints are discussed intelligently. The reader can then apply these insights to real-life situations.

Arguments can go on for quite a while—certainly much longer than can fit on a page. The purpose of the diagrams is not to exhaustively explore every possible aspect of an argument. Rather, the diagrams are meant to help us think critically, understand opposing viewpoints, and make the case for our position in a way that is sensible. Commitment to any worldview of substance is not a frivolous endeavor, especially when the worldview in question encompasses high-stakes beliefs. Therefore, it is to our benefit to think critically about the claims of viable worldview options, learning to accurately assess the points made on their behalf as well as opposing arguments.

Further, we must seek to understand other perspectives and not simply conclude they are flawed or false on the basis of our own limited understanding, brief exposure to their beliefs, or hearsay. Understanding often involves the ability to listen combined with a degree of humility in desiring to truly comprehend opposing viewpoints.

Our purpose also involves demonstrations of how to make our case sensibly in dealing with ideas that often conflict diametrically with our own understanding of reality. All too often, contemporary disagreements quickly fall into heated linguistic fistfights involving bluster, name-calling, and rhetorical posturing rather than calm, precise, and well-reasoned presentation and assessment. This is not to say that we must leave all emotion out of worldview analysis; that is untenable, given human nature. Nevertheless, we should strive to think clearly and set forth our case in a reasonable manner that invites discussion.

The arguments set forth in the previous pages are heady matters, requiring concentrated thought and effort. Some of the points made may have made us uncomfortable, perhaps causing us to doubt our own perspective. As a Christian theist, my intention in these pages has not been to tear down the faith, leaving adherents in disarray and confusion. Yet neither has my purpose been to avoid tough challenges to the faith. Those with doubts about the faith may consult the many additional resources listed in the annotated bibliography. These will offer robust intellectual evidences for faith and will also benefit non-Christians who have doubts about their worldview.

Finally, it is my evidence-supported conviction that Christianity is "true and reasonable" (Acts 26:25 NIV), offering the best explanation of reality and able to withstand the serious criticisms leveled against it. God exists, objective moral values are rooted in his nature, real truth can be grasped, and Christ is indeed "the way and the truth and the life" (John 14:6 NIV). Arguments and worldviews opposed to Christianity fall short not only in their assessment of the faith, but also in their own ability to adequately explain reality and respond to challenges.

Life is more than arguments and diagrams, but this does not mean such tools are of little value in the quest for truth about reality. Indeed, they can serve as beneficial tools in the search for ultimate meaning about ourselves and the world around us. We all long for explanations regarding our existence and purpose. Transcendent meaning is either real or it is not. If it is not real, then we had better come to grips with this harsh truth despite the consequences. But if transcendent meaning is real—if a loving God exists and if Christ is truly the way—then we had better take it seriously, doing our best to discern truth from error, and come to grips with the God of the universe, who is "not far from each one of us" (Acts 17:27 NASB).

Glossary

abductive reasoning. Reasoning to the best explanation; often used in scientific endeavors. Some classify it as a form of inductive reasoning.

ad hominem. Literally, attacking the man or person. An ad hominem argument is a fallacious form of argumentation that attacks the person rather than the substance of the person's argument, thus often resorting to name-calling rather than reasonable criticism.

Advaita Vedanta. An Eastern form of monistic pantheism popular in various iterations in the West. Monism means that all reality is one, while pantheism holds that everything is divine.

a fortiori. A logical argument form literally meaning "from the stronger." In brief, this kind of argument form states that if A is true, the truth of B is even stronger. Consequently, if one accepts A, then B must also be accepted.

annihilationism. The theistic belief that God will not allow those who reject him to suffer in eternal hell but will instead annihilate (utterly destroy) them.

anthropological argument. As used in this book, the term refers to Blaise Pascal's anthropological argument. Pascal argued that only Christianity can explain the seeming paradox of human greatness (via the *imago Dei*) and human wretchedness (via the Fall of man).

apologetics. The rational defense of Christianity as "true and reasonable" (Acts 26:25 NIV), typically taking positive and negative forms. Positive apologetics makes a positive case for faith, while negative apologetics critiques competing beliefs. See 1 Peter 3:15.

argument from desire. An argument, popularized by C. S. Lewis but with roots in Augustine and Pascal, that argues from desire to the reality of God and heaven. If we have a desire that nothing in this world can satisfy, then this desire must find its fulfillment in another world.

argument map. A logical diagram indicating argument conclusion, supporting premises, rebuttals, and objections. While the professional study of logic employs certain techniques in diagramming arguments, the diagrams in this book are modified to be more popularly accessible.

assumptions. Presuppositions, often unstated, that are presumed by someone making an argument.

atheism. The denial of the existence of any supernatural being or beings (i.e., the denial of the existence of God).

atonement. In Christian theology atonement refers to what Christ's death and resurrection accomplished in relation to human salvation. There are multiple theories of the atonement including the ransom view, penal substitution, moral example theory, necessary satisfaction view, and others.

best way defense. Rooted in Augustinianism, the best way defense is a theodicy in response to the problem of evil. It claims that although this world is not the best possible world, it is the best way to the best possible world. Ultimately, evil will be decisively overcome.

circular reasoning. Arguing in a circle—trying to prove a point by making the point. Also called a *tautology*.

classical apologetics. A form of apologetics that first seeks to make a case for the existence of God, then demonstrate that Christianity is true. Classical apologetics emphasizes logic (right reasoning) but is not to be equated with rationalism as a philosophical movement.

coherence view of truth. A theory of truth that sees truth as a web of coherence. A proposition is considered true so long as it is consistent with other propositions within this web of coherence. However, even if a web of coherence is consistent within itself it may still contradict known truths beyond its own web of coherence.

conclusion. The final point an argument is attempting to make.

correspondence view of truth. See **truth, correspondence view of**.

cosmological arguments. A traditional family of arguments for the existence of God based on the existence and origins of the universe. An example is the *kalam cosmological argument*. Some theistic proponents of cosmological arguments believe that modern scientific evidence such as the Big Bang theory lend credence to cosmological arguments. The broad point is that given a universe, its cause must be reasonably explained. And all things considered, God is the best explanation of the cause of the cosmos.

critical thinking. Logical thinking that seeks to understand and evaluate any given intellectual argument, proposition, or position.

cumulative case apologetics. An apologetic methodology that seeks to build a cumulative case in support of Christianity by drawing from various sources such as logic, historical evidence, and so forth. Taken together, the various arguments support the truth of the Christian worldview.

deductive reasoning. Reasoning that draws inferences from the general to the particular, drawing conclusions before it evaluates experience. Deductive arguments result in absolute conclusions provided all the parts of the argument are true.

deism. The belief that God exists and created the universe but is not interested in his creation or the creatures that inhabit it. Consequently, deists deny the possibility of miracles.

doctrine, essential Christian. Refers to the core Christian beliefs that the church has held to throughout its history including the deity of Christ, the bodily resurrection, the Trinity, and so on.

empiricism. A view of knowledge that values sensory experience over reason in determining truth.

epistemology. The branch of philosophy concerned with what knowledge is, how it can be acquired, and how it can be justified.

ethics. The branch of philosophy concerned with moral right and wrong.

evidential apologetics. A form of Christian apologetics that emphasizes a congruence of various evidences in support of Christianity. Typical evidences include arguments from the reliability of the New Testament documents, archaeological support for the Bible, and arguments in support of the reality of the bodily resurrection of Christ. Some classical apologists may employ evidential techniques (and vice versa).

evil, problem of. Considered a problem for theists because of the seeming difficulty in reconciling the reality of a good, all-powerful God with the reality of evil and suffering. The problem of evil is also a problem for those who hold other worldviews, such as atheism and pantheism, since they, too, must explain evil and suffering.

fallacy. A logical error in reasoning or in an argument.

fideism. The philosophical position that religious belief is based solely on faith apart from reason.

free will defense. A theodicy in response to the problem of evil. It posits that God granted human beings free will, and the possibility of humans choosing to do evil was justifiable because of the greater good of human freedom.

genetic fallacy. Rejecting a conclusion on the basis of its origins or source rather than evaluating it on its own merits. However, the origin of an idea is not relevant regarding whether or not it is true.

image of God. Also, *imago Dei.* The image of God (Gen. 1:26–27) within Christian theology argues that human beings are not replicas of God, but since they are made in his image they possess unique qualities such as creativity, intellect, and moral will.

inductive reasoning. Reasoning from the particular to the general, making inferences on the basis of examining the evidence. Induction yields probable conclusions, not absolute ones.

kalam argument. A form of the cosmological argument for God's existence first developed by Muslim apologists and more recently deftly articulated and defended by Christian apologist William Lane Craig. In short, the kalam argument claims that if the universe had a beginning, then the best explanation of the cause is God.

law of noncontradiction. A foundational principle of logic often stated as A is not non-A, meaning that contradictory truths cannot both be true in the same way at the same time.

metanarrative. A broad "story" or worldview that seeks to explain reality. Often used by postmodernists, who deny the validity of any one metanarrative, in reference to worldviews that seek to provide an overarching understanding and explanation of all of reality, such as Christian theism.

moral arguments. A family of traditional arguments for God. They claim that human moral standards support belief in the existence of a moral lawgiver (i.e., God).

naturalism. The belief that only the material world exists, thus ruling out anything supernatural. Also known as philosophical naturalism or philosophical materialism.

natural theology. Belief that successful arguments for the existence of God may be found in nature via such ways as design or moral arguments. Some Christian theists reject or minimize the value of natural theology on the basis of human depravity and inability to discern God via natural theology arguments.

New Age spirituality. Popular Westernized forms of Eastern religious beliefs such as monistic pantheism and reincarnation.

nihilism. The belief that the universe as a whole, and human life in particular, is without meaning or purpose in the broad scheme of reality. True nihilism ends in despair.

objection. An opposing point of view expressing disagreement with one or more points of a logical argument or position.

OMVs. Objective moral values. Moral values that are viewed as objective rather than relative or subjective.

ontological arguments. Arguments from being for the existence of God, typically following Anselm's versions or modern variations such as Alvin Plantinga's defense of the ontological argument. The standard Anselmian version is usually presented as reasoning to the existence of God on the basis of his status as the greatest conceivable being.

ontology. In philosophy, ontology, which is related to metaphysics, has to do with the nature of being, such as what constitutes human existence, meaning, and essence. See **ontological arguments**.

panentheism. Similar but distinct from pantheism, panentheism joins God with his creation such that the universe is in a sense God's body.

pantheism. Although there are many forms of pantheism, the standard definition is that pantheism believes that all is divine. Everything has a divine, typically impersonal, force flowing through it; thus, there are no distinctions between the divine and creation since all is divine. Advaita Vedanta (monistic pantheism) is the most common popular form of pantheism in the West.

philosophy. The love of wisdom. Philosophy touches on many areas of human existence including ultimate reality (metaphysics), right and wrong (ethics), and knowledge (epistemology).

pluralism, religious. The belief in the ultimate unity of all religions as essentially teaching the same core truths. Thus, religious pluralists believe that all roads lead to God.

polytheism. Belief in more than one deity. Forms of Hinduism and neopaganism, for instance, are polytheistic.

postmodernism. A cluster of philosophical ideologies with no official list of beliefs. Some postmodernists deny objective truth and any overarching metanarrative or explanation of reality. See **truth, postmodern view of.**

pragmatic view of truth. A theory of truth that is concerened with the pragmatism of claims and whether or not they result in positive effects. If something "works," that is sufficient for the pragmatic view of truth to see a claim as true. However, what "works" may not necessarily correspond with what is true.

premise. Supporting evidence for a logical conclusion in an argument.

presuppositional apologetics. A form of apologetics that believes essential Christian truths must be presupposed in order for anyone to truly understand reality.

rationalism. The belief that reason alone is the means of accurately understanding reality. Note that classical apologists may incorporate reasoning without being strict rationalists.

realism. An approach to understanding reality that views it as external, existing beyond just the mind.

reductio ad absurdum. Literally, to reduce an argument to absurdity, thus demonstrating that the argument in question is flawed.

Reformed epistemology. A form of apologetic methodology that considers belief in God to be *properly basic*, meaning that no arguments are needed to justify a belief in God. Key proponents include Alvin Plantinga, William Alston, and Nicholas Wolterstorff.

relativism. The belief that there are no absolutes. Moral relativism, for instance, believes that moral standards are relative not absolute, defined for instance by culture, individuals (subjectivism), and so forth.

resurrection. As applied to the Christian doctrine of the resurrection of Christ, it refers to Christ's physical, bodily resurrection from the dead as recorded in the New Testament. As the cornerstone doctrine of Christianity (1 Cor. 15), it stands in opposition to denials of the bodily resurrection, liberal spiritualizations of it, and other distortions of the doctrine.

secular humanism. An optimistic form of naturalism that sees hope for humanity despite secular humanism's denial of the supernatural.

soul-making theodicy. A response to the problem of evil that explains evil as necessary to help develop human character.

teleological arguments. A family of traditional arguments for God based on design in nature. If we can detect design, then there must be a designer (i.e., God).

theism. The belief in a personal God transcendent from his creation but active in it via providence, miracles, and other ways.

theodicy. Literally, "God's justice." A theodicy attempts to justify the ways of God toward man in relation to the problem of evil and suffering.

Trinity. Distinct Christian belief that although there is only one God, he has revealed himself as three distinct persons who are one in nature and essence, coequal and coeternal. Trinitarianism is, as such, not polytheism, tritheism (three gods), or modalism (one God changing masks so to speak). Neither does Christian theology view the Trinity as a logical contradiction, though it is in many respects a mystery.

truth. That which corresponds to reality.

truth, coherence view of. The view that truth is what coheres with or is consistent with other beliefs. However, coherent views of truth may cohere within themselves but still be false.

truth, correspondence view of. Argues that truth is what corresponds to reality.

truth, postmodern view of. A denial that one overarching "story," truth, or worldview exists that will explain all reality. Instead, many postmodernists view truth as a matter of perception and perspective rather than as absolute.

truth, pragmatic view of. Views truth as that which results in what "works" or is beneficial.

worldview. The way in which one views and interprets reality.

Annotated Bibliography

Anderson, Paul M., ed. *Professors Who Believe: The Spiritual Journeys of Christian Faculty*. Downers Grove, IL: InterVarsity, 1998. A collection of testimonies from Christian professors.

Beckwith, Francis and Gregory Koukl. *Relativism: Feet Firmly Planted in Mid-Air*. Grand Rapids: Baker, 1998. Are truth and morality relative? Beckwith and Koukl answer with a resounding, "No," as they explore in popular fashion questions regarding moral relativism.

Beckwith, Francis J., William Lane Craig, and J. P. Moreland, eds. *To Everyone an Answer: A Case for the Christian Worldview*. Downers Grove, IL: InterVarsity, 2004. This collection of essays addresses a number of issues related to apologetics including faith and reason, the existence of God, Christ, philosophy, Christianity and culture, pantheism, Islam, and more. Contributors include the well-known editors as well as figures such as Craig Hazen, William Dembski, Paul Copan, Gary Habermas, Ravi Zacharias, and others.

Boa, Kenneth D. and Robert M. Bowman Jr. *Faith Has Its Reasons*. Carlisle, UK: Paternoster, 2005; Downers Grove, IL: InterVasity Press, 2012. This second edition includes numerous refinements and improvements, making it far preferable to the first edition. Boa and Bowman present and assess apologetic methods within four broad categories: classical apologetics, evidential apologetics, Reformed apologetics, and fideist apologetics. Even where I disagree with this work, I find it eminently useful nonetheless.

———. *Twenty Compelling Evidences That God Exists*. Tulsa, OK: River Oak, 2002. Boa and Bowman offer numerous arguments for God's existence ranging from the traditional (cosmological, design) to specific arguments in favor of Christianity such as Christ and his resurrection and the reliability of the Bible.

Budziszewski, J. *Written on the Heart: The Case for Natural Law*. Downers Grove, IL: InterVarsity, 1997. A contemporary Christian defense of natural law which can be integrated into a moral argument for God's existence.

Campbell-Jack, W. C. and Gavin McGrath, eds. *New Dictionary of Christian Apologetics*. Downers Grove, IL: InterVarsity, 2006. A helpful apologetics reference work featuring a number of contributors. A notable omission is a lack of an entry on pantheism, but on the whole this is a useful work.

Carroll, Vincent and David Shiflett. *Christianity on Trial: Arguments Against Anti-Religious Bigotry*. San Francisco, California: Encounter, 2002. Carroll's journalistic writing style shows in this readable defense of Christianity which highlights its roles in Western culture, slavery, science, charity, and other areas.

Carson, D. A. *How Long, O Lord? Reflections on Suffering and Evil*. Grand Rapids: Baker, 1990. Carson methodically explores the problem of evil and suffering in relation to the Christian worldview, avoiding the common free will defense but at times appealing to mystery.

Clark, David K. and Norman L. Geisler. *Apologetics in the New Age: A Christian Critique of Pantheism*. Grand Rapids: Baker, 1990. One of the most thoughtful and accessible Evangelical critiques of pantheism, emphasizing Suzuki, Shankara, Radhakrishnan, Plotinus, and Spinoza. If Christians are able to thoughtfully understand and rebut intellectual forms of pantheism, the popular "New Age" forms should pose little or no problems by comparison.

Clark, Gordon H. *Logic*. Jefferson, MD: Trinity Foundation, 1985. Presuppositionalist Christian thinker Gordon Clark offers an introduction to logic including coverage of topics such as informal logical fallacies, formal logic, and the syllogism.

Clark, Kelly James, ed. *Philosophers Who Believe: The Spiritual Journeys of 11 Leading Thinkers*. Downers Grove, IL: InterVarsity, 1993. A collection of testimonies from notable Christian philosophers including Mortimer Adler, Richard Swinburne, Alvin Plantinga, and more.

Corduan, Winfried. *No Doubt About It: The Case for Christianity*. Nashville: B&H, 1997. Corduan offers a thoughtful-yet-accessible guide to key apologetic issues including faith and reason, truth, epistemology, worldviews, God's existence, the question of miracles, the New Testament, and questions about Jesus. Opening vignettes engage the reader.

Cowan, Steven B., ed. *Five Views on Apologetics*. Grand Rapids: Zondervan, 2000. Five authors defend different approaches to Christian apologetics: the classical method (William Lane Craig), the evidential method (Gary Habermas), the cumulative case method (Paul Feinberg), the Reformed epistemological method (Kelly James Clark), and the presuppositionalist method (John Frame).

Craig, William Lane. *Reasonable Faith: Christian Truth and Apologetics*. Wheaton, IL: Crossway, 2008 (third edition). Craig's masterful defense of the Christian worldview includes material on the existence of God, the meaning of life, historical knowledge, miracles, Jesus, and the resurrection. This is a must-read for the serious apologist. The second edition includes a helpful chapter on the reliability of the New Testament by scholar Craig Blomberg.

Craig, William Lane and Chad Meister, eds. *God Is Great, God Is Good: Why Believing in God Is Reasonable and Responsible*. Downers Grove, IL: InterVarsity, 2009. Essentially a collection of essays by Christian apologists responding to critiques of the New Atheists, this volume includes some notable essays including a response to *The God Delusion* by Richard Dawkins from Christian philosopher Alvin Plantinga.

Craig, William Lane and Walter Sinnot-Armstrong. *God? A Debate Between a Christian and an Atheist*. New York: Oxford, 2004. One of the finest recent books representing an intelligent dialogue between a Christian and an atheist. Craig makes a cumulative case for the truth of Christianity utilizing a form of the cosmological argument, a fine-tuning (design) argument, a moral argument, an argument from Christ, and an appeal to religious experience.

D'Souza, Dinesh. *What's So Great About Christianity?* Carol Stream, IL: Tyndale House, 2008. A highly readable tour of Christianity's benefits to the world, which also includes material responding to contemporary atheism. D'Souza defends theistic evolution and also values Kant's epistemology (this latter point is somewhat perplexing given that Kant's view of knowledge leads to metaphysical skepticism).

Engel, S. Morris. *With Good Reason: An Introduction to Informal Fallacies*, 6th ed. New York: St. Martin's, 1999. An entertaining and informative tour of logic and specifically, a number of informal fallacies such as hasty generalization, bifurcation, begging the question, complex question, false analogy, irrelevant thesis, and so on.

France, R. T. *The Evidence for Jesus*. Downers Grove, IL: InterVarsity, 1986. France explores a variety of evidences for the historicity of the person of Christ including evaluations of non-Christian evidence, Christian evidence beyond the New Testament, the New Testament documents, archaeological evidence, and Jesus in history.

Geisler, Norman L. *Baker Encyclopedia of Christian Apologetics*. Grand Rapids: Baker, 1999. In many ways this work is the culmination of Geisler's lifetime of research and writing on apologetics. A number of helpful entries cover worldviews, apologetic methodology, and much more.

———. *Christian Apologetics*. Grand Rapids: Baker, 1976. Geisler offers a textbook on apologetics, emphasizing worldviews such as deism, pantheism, panentheism, atheism, and Christian theism.

———. *Miracles and the Modern Mind: A Defense of Biblical Miracles*. Grand Rapids: Baker, 1992. Philosopher, theologian, and apologist Norman Geisler explores a number of questions about the biblical miracles, asking whether or not they are impossible, incredible, irrational, unscientific, mythological, historical, actual, and more. Two helpful appendices cover the historicity of miracles in the Old Testament and a comprehensive listing of miracles in the Bible.

———. *The Roots of Evil*. Eugene, OR: Wipf and Stock, 2002. A reissue of the 1978 Zondervan book, *The Roots of Evil* offers a short presentation and response to the problem of evil which relies on aspects of Thomism, the free will defense, and more.

———. *Systematic Theology: In One Volume*. Minneapolis: Bethany House, 2011. A compilation of Geisler's earlier four-volume systematic theology, covering essential Christian doctrine while offering a uniquely philosophical and apologetic approach. The section on the attributes of God is thorough and profound.

Geisler, Norman L., and Ronald M. Brooks. *Come, Let Us Reason: An Introduction to Logical Thinking*. Grand Rapids: Baker, 1990. A unique introduction to logic in that the examples are all based on Christian theology and concepts. Includes discussion of induction, deduction, formal fallacies, informal fallacies, and advice for logically evaluating literature and scientific thought.

————. *When Skeptics Ask*. Wheaton, IL: Scripture Press, 1990. An accessible introduction to defending the faith covering the need for apologetics, the existence of God, competing worldviews such as atheism and pantheism, the problem of evil, miracles, Christ, truth, science and faith, and more.

Geisler, Norman L., and Paul Hoffman, eds. *Why I Am a Christian: Leading Thinkers Explain Why They Believe*, rev. ed. Grand Rapids: Baker, 2006. A number of Christian thinkers present reasons for their faith. Some notable contributors include Francis Beckwith, William Lane Craig, Gary Habermas, Peter Kreeft, J. P. Moreland, and Ravi Zacharias.

Geisler, Norman L., Alex McFarland, and Robert Velarde. *10 Questions and Answers on Atheism and Agnosticism*. Torrance, CA: Rose, 2007. A booklet highlighting a classical apologetics approach in defense of the existence of God including the cosmological argument, moral argument, discussion of science and faith, the problem of evil, the reliability of the Bible, and other topics.

Geisler, Norman L., and Frank Turek. *I Don't Have Enough Faith to Be an Atheist*. Wheaton, IL: Crossway, 2004. A popular-level classical approach to defending the faith which reasons to the truth of Christianity in logical progression. Truth and knowledge are addressed as well as arguments for God's existence, the reliability of the New Testament, the person of Christ, and more.

Geisler, Norman L., and Patrick Zukeran. *The Apologetics of Jesus: A Caring Approach to Dealing with Doubters*. Grand Rapids: Baker, 2009. A helpful overview of how Jesus defended the faith by using reason, appealing to evidence, telling stories, and more.

Geivett, R. Douglas, and Gary R. Habermas, eds. *In Defense of Miracles: A Comprehensive Case for God's Action in History*. Downers Grove, IL: IVP Academic, 1997. In this volume, several contributors address questions of miracles, responding to Hume, and more recently, Anthony Flew, demonstrating that miracles are viable.

Gish, Duane T. *Evolution: The Challenge of the Fossil Record*. El Cajon, CA: Creation-Life Publishers, 1985. Gish, a young earth creationist and scientist, takes a look at the fossil evidence for Darwinism and finds it significantly lacking. His material on the alleged evolution of flight in birds, mammals, insects, and reptiles is particularly thought-provoking. It is far more a negative critique of Darwinism than it is an apologetic for Christianity.

Groothuis, Douglas. *Are All Religions One?* Downers Grove, IL: InterVarsity Press, 1996. A reader-friendly introduction to religious pluralism from a Christian perspective, comparing Christianity, popular forms of Hinduism, and Islam. Groothuis includes a more thorough critique of religious pluralism in chapter 23 of his more recent work *Christian Apologetics*.

————. *Christian Apologetics: A Comprehensive Case for Biblical Faith*. Downers Grove, IL: InterVarsity, 2011. This is the definitive contemporary apologetics text, addressing apologetic methodology, truth, the existence of God, and three major objections to Christianity (religious pluralism, Islam, and the problem of evil). The author describes himself as a cumulative case apologist, though much of the approach is compatible with classical apologetics and, at times, evidentialism.

———— *On Jesus*. Belmont, CA: Wadsworth, 2003. A short defense of Jesus as a philosopher including chapters on his use of logical argument forms, metaphysics, epistemology, and ethics.

———— *On Pascal*. Belmont, CA: Wadsworth, 2003. A brief look at the philosophy of Blaise Pascal including his wager argument, his anthropological argument, and more.

———— *Truth Decay: Defending Christianity Against the Challenges of Postmodernism*. Downers Grove, IL: InterVarsity, 2000. A solid defense of the biblical, correspondence view of truth, particularly in relation to postmodern challenges.

———— *Unmasking the New Age*. Downers Grove, IL: InterVarsity, 1986. Perhaps the best evangelical Christian response to the rise of the New Age movement in the 1980s, Groothuis thoughtfully engages and refutes monistic pantheism and related Westernized ideas.

Habermas, Gary. *The Historical Jesus: Ancient Evidence for the Life of Christ*. Joplin, MO: College Press Publishing, 1996. A thoughtful look at the evidence for Christ from one of evangelicalism's leading scholars on the resurrection of Christ.

Habermas, Gary, and Michael Licona. *The Case for the Resurrection of Jesus*. Grand Rapids: Kregel, 2004. Offers a robust yet accessible defense of the resurrection of Jesus and is especially helpful in presenting Habermas's unique "minimal facts" approach, as well as addressing alternative theories of the resurrection.

Hill, Jonathan. *What Has Christianity Ever Done for Us?* Downers Grove, IL: InterVarsity, 2005. Hill offers a witty exposition of the benefits of Christianity in a variety of areas such as literature, education, and more.

Hitchens, Christopher. *God Is Not Great: How Religion Poisons Everything.* New York: Twelve/Hatchette Book Group, 2007. The late Christopher Hitchens, one of the so-called "new atheists" implements one logical fallacy after another in this hyperbolic attack on religion, particularly Christianity. See Craig and Meister, *God Is Great, God Is Good* for a helpful response to Hitchens and other New Atheists.

House, H. Wayne, and Joseph M. Holden. *Charts of Apologetics and Christian Evidences.* Grand Rapids: Zondervan, 2006. Helpful charts (not argument diagrams) on apologetics and apologetics issues such as apologetic methodology, philosophical apologetics, theistic apologetics (worldviews, arguments for God), revelation, religion, the resurrection, manuscript evidence for the Bible, and more.

Kennedy, D. James, and Jerry Newcombe. *What If Jesus Had Never Been Born?* Nashville: Nelson, 1994. Posing a unique question, Kennedy and Newcombe reveal the major positive impact Christianity has had on the world in areas such as compassion, education, government, science, medicine, and other topics. A shorter and more accessible work than Schmidt's similar work *How Christianity Changed the World.*

Kreeft, Peter. *Making Sense Out of Suffering.* Ann Arbor, MI: Servant Books, 1986. In a readable style apologist Peter Kreeft explores the problem of evil from philosophical, artistic, and prophetic perspectives.

Kreeft, Peter, and Ronald K. Tacelli. *Handbook of Christian Apologetics.* Downers Grove, IL: InterVarsity, 1994. A witty exposition of common apologetics issues which includes no less than twenty arguments for God's existence, questions about the problem of evil, issues regarding the person of Christ, questions about heaven and hell, material on Christianity in relation to other faiths, and a chapter on objective truth.

Lewis, C. S. *The Abolition of Man.* New York: Macmillan, 1943. Lewis's masterful defense of natural law, which he calls the Tao, serves as an important stepping-stone in his later development of a moral argument for God.

———. *Mere Christianity.* New York: Macmillan, 1952. Book 1 in particular serves as a relevant popular presentation of a moral argument for the existence of God.

———. *Miracles.* New York: Macmillan, 1960. For the 1960 edition, Lewis revised chapter 3 following criticism by Christian philosopher Elizabeth Anscombe. Note that on the whole, *Miracles* offers excellent arguments, but at times Lewis strays into neoorthodoxy.

———. *The Problem of Pain.* New York: Macmillan, 1943. Lewis's thoughtful approach to the intellectual problem of evil and suffering addresses questions of God's goodness and omnipotence in relation to the problem, with Lewis settling, on the whole, on a free will defense to the challenge.

Lewis, Gordon R. *Testing Christianity's Truth Claims.* Lanham, MD: University Press of America, 1990. Originally published in 1976 (Moody), this book tackles several approaches to apologetics, defending the approach of Edward John Carnell, which Lewis dubs the verificational approach.

Mangalwadi, Vishal. *When the New Age Gets Old: Looking for a Greater Spirituality.* Downers Grove, IL: InterVarsity, 1992. A Christian Indian, Mangalwadi offers a unique perspective as he evaluates a variety of New Age ideas.

McDowell, Josh. *The New Evidence That Demands a Verdict.* Nashville: Thomas Nelson, 1999. Combining McDowell's earlier works (*Evidence That Demands a Verdict* and *More Evidence That Demands a Verdict*) this collection offers McDowell's trademark evidentialist apologetic for Christianity, offering both positive evidence for Christ and the biblical record, as well as critiques of views such as the documentary hypothesis and form criticism. Includes many documented quotations of interest.

McDowell, Josh, and Bill Wilson. *He Walked Among Us: Evidence for the Historical Jesus.* San Bernardino, CA: Here's Life Publishers, 1988. A popular look at the evidence for the historical Christ covering extrabiblical evidence and the reliability of the New Testament.

McGrath, Alister. *The Twilight of Atheism: The Rise and Fall of Disbelief in the Modern World.* New York: Doubleday, 2004. McGrath explores the tenacity of religious worldviews despite the challenge of atheism.

Moreland, J. P. *Christianity and the Nature of Science: A Philosophical Investigation*. Grand Rapids: Baker, 1989. Moreland offers a thoughtful look at the philosophy of science from a Christian perspective, addressing the meaning of science, its methodology, and its limits.

————. *Love Your God with All Your Mind: The Role of Reason in the Life of the Soul*. Colorado Springs: NavPress, 1997. Moreland makes a compelling case for the value of the intellect in the Christian life.

————. *Scaling the Secular City*. Grand Rapids: Baker, 1987. A robust apologetic work addressing traditional arguments for God's existence (cosmological, design), as well as addressing the argument from mind, the meaning of life, the reliability of the New Testament, Christ's resurrection, thoughtful insights on science and Christianity, and useful material on moral relativism and the value of religious experience within a Christian context.

Moreland, J. P., and William Lane Craig. *Philosophical Foundations for a Christian Worldview*. Downers Grove, IL: InterVarsity Press, 2003. An impressive textbook by two noteworthy evangelical apologists. The emphasis is on philosophy including epistemology, metaphysics, ethics, philosophy of science, philosophy of religion, and philosophical theology.

Moreland, J. P., and Kai Nielsen. *Does God Exist? The Great Debate*. Nashville: Nelson, 1990. A helpful structured debate between a Christian theist (Moreland) and an atheist (Nielsen). Includes responses by individuals such as Peter Kreeft, Antony Flew, and Dallas Willard.

Morgan, Christopher W., and Robert A. Peterson, eds. *Faith Comes by Hearing: A Response to Inclusivism*. Downers Grove, IL: InterVarsity, 2008. A response to Christian inclusivism, relevant to our studies in reference to claims of religious pluralism and Christian exclusivity.

Morris, John and Frank Sherwin. *The Fossil Record*. Dallas: Institute for Creation Research, 2010. Young earth creationists explore the fossil record and conclude that Darwinism falls far short of the anticipated evidence supposedly in its favor.

Netland, Harold. *Encountering Religious Pluralism: The Challenge to Christian Faith and Mission*. Downers Grove, IL: InterVarsity, 2001. A thoughtful and at times challenging work addressing questions about religious pluralism. Includes a compelling chapter on developing an evangelical theology of religions.

Pearcey, Nancy. *Total Truth: Liberating Christianity from Its Cultural Captivity*. Wheaton, IL: Crossway, 2004. In the spirit of Francis Schaeffer (an influence on Pearcey), *Total Truth* thoughtfully addresses a number of topics in relation to worldviews, religion, science and faith, the intellectual life and Christianity, and much more.

Pearcey, Nancy, and Charles Thaxton. *The Soul of Science: Christian Faith and Natural Philosophy*. Wheaton, IL: Crossway, 1994. A survey of the progression of science in relation to faith, emphasizing the importance of Christianity in relation to the scientific revolution.

Reisser, Paul, Dale Mabe, and Robert Velarde. *Examining Alternative Medicine: An Inside Look at the Benefits and Risks*. Downers Grove, IL: InterVarsity, 2001. A thoughtful critique of alternative medicine including an evaluation of monistic pantheism, energy-based medicine, and postmodern thought's influence on medicine. Includes a thorough analysis and response to the teachings of Deepak Chopra.

Rhodes, Ron. *Answering the Objections of Atheists, Agnostics, and Skeptics*. Eugene, OR: Harvest House, 2006. In popular fashion, apologist Ron Rhodes addresses a number of common objections to the Christian worldview.

Samples, Kenneth Richard. *Without a Doubt: Answering the 20 Toughest Faith Questions*. Grand Rapids: Baker, 2004. A keen thinker, Samples defends the Christian worldview by addressing a number of apologetic questions regarding the existence of God, the reliability of the Gospels, religious pluralism, science and Christianity, ethics, and more.

————. *A World of Difference: Putting Christian Truth-Claims to the Worldview Test*. Grand Rapids: Baker, 2007. Another helpful defense of the faith from Samples, this work is notable for its emphasis on testing truth claims and, as a result, offers nine criteria for evaluating claims.

Schaeffer, Francis A. *The God Who Is There*, 30th anniv. ed. Downers Grove, IL: InterVarsity, 1998. A classic work defining the Christian worldview and its relevance to all of life in comparison to competing ideologies—thoughtful and potentially life-changing.

Schmidt, Alvin J. *How Christianity Changed the World*. Grand Rapids: Zondervan, 2004. A robust and well-documented look at Christianity's positive influence on many areas including morality, compassion, women's rights, labor, science, liberty, the fine arts, literature, and several other subjects. The narrative is a bit dry, but the information is fascinating.

Sire, James. *Habits of the Mind: Intellectual Life as a Christian Calling*. Downers Grove, IL: InterVarsity, 2000. Sire presents the case for the value of intellectualism in the Christian life.

———. *A Little Primer on Humble Apologetics*. Downers Grove, IL: InterVarsity, 2006. Sire offers some much-needed advice on the role of humility in the Christian life in relation to the defense of the faith. Includes wonderful advice on the calling and apologetics, as well as key character attributes necessary to defending the faith biblically.

———. *The Universe Next Door: A Basic Worldview Catalog*, 5th ed. Downers Grove, IL: InterVarsity, 2009. The classic Christian work assessing competing worldviews such as Christian theism, deism, naturalism, nihilism, existentialism, monistic pantheism, and postmodernism.

———. *Why Good Arguments Often Fail: Making a More Persuasive Case for Christ*. Downers Grove, IL: InterVarsity, 2006. Apologetics is about far more than arguments for the faith. Sire explores a number of reasons why someone may reject our arguments in defense of Christianity.

Sproul, R. C. *The Holiness of God*. Second edition. Nashville: Tyndale House, 2000. Sproul's classic work, first published in 1985, explores a key facet of God's nature. An engaging and moving work.

Sproul, R. C., John Gerstner, and Arthur Lindsley. *Classical Apologetics: A Rational Defense of the Christian Faith and a Critique of Presuppositional Apologetics*. Grand Rapids: Zondervan, 1984. As the title suggests, this work features a presentation and defense of classical apologetics and a critique of presuppositionalism. Traditional natural theology arguments for God are included, such as the cosmological argument and teleological argument.

Stark, Rodney. *For the Glory of God: How Monotheism Led to Reformations, Science, Witch-Hunts, and the End of Slavery*. Princeton, NJ: Princeton University Press, 2003. Stark's engaging historical overview of the influence of Christianity is particularly interesting in relation to its explanation of the key role of Christianity in the rise of modern science.

———. *The Victory of Reason: How Christianity Led to Freedom, Capitalism, and Western Success*. New York: Random House, 2006. Shorter than *For the Glory of God*, this work addresses similar topics, covering the important role Christianity played in the rise of capitalism, science, and other areas of Western culture.

Story, Dan. *Engaging the Closed Minded: Presenting Your Faith to the Confirmed Unbeliever*. Grand Rapids: Kregel, 1999. In this short work, Story approaches apologetics from the evidentialist perspective, offering numerous tips and general advice for engaging non-Christians with gentleness and with respect.

Strobel, Lee. *The Case for the Resurrection: A First-Century Investigative Reporter Probes History's Pivotal Event*. Grand Rapids: Zondervan, 2010. A booklet excerpted from *The Case for Christ Study Bible*. Offers a good popular summary of the evidence for the resurrection. Like Habermas, Strobel incoporates a minimal-facts approach.

Taylor, James E. *Introducing Apologetics: Cultivating Christian Commitment*. Grand Rapids: Baker, 2006. A helpful textbook approach to Christian apologetics addressing apologetic methodology, worldviews, Christ, and challenges to the faith such as natural selection, postmodernism, and moral relativism. It includes discussion questions and suggestions for further reading.

Velarde, Robert. *Conversations with C. S. Lewis: Imaginative Discussions About Life, Christianity, and God*. Downers Grove, IL: InterVarsity, 2008. Features a series of fictional conversations between C. S. Lewis and a contemporary atheist, addressing topics such as the existence of God, morality, the problem of evil, and other apologetics matters.

———. *What Christianity Has Done for the World*. Torrance, CA: Rose, 2007. A booklet presenting a summary of Christianity's contributions in areas such as compassion, human life, education, science, medicine, the fine arts, literature, and philosophy. Consider it a highly condensed presentation of material in books such as Schmidt's *How Christianity Changed the World*.

Wells, Jonathan. *Icons of Evolution: Science or Myth?* Washington, DC: Regnery, 2000. A proponent of Intelligent Design, Wells debunks many "icons" of evolution including the Miller-Urey experiment that allegedly created life in the laboratory, Darwin's tree of life, Haeckel's embryos, peppered moths, Galapagos finches, and more. A documentary video of the same title is also available.

Subject Index

abductive reasoning, 95, 104, 105, 108, 158, 176, 195
Abolition of Man, The, 74, 202
Advaita Vedanta, 110, 162, 195, 197
Akashic Records, 165–66
altruism and morality, 72–73, 104, 107, 177
annihilationism, 118, 121, 195
Apologetics in the New Age, 166, 199
Apologetics of Joy, The, 101
argument from reason, 53, 57, 72
ascended masters, 165
atonement, 92–95, 168, 195

Baker Encyclopedia of Christian Apologetics, 175, 200
best way defense, 111, 113, 115, 120, 129, 149–50, 195
blind men and elephant illustration, 169
brain chemistry (atheism), 139, 142, 143, 190
Brhaman, 174

Cambrian explosion, 136–37
Christ-consciousness, 169
Christian Apologetics, 51, 63, 65, 158, 188, 191, 201
Christianity and the Nature of Science, 81, 202
Christianity on Trial, 78, 199
Christian Science, 116, 177
City of God, 78
Confessions, 78
Crusades, 154, 155, 160

Darwinism, 77, 134–38
delusion, God as, 140
depravity, 143
Divine Comedy, 78
Does God Exist?, 127, 203

Encountering Religious Pluralism, 169, 172, 203

Euthyphro dilemma, 70, 74
Evidence for Jesus, The, 89, 90, 200
evil, as mystery, 147
evil, as privation, 113, 129
evolution, evidence for
    archaeopteryx, 136
    finch beaks, 137
    fruit flies, 137
    IDA (fossil), 136
    mutations, 134, 135
    peppered moths, 137
Examining Alternative Medicine, 165, 166, 203

Faith Comes by Hearing, 92, 96, 203
fideism, 35, 142, 196
For the Glory of God, 76, 160, 204
Fossil Record, The, 138, 203

general revelation, 42, 95, 127
genetic fallacy, 150, 196
God, as moral lawgiver, 53, 110, 129, 197
God Delusion, The, 144, 200
God Is Great, God Is Good, 144, 200
God of the gaps, 131
gratuitous evil, 46, 115, 130, 150

Handbook of Christian Apologetics, 98, 100, 202
hasty generalization, 128, 160
haunted universe, 127
hiddenness of God, 127, 143
Hinduism, 168
Holiness of God, The, 96, 204
How Christianity Changed the World, 78, 81, 203

Icons of Evolution, 137, 204
image of God (imago Dei), 24, 195, 196
Incarnation, 119
ineffable experience, 164

Inquisition, 154, 155, 160
Intelligent Design, 52, 134, 135, 138, 159, 204
irreducible complexity, 135
irrelevant thesis, 129
Islam, militant, 155

karma, 105, 107, 156

libertarian freedom, 118–19
limited knowledge response to evil, 150–51
logic, "Western," 173, 176

macroevolution, 134, 137
Making Sense Out of Suffering, 152, 202
maya, 174
metaphysical dualism, 162
microevolution, 137
mithya, 174

natural theology, 95, 126, 197
Nazis, 154, 155
negative apologetics, 141
New Age, 62–64, 94, 116, 166, 168, 169, 174, 177, 197
New Evidence That Demands a Verdict, The, 172, 202

Occam's razor, 134
On Pascal, 108, 201

Paradise Lost, 78
Pilgrim's Progress, 78
polytheism, 50, 70, 168, 197, 198
positive apollogetics, 141
post hoc fallacy, 104
principle of credulity, 185–86
Problem of Pain, The, 152, 202
properly basic beliefs, 72, 189, 198

quantum physics, 165

Reformed epistemology, 8, 72, 198
repentance, 168
Roots of Evil, The, 115, 200

Salem witch trials, 154
salvation, 168
Scaling the Secular City, 187, 188, 203
science, and Christianity, 159
science, limits of, 185, 190, 191
Socratic method, 130

soul-making theodicy, 112, 113, 115, 129, 150, 198
Soul of Science, The, 81, 203
special revelation, 42, 50, 95, 127, 164
specified complexity, 135

tertium quid, 70
testing truth claims/worldview tests [158]
theistic evolution
theodicy
tolerance, 156–57, 171–72

transitional forms, 135
Trinitarianism, 168

Unmasking the New Age, 166, 201

What If Jesus Had Never Been Born?, 81, 202
What's So Great About Christianity?, 81, 138, 160, 200
When Bad Thins Happen to Good People, 149
World of Difference, A, 158, 203

Name Index

Alston, Wiliam, 198
Anselm, 51, 197
Aquinas, 35, 65, 79, 113
Augustine, 35, 54, 65, 78, 79, 98, 113, 195

Beckwith, Francis, 65, 199, 201
Boa, Kenneth, 22, 199
Bonhoeffer, Dietrich, 155
Bowman, Robert, 22, 199
Bruce, F.F., 20
Bunyan, John, 78

Carroll, Vincent, 78, 199
Chopra, Deepak, 166, 203
Clark, David, 166, 199
Collins, Francis, 138
Copan, Paul, 74, 199
Craig, William Lane, 65, 86, 189, 191, 196, 199, 200, 201, 202, 203

Dante, 78
Dawkins, Richard, 131, 138, 144, 200
Dembski, William, 138, 199
D'Souza, Dinesh, 81, 138, 160, 200
Dulles, Avery Cardinal, 22

Edgar, William, 22

Feuerbach, Ludwig
France, R.T., 89, 90, 200
Freud, Sigmund, 142

Geisler, Norman, 20, 27, 45, 51, 90, 96, 115, 166, 174, 175, 199, 200, 201
Geivett, R. Douglas, 45, 90, 201
Gish, Duane, 138, 201
Groothuis, Douglas, 13, 27, 51, 62, 63, 65, 108, 158, 166, 172, 187, 188, 191, 201

Habermas, Gary, 45, 90, 199, 200, 201, 204
Harris, Sam, 131
Hick, John, 150
Hill, Jonathan, 81, 201
Hitchens, Christopher, 131, 160, 202

Job, 151
Johnson, Phillip E., 138

Kennedy, D. James, 81, 202
Kierkegaard, Søren, 35, 65
Koukl, Greg, 65, 74, 199
Kreeft, Peter, 55, 98, 100, 101, 152, 201, 202, 203
Kushner, Harold, 149

Lewis, C.S., 8, 19, 45, 53, 54, 57, 65, 68, 73, 74, 90, 98, 101, 113, 119, 152, 195, 202, 204
Licona, Michael, 90, 201

Mabe, Dale, 165, 166, 203
Macdonald, Michael, 98
McDowell, Josh, 90, 172, 202
Meister, Chad, 22, 200
Milton, John, 78
Moreland, J.P., 29, 81, 127, 187, 188, 199, 201, 202, 203
Morgan, Christopher, 92, 96, 203
Morris, John, 138, 203
Mother Teresa, 180

Netland, Harold, 169, 172, 203
Newcombe, Jerry, 81, 202
Nielsen, Kai, 127, 203

Oliphint, K. Scott, 22

Parmenides, 174
Pascal, Blaise, 7, 54, 65, 98, 104–108, 195, 201

Pearcey, Nancy, 48, 81, 203
Peterson, Robert, 92, 96, 203
Plantinga, Alvin, 51, 65, 72, 197, 198, 199, 200
Plato, 70, 74, 79
Puckett, Joe, 101

Rae, Scott, 74
Reisser, Paul, 165, 166, 203
Reppert, Victor, 57

Samples, Kenneth, 158, 203
Schaeffer, Francis, 48, 65, 203
Schmidt, Alvin, 78, 81, 202, 203, 204
Sherwin, Frank, 138, 203
Shiflett, David, 78, 199
Sinnott-Armstrong, Walter, 189, 191
Sire, James, 27, 29, 203, 204
Sproul, R.C., 96, 204
Stark, Rodney, 76, 160, 204
Stenger, Victor, 165
Strobel, Lee, 19, 90, 204
Sweis, Khaldoun, 22

Tacelli, Ronald, 55, 98, 100, 202
Tadie, Andrew, 98
Thaxton, Charles, 81, 203

Velarde, Robert, 104, 165, 166, 200, 203, 204

Wells, Jonathan, 137, 204
Willard, Dallas, 13, 127, 203
Wilson, Bill, 90, 202
Wolterstorff, Nicholas, 198

Zukeran, Paul, 20, 27, 201

About the Author

Robert Velarde (MA, Southern Evangelical Seminary) is an author, educator, and philosopher. In addition to serving as a curriculum writer, he is also an adjunct faculty member of Denver Seminary. He is a member of the Evangelical Theological Society, the Evangelical Philosophical Society, the Society of Christian Philosophers, and the International Society of Christian Apologetics. A regular contributor to *Christian Research Journal*, Robert has published numerous articles on topics that include philosophy, theology, technology, apologetics, and popular culture. His books include *Conversations with C. S. Lewis* (InterVarsity), *The Heart of Narnia* (NavPress), *The Wisdom of Pixar* (InterVarsity), *Inside the Screwtape Letters* (Baker), and *Examining Alternative Medicine* (InterVarsity). He resides in Colorado with his wife and four children. Robert maintains a blog, *A Reasonable Imagination*, at http://areasonableimagination.com and a Twitter account @robert_velarde.